College Life
and the Mores

By JANET AGNES KELLEY, Ed.D.

SCHOOL OF EDUCATION, THE CITY COLLEGE OF NEW YORK

BUREAU OF PUBLICATIONS

TEACHERS COLLEGE

COLUMBIA UNIVERSITY

NEW YORK, 1949

To My Father and Mother
John T. and Jane E. Maclay Kelley

PREFACE

$\mathbf{M}$Y interest in this study began when I went from guidance work in a public school system to personnel work in a college. From the beginning I was impressed with the striking differences between the two kinds of institutions. The college was an institution with a society of its own; there was a culture in this college society which was different from that of the public school. Early in my work I was also impressed with the power of tradition on the college campus and its influence in forming the mores of students as well as faculty. The campus was a veritable culture complex. Tradition played a constructive role but also had its destructive effects. The difficulty in working with the destructive elements led me into an understanding of the complexities of a social system strongly conditioned by the past. I began early to see the importance of a study of the dynamics of social behavior which led to the mores of a college campus.

In their attempts to understand the dynamics of social behavior, workers in this area of research have taken into consideration the interrelations of the individual, society, and culture. These attempts indicate that there are meeting points among three long-established scientific disciplines: psychology, sociology, and anthropology. As Linton states:

Following the earlier atomistic trends of scientific research, each of these [psychology, sociology, and anthropology] has been treated as a separate field of investigation and made the subject of a distinct discipline. The individual has been assigned to Psychology, society to Sociology, and culture to Cultural Anthropology, although the last two sciences have shown a constant tendency to overlap in their investigations.[1]

"But," he continues, "it seems safe to say that the next few years

[1] Ralph Linton, *The Cultural Background of Personality*, p. 4–5. Copyright, 1945, by Appleton-Century-Crofts, Inc.

will witness the emergence of a science of human behavior which will synthesize the findings of Psychology, Sociology, and Anthropology."[2]

Authorities in all three areas are agreed on three basic elements in the study of social behavior:

First, the individual, his needs, potentialities, and mechanisms of learning are at the base of all social and cultural phenomena. Individuality, however, is achieved in and through social contacts; an individual's drives are satisfied within the frame of social interaction. According to Mead,

The individual possesses a self only in relation to the selves of the other members of his social group; and the structure of his self expresses or reflects the general behavior pattern of this social group to which he belongs, just as does the structure of the self of every other individual belonging to this social group.[3]

Second, a conception of social behavior implies the interaction of individuals. Or, as Young says:

Society depends essentially upon what George H. Mead called the "social act." That is, a social configuration is present whenever any given action tendency is modified by, or is not completed without, the intercession of another human being.[4]

The third basic element in the study of social behavior is culture. Young defines culture thus:

The term refers to the more or less organized and persistent patterns of habits, ideas, attitudes, and values which are passed on to the newborn child from his elders or by others as he grows up. It provides a large part of the content of our beliefs and convictions, of our prejudices, of our affections, and of our antagonisms. . . .[5] In terms of what others demand or accept of us, we may say that some aspects of culture represent complete expectancies, such as are found in the law, the mores, and the necessitous compliance with the operations of physical nature as they become integrated into culture.[6]

---

[2] *Ibid.*, p. 5.

[3] George H. Mead, *Mind, Self, and Society,* p. 164. Copyright, 1934, by The University of Chicago Press.

[4] Kimball Young, *Social Psychology,* p. 5. Copyright, 1946, by Appleton-Century-Crofts, Inc.

[5] *Ibid.*, p. 7–8.

[6] *Ibid.*, p. 8.

Culture, however, has never been able to determine completely the life organization of individuals. There will always be differences in learning potentialities, in interpretation of experience, which, though culturally qualified, still remain individualized.

Personnel workers have long recognized this uniqueness of the individual and have drawn heavily upon the findings of psychology as a base for their work with the individual student. All authorities recognize that the individual is not putty in the hands of the social forces. Only within the limits set by heredity is an individual adaptable to new situations and new demands. As there are physiological constants which come to the individual from his family ancestry, so, too, is the degree of learning ability determined by organic hereditary forces. Students in the same college are confronted by the mores of that college but they do not all have the same problems of adjustment. The psychology of adjustment is the psychology of learning. Insight, purpose, practice, are essential in adjustment as in learning.

The writer does not wish to deny or minimize the importance of the psychological aspect of the study of an individual. The findings of psychology have been vastly important to personnel work. It is the purpose of this study, however, to describe some of the contributions from the fields of sociology and anthropology which likewise are important to an understanding of student life. A proper integration of all three fields may be successfully achieved.

The writer sought enlightenment from the beginning of this study in Sumner's position that an understanding of social behavior must be found in the usages, mores, and institutions of society. Sumner holds: "The mores are the ways of doing things which are current in a society to satisfy human needs. . . ."[7] He notes also in his definition "the faiths, notions, codes, and standards of well-living which inhere in these ways, having a genetic connection with them."[8] A study of faiths, notions, beliefs, and customs leads one into a better understanding of the culture. The college culture, as any other, presents certain expectancies concerning a student's position in the social system of the campus—his role, prestige, and status. Because of these expectancies a social struc-

[7] W. G. Sumner, *Folkways*, p. 59. Copyright, 1906, by Ginn and Company.
[8] *Ibid.*, p. 59.

ture takes place which leads to various types of social behavior. The student's needs are satisfied also within the framework of social interaction and social interrelationships among all the personalities of a college campus. Finally, each student on the college campus, to satisfy certain needs, usually becomes a member of a group. Every group has a particular style of action, manner of living, and certain mores, depending upon the organization, structure, and functions of its members.

With basic material drawn mainly from authorities in the fields of sociology and anthropology, the five premises of the study then become:

1. The mores are ways of doing things to satisfy needs.

2. Culture sets the framework within which the student learns to function with his fellows; the mores grow out of this culture.

3. The mores are structured by a college social system which defines the position, status, and prestige of its members and the culturally patterned behavior expected of these positions.

4. The mores are strongly conditioned by the interrelationships of persons and groups on a campus.

5. The mores spring from the organization, structure, and functioning of groups.

The purpose of this study, then, is to define the mores, their content and scope, through a development of the above premises. In this development, it proposes also to show how the mores arise, function, and, if necessary, can be changed in a college community. In addition, it aims to point out the importance of this rather intangible, yet dynamic and living, phase of student life; to point out certain differences in student mores throughout American colleges and the factors which underlie these differences; to draw implications for educators and personnel workers as to ways in which the mores can be constructively used for the social control of student life; and to present plans and techniques for a better understanding of their functioning on the campus. Finally, it aims to describe the present-day impacts on the campus and to point out the need for a reassessment and re-evaluation of the mores to meet current conditions.

The method by which the writer prepared this study consisted, first, of the development of a theoretical framework based on (1) the literature in the field of sociology and anthropology, (2) personal experience on a college campus, and (3) discussions with sociologists, anthropologists, and personnel workers. Second, in order to test this theoretical framework and to enrich the content of the above premises by means of illustrations, conferences were held with forty personnel workers who attended the 1946 summer session at Teachers College, Columbia University, and who represented colleges located in different geographical areas of the United States. To become informed about the impact of the veteran on the campus, conferences were held with fifty college veterans who had served in various divisions of the Army, Navy, and Air Corps. At least fifty other conferences were held with students from various colleges.

Third, various surveys and pieces of research were undertaken. To discover patterns of stability or change the catalogues of one college covering a period of twenty years were studied. The handbooks, yearbooks, and student newspapers of another college, covering a period of twenty years, were analyzed. For a period of six months an analysis was made of the current social behavior on college campuses, by a systematic following of the weekly and daily student newspapers of some twenty colleges located in different parts of the United States. For six months in 1946 the "Education in Review" section of the Sunday edition of *The New York Times* was noted for innovations and new impacts caused by students on present-day college campuses.

Fourth, literature and research in the field of campus life were studied, and from time to time research studies made by others were used to document and illustrate certain areas of the study.

There are limitations to this study. First, only recently have the mores and the social system of the college campus been given attention as a field for study in personnel work. Little has been written and little research has been done in this area. Although this fact may indicate the need for more work, it has also deprived this study of a rich background of research on which to develop the subject further.

Second, the necessity for creating a general framework adequate to treat the more important aspects of this social and cultural area has required much time and thought. A more complete development of the area would require more time than could be given in this one study.

Third, in the interviews it was found difficult to ask direct objective questions. However, the total picture which each personnel worker gave of the social behavior on his or her campus seemed more important for a study of this kind.

For personnel workers and educators interested in starting a study of their own college social system and of the mores of their students, suggestions for carrying on such research are presented in the Appendix. Detailed outlines and schedules are included there for that purpose. Personnel workers and educators may be interested in starting their study with only one phase of student life and carrying on a definite study in that one area. By beginning a research in one small phase of the social behavior of a student body, a trend may be discovered which will reveal the whole pattern of the campus.

Sincere appreciation and acknowledgments are extended to Professors R. Freeman Butts, Esther Lloyd-Jones, and Donald G. Tewksbury, all of Teachers College, Columbia University, for their genuine interest in this study and for their constructive guidance and kindly supervision. To Professor Lloyd-Jones, major adviser for the study, the author is especially grateful for hearty support and encouragement in exploring the fields of sociology and anthropology for an interpretation of personnel work.

In preparing a theoretical framework for this study valuable aid was received from Professor Ralph Linton, then of the Department of Anthropology, Columbia University, and now at Yale University. Appreciation is expressed to him for the helpful suggestions he gave to the author in conferences.

Sincere thanks are also expressed to the personnel workers, the student veterans, both men and women, and other college students who gave generously of their time to acquaint the writer with student life, customs, and mores, and with postwar adjustments and problems on the present-day campus.

JANET AGNES KELLEY

New York, N. Y.
January, 1948

CONTENTS

                                                                    PAGE

I. THE MORES AND THEIR FUNCTION IN SOCIAL CONTROL . .   1

What Are the Mores?   2
    Mores and Man's Needs   2
    Mores: the Product of the Culture   5
    Mores: the Mechanics of a Social System   5
    Mores: the Functioning of Groups   5
    Again—What Are the Mores?   6
    The Mores and the Whole Social Configuration . .   7
Where Do the Mores Come From?   8
    Emergence from the Culture and History of the
        College   8
    Formation by Cultural Controls and Processes . . .   9
How Do the Mores Change?   11
    Discovery and Invention   11
    Diffusion   14
    Borrowing   15
    Who Changes the Mores?   17
Do the Mores Control Student Life on a College Campus?   23
Whither the Mores?   24
Bibliography   25

II. THE COLLEGE AS A CULTURE-MATRIX   27

The Culture Which the Student Brings   28
    Implications for Personnel Workers and Educators .   33
Traditional and Established Culture of the College . .   34
    The Mores of Control in the Social Heritage . . .   34
        Traditions   35
        College Spirit   41
        Folkways and Customs   45
        Implications for Personnel Workers and Educators   48
    Further Mores of Control in an Established Institu-
        tional Culture   51
        Regulative and Suggestive Control   51

  PAGE

        Indoctrination, Assimilation, Culturally Transmit-
            ted Attitudes   56
        Ceremony and Ritual   58
        Student Government   61
        Implications for Personnel Workers and Educators .   65
    Physical and Material Culture   68
        Implications for Personnel Workers and Educators .   74
    Summary   74
    Bibliography   76

III. THE CULTURE OF THE WIDER COMMUNITY   79

    Influence of the Alumni   79
        Implications for Personnel Workers and Educators .   85
    Influence of the Local Community   85
        Implications for Personnel Workers and Educators .   91
    Influence of National Organizations   93
        Implications for Personnel Workers and Educators .   96
    Influence of Society at Large   98
        Implications for Personnel Workers and Educators .   102
    Bibliography   103

IV. SOCIAL STRUCTURING: STATUS, ROLE, AND PRESTIGE IN COL-
    LEGE SOCIETY   106

    Academic Structuring   108
        Status in the Academic Structure   110
    Student Structuring   115
        Age-Sex and Social Group System   116
        Occupational Choice   118
        Optional Relationships and Residential Social Group-
            ings   119
            Social Stratification 120
            Social Cleavages   122
            Racial, Religious, and National Discriminations .   123
            Selective Mechanism Structuring 125
    Social Structuring Due to Material Equipment . . .   130
    Status, Role, and Prestige on a College Campus . . . 132
    Implications for Personnel Workers and Educators . . 139
    Bibliography   143

PAGE

V. THE COMPLEX OF INTERRELATIONS ON THE CAMPUS . . . 145

Campus Interrelations and the Total Social Configuration 146
General Interrelations—Student, Faculty, Administration, Parent, Community 146
Parental Letter 148
Totality of Interrelations 150
Campus Situations for Constructive Mores in Interrelations 153
Interpersonal Relationships 154
Importance of Interpersonal Effectiveness 155
Leadership 155
Criteria for Evaluation of Leadership 157
Leadership Techniques 160
The Sociometric Test 161
Choice Analysis 162
Other Aids . . . . , . . 163
Leadership and Dominance 163
Individual Status Dominance 164
The Followers 165
Implications for Personnel Workers and Educators . . 166
Bibliography 169

VI. THE ROLE OF GROUPS IN THE CAMPUS MORES 172

Social Grouping 174
Formal Organization 177
Informal Organization 179
Informal Clique Structure 183
Plan for Study of Informal Groups 186
Organization, Functioning, and Structure of Groups . 188
Social Status and Role within Each Group 191
Intergroup Relations 193
Specific Techniques in Studying Groups 195
Group Description 196
Group Record 198
Group Diaries 199
Social Processes in Group Work 200
Implications for Personnel Workers and Educators . . 202
Bibliography 207

  PAGE

VII. THE COLLEGE IN TRANSITION 210
    Impact of the Culture Which the Student Brings with
        Him 211
    The Heterogeneity in Composition of the Student
        Body 212
    Needs of a Heterogeneous Student Body 214
    Status and Role on the Present-day Campus 215
    Impact of the Veteran 219
        The Conditioning from Military Mores 219
        Adjustment of the Veteran on the Campus . . . 221
        Veterans' Groups 227
    Impact of the Present-day Campus on the Traditional
        Established Culture of the College 229
    Curricular Innovations 229
    Student Impact on Administrative Measures . . . 234
    The New Impact of Student Government 235
    Impact of a New Social System 239
    Present-day Impact of Campus Politics 246
    Housing Problems 248
    Impact of Campus Thought and Action on the Wider
        Community 257
    Implications for Personnel Workers and Educators . . 259
    Bibliography 262

VIII. CONCLUSION 264
    Bibliography 276

APPENDIX: Plans and Techniques for Research on the Mores of
    Students on a College Campus 279

INDEX 293

*College Life
and the Mores*

I

THE MORES AND THEIR FUNCTION
IN SOCIAL CONTROL

"We don't do it like that on our campus," "We have this custom over our way," "We did it that way when I went to college." Such statements as these show that different ways of doing things become ingrained in students on various campuses throughout the college world. They also show that these different ways of doing things embody a set of mores peculiar to each campus community, and exercise a social control over students, becoming regulators of their behavior.

Very little attention has been given to the social organization of the college community as it affects the students and the faculty. In all angles of life more thought is given to technical organization than to human organization or to the fine shadings of social relations that are important in helping individuals to cooperate and to set acceptable standards of social behavior. One wonders why more effort has not been spent by educators in discovering the motivations for these different ways of doing things, the processes by which they are developed, from what source they come, what they are, how they can be changed, and their importance to constructive living on the campus and in later life.

The purpose of this chapter is to define the scope and function of the mores, to describe how they develop and operate consciously and unconsciously in student life, and to point out how they may be changed, if necessary. It aims to emphasize the importance of a knowledge of the mores in meeting the new conditions and changing interests on the present-day campus, which, since the war, has been in the process of reconstruction. It also stresses the necessity of re-evaluating the mores in order to meet the present-day needs.

1

What Are the Mores?

Sumner has defined the mores as

The ways of doing things which are current in a society to satisfy human needs and desires, together with the faiths, notions, codes, and standards of well living which inhere in those ways, having a genetic connection with them.[1]

Can a college community be thought of as a society? According to Linton, "A society is any group of people who have lived together and worked together long enough to get themselves organized and to think of themselves as a social unit with well-defined limits." [2] MacIver says, "Society is the system of social relationships in and through which we live."[3] Both of these statements confirm the opening sentences of this chapter which indicate rather clearly that each college is a society with its own particular social limits and its own system of relationships. The "human needs and desires" which have brought about "ways of doing things" on the part of students on the college campus are factors which have long been unrecognized, or recognized too seldom, by personnel workers and educators as the heart of social behavior in the college social system.

MORES AND MAN'S NEEDS

What are the needs of college youth which they are trying to express in their ways of doing things? How can a personnel worker utilize these needs for constructive mores? In attempting to discern the desires and needs which eventuate in mores, one might examine the four general patterns of wishes which Thomas and Znaniecki suggest, namely: wishes (1) for new experiences, (2) for stability, (3) for response, and (4) for recognition.[4] Or one might look to the social status, ego-integrative, and physical needs which Prescott[5] proposes.

[1] William G. Sumner, *Folkways*, p. 59. Copyright, 1906, by Ginn and Company.
[2] Ralph Linton, *Study of Man*, p. 91. Copyright, 1936, by Appleton-Century-Crofts, Inc.
[3] R. M. MacIver, *Society, Its Structure and Changes*, p. 9.
[4] W. I. Thomas and F. Znaniecki, *The Polish Peasant in Europe and America*, Vol. III, Introduction.
[5] Daniel A. Prescott, *Emotion and the Educative Process*, p. 114.

The fulfillment of the social status needs of a college student may depend upon the particular relationships that are essential for him to establish with other persons in the college culture. Only by maintaining satisfactory relationships with other persons and organizations can these needs be satisfied. He must become a member of some of the social groupings on the campus, and his functioning and that of others must be such that he will have a sense of belonging, a feeling of security, ties of friendship, and acceptance by the group.

Each freshman is already a group product when he enters college. Almost immediately he becomes a member of one or more college groups and is conditioned by the particular mores of these new environing groups. The individual has long been appreciated by personnel workers as a group product, but the data which they have collected have too often been used to understand his functioning as an individual rather than as a group product. Witness the information for which personnel staffs traditionally have been asking: father's occupation, mother's occupation, father's nationality, mother's nationality, number of self-supporting members of family, citizenship, church preference, member of what activities in high school, location of home, population of home town, etc. Too often personnel workers in colleges have studied these items in the light of the isolated individual, not recognizing that a student's mores, in whatever groups he is functioning in the college, may be to a large extent the result of all the groups which have molded him. In the social system of a campus, the particular ways of doing things to achieve prestige, esteem, social status, and a role on the campus may have evolved from an effort to satisfy not only social status needs but also the need for stability or ego-integrative needs. Because of competition on the campus, of ways of acquiring prestige, often the need for social status operates in a restrictive, discriminatory manner, bringing about selective mechanisms and social stratification. Often without the college community being aware of it, certain physical conditions and material equipment affect the satisfaction of student needs in unique ways, as will be noted in later chapters.[6]

Students have ego-integrative and physical needs which must be

[6] See Chapters II and IV of this study.

satisfied; it is important that they be satisfied in constructive "ways of doing things." A student's ego-integrative needs may be quite evident when he is striving to discover his role on the campus and to play it in a way that will bring him satisfying prestige. He cannot become adjusted unless he feels that he has attained selfhood in some degree as he lives in the college community. The experiences which a college community offer mold this selfhood. If the experiences on a college campus are too limited or too restricted, the behavior patterns of individuals having these experiences will be inadequate. If an individual student is not given responsibility for regulating his own behavior, his ways of doing things may lack independence or may become defiant. Also, from the standpoint of the preservation of physiological equilibrium—physically and emotionally—certain destructive ways of doing things may develop in individuals unless personnel workers recognize the need for proper food, physical exercise, rest, relaxation, and constructive tension-relieving activities. Too, food and eating habits, sex habits, recreational patterns, and other physical habits will be conditioned by the mores of the student's family and the community culture. It is only by working with the mores of a conditioned student culture and attempting to establish an integration with the educational aims within that culture that desirable mores can be built to satisfy physical needs.

The satisfaction of the needs for security and response on the part of students usually is achieved through interrrelations among all persons in the college community. There is always the potential for good interrelations on the campus. The attitudes built up through such interrelations sustain and modify the affective tone of a campus and of a social system. It is in constructive working through of all these interrelationships that desirable mores can be built. Each college campus represents a social unit with a particular system of relationships, structure, and organization. Groups are a part of the social unit; their ways of functioning usually depend upon the composition of the student body, various cultural factors, and the needs to be satisfied. The desire to organize groups, belong to groups, function in groups, and develop group folkways and other social techniques for group living attests, as has been mentioned before, the need to satisfy social status, as well as the need for security, response, and new experiences. Thus, in all types of behavior observed on a college campus one can see the efforts of students to satisfy one or more of these types of needs.

MORES: THE PRODUCT OF THE CULTURE

To return to Sumner's definition of the mores: "The mores are the ways of doing things . . . to satisfy human needs and desires, together with the faiths, notions, codes, and standards of well-living which have inhered in these ways of doing, having a genetic connection with them."[7] It is necessary, then, to seek an understanding of the mores also in the culture and history of the college community. Faiths, beliefs, codes, which have a genetic connection with ways of doing things on the campus go back to the origins, and above all to the culture of the college community. Established customs, rules and regulations, traditions, and group folkways that have arisen to satisfy some need—the need for stability and security, perhaps more than any other—these become the mores.

MORES: THE MECHANICS OF A SOCIAL SYSTEM

Through the workings of the mores there usually results a well-defined structure of positions peculiar to each campus in regard to age, sex, class, and common interests. The mores are also the cultural expectancies of the college community with regard to these positions. Included in the mores are also the patterns of interactions and interrelations among the individuals in the college system.

MORES: THE FUNCTIONING OF GROUPS

The mores are the modes of behavior of college students as individuals or as groups. It appears, however, that individual ways of doing things are not independent, self-contained modes of behavior but are responsive to the group-sustained mores. The mores imply which standards of group well-being groups select, consciously and unconsciously. They imply on the part of the total group the tendency "to do as all do." Some mores are common to the whole college; others are peculiar to a group or groups on the

[7] Sumner, op. cit., p. 59.

campus. "If we name the whole system of behavior patterns characteristic of a group, its folkways, then this system regarded as a regulator of conduct may be termed the mores."[8]

AGAIN—WHAT ARE THE MORES?

In summary, the college mores include the ways students do things to satisfy their needs, particularly such personality needs as prestige, superiority, social status, security, and response. Also, in the process of satisfying these needs, the mores comprise the patterns of interactions and interrelations among persons in the college community, the "rating and dating" complexes, the prestige systems, and the techniques of group living. The mores also include the entire system of relationships arising from the organization, structure, and functioning of a student body. They represent systems of control and elements of force, and such factors as submission and dominance. The mores include reactions due to the cultural processes of change, such as invention and diffusion. They are the traditions, customs, folkways, fads, usages of a college culture; they are the attitudes, sentiments, and life philosophies of all who are in any way part of the campus organization and community. The mores also are a *product* of the total culture; individuals not only *acquire* their family culture but are *molded* by variations and differences as they move from group to group, and when they enter college they do so with all these imprints upon them. The mores concern the whole of life and serve all interests, political, social, religious—the ways of governing, the ways of sociality, the morals. The mores are social ritual in which all participate unconsciously—the current habits as to social life between the sexes, propriety, amusements, or reading materials. The mores are the manners, the styles, and the codes of group living. The mores also necessarily consist, in a large part, of taboos, which indicate the things that must not be done. According to Sumner, "Taboos may be divided into two classes, (1) protective and (2) destructive."[9]

In other words, the mores bring to an individual codes of action, standards, and rules of ethics. They represent the *living* char-

---

8 MacIver, *op. cit.*, p. 17.
9 Sumner, *op. cit.*, p. 31.

acter of a group or community, operative in conscious or unconscious control over its members.

THE MORES AND THE WHOLE SOCIAL CONFIGURATION

A significant way to discover the mores on any one campus is to make a study of the total picture of student life and of the college community as well as separate analyses of the various parts of student life, such as the study of particular groups, individuals, or interpersonal relationships. It is the interaction of all parts of student life that is important—the interaction between faculty, administration, students, groups, and community. According to Gestalt psychology, the whole determines its parts. If two wholes function on a campus, for example, a faculty world and a student world, then there is discontinuity, and any understanding must take account of the differences rather than the similar elements of the two. That the psychological traits of college students are not inherited but are molded and created by their experiences has great significance to personnel workers. Thus, the basic psychological needs; administrative, faculty, and student standards and interrelations; group standards, group organization and functioning; cultural conditioning, social rituals, taboos, parent expectancies, alumni progressive and regressive tendencies, and societal influences—all function in the motivation of behavior and in the student mores peculiar to each college community.

The preceptorial plan at Princeton, the tutorial program at Harvard, the honors courses at Swarthmore, the faculty-student congress at Bucknell, the community plan at Bennington, the study-work plan at Antioch, the cooperative plan at Sarah Lawrence, and the various counseling and curricular developmental plans of other colleges and universities throughout the country attest the humanization of higher education and the building of new mores through effective interactions of all elements on a campus. They also attest the evolution of programs that meet the needs of students, each peculiar to the culture of a campus, its location, and the organization, structuring, and functioning of its clientele. Constructive mores are likely to develop through such educational goals.

Where Do the Mores Come From?

EMERGENCE FROM THE CULTURE AND
   HISTORY OF THE COLLEGE

Certain traditions have been handed down entirely from outside the college community. Others may be entirely indigenous to the culture of the particular college community concerned. The college as an institution and the student clientele, in order to satisfy their needs for security and stability and to establish standards of well-being and of college welfare, have continued to extend old mores to meet new. A veritable culture-matrix, peculiar to each college community, is thus developed. Above all, the culture-matrix is strongly conditioned by the type of college in which it has developed.

One should be mindful that the cultural factors in a college community, the composition of this particular student body, the geographical location, its particular history, different kinds of structuring, special social heritage, all create mores indigenous to that culture. This fact is strikingly apparent when one considers the differences in colleges throughout the United States. A few colleges date back to the seventeenth century, some to the eighteenth, many to the nineteenth, and a few others to the twentieth. Culturally, the colleges of the West are different from those of the East, and those of the North from those of the South. Among the types of colleges are, to mention a few, liberal arts, state, denominational, agricultural, technical. In size of student population, some colleges are large, others medium, and many small. From the standpoint of type of community, students come from rural, small town, and cosmopolitan areas; as to background, students come from homes and families of high, middle, and low socio-economic status; from the standpoint of transportation, most of the student body commute daily or live in college dormitories; as to institutional control, it may be private, public, or denominational.

It is not difficult to realize from these differences that each college has a culture complex of its own and the customs, beliefs, faiths, and patterns of behavior or the mores will be different for the students on each campus, these patterns being conditioned by the past history and particular culture of the college concerned.

If a college is strongly conditioned by the past, many customs, traditions, and beliefs will be handed down from generation to generation.

Also, a college is conditioned psychologically. It is an area of local association, and is made up of a group of people in primary, personal, face-to-face contacts. Because of this particular cultural conditioning, one college may develop a well-integrated program and a homogeneous structure; another may be disintegrated and heterogeneous; another may be heterogeneous, yet closely integrated. The students in one college may have the attitude that the college "owes them a living"; in another, the students may feel that they owe the college every ounce of effort that they can contribute. A pattern of individualism may flourish on one campus, a pattern of conformity on another; a pattern of liberality on one, and a pattern of conservatism on another; a pattern of cooperation on one, and non-cooperation on another. Also, in any campus life, students are influenced by pressures from the outside—the influence of alumni, of the local town, of national organizations, of the wider culture—all of which interrelate with the campus life and exert social control on student patterns.

FORMATION BY CULTURAL CONTROLS AND PROCESSES

How are mores established and handed down? Sociologists state that mores are formed by ritual, by ceremonies, by various forms of control—the element of force, indoctrinations, coercions, or selective mechanisms. They are also developed through group interests. No single cause can be assigned to explain the way mores form. New faculty, new administration, new elements in the student body, policies of administration, individual culture of students—all bring into being and continue to influence the changeful fabric of college society. The cultural processes of change, such as invention, imitation, innovation, and diffusion, likewise bring new mores into a college social system. In every college community before change takes place, one can observe a patterning of culture, that is, characteristic schemes of social relationships, and institutional complexes. The social scheme, in brief, is closely tied with the dominant cultural pattern.

Although the process of making folkways and establishing mores is going on all the time, it is difficult to analyze. The personalities on a college campus, in their efforts to maintain status, each struggling unconsciously to satisfy his own human needs and desires, inevitably bring about, according to Sumner's position, ". . . mutual reactions (antagonisms, rivalries, alliances, coercions, and cooperations) . . . From these result configurations in a college community, i.e., more or less fixed positions of individuals and subgroups towards each other with more or less established methods of interaction between them." [10]

Among the processes by which mores may be formed are: (1) competition, which may lead to a whole prestige system; (2) conflict, in which the more dominant are likely to prevail; (3) assimilation built up through various coercions; (4) exploitation, in which the more dominant groups take advantage of the weaker; or (5) differentiation, as is shown by selective mechanisms, such as social stratification. Personalities, however, often cooperate to build up associations, organizations, customs, and institutions which appear full-grown, although no one intended or planned them so in advance. Every action of every individual in the college community fixes an atom in this structure; the structure thus built up becomes societal and institutional. Sumner says of this structure that "It is a category in which custom produces continuity, coherence, and consistency. . . ."[11]

Continuity, coherence, and consistency are therefore characteristics of the mores. According to sociologists, the mores have also a persistency which shows inertia and a rigidity against social change. On the other hand, they have variability, inasmuch as they are not perpetuated just as they are received. Conditions of student living on a campus change, and interests change. Although the mores do have a degree of firmness, they are flexible enough to conform to changes in the interests and life conditions of students on the campus. Errors sometimes enter into the mores and become a part of them. In the main, the mores have the authority of facts; they come down from the past and each individual is born into them. They are unformulated and undefined, but nevertheless exert a force as strong as written law.

10 Sumner, *op. cit.*, p. 34.
11 *Ibid.*, p. 35.

How Do the Mores Change?

Growth and change on a college campus take place through a strange mélange of cultural processes. Some of these processes will be developed in the following pages.

DISCOVERY AND INVENTION

Linton writes that discovery and invention are

. . . the obvious starting points for any study of cultural growth and change, since it is only by these processes that new elements can be added to the total content of man's culture. . . . Every culture element can ultimately be traced to a discovery or invention, or to a more or less complex combination of various discoveries and inventions which arose at a particular time and place.[12]

The football movement is an outstanding example of a cultural pattern which has been shaped by the process of discovery and invention in the college world. Inventions were made as the game progressed; rules were invented and skill became relative to the game's cultural pattern. As Waller notes:

It is interesting, too, that a "form" which is partly cultural comes to reside in every feature of competitive athletics. . . . It is possible that an athlete, by long practice, might develop this form through trial and error and the gradual removal of imperfections in his performance. But it is more likely that the athlete gets this form through cultural diffusion.[13]

Form in athletics has a cultural character in that it may represent the accumulated improvements and inventions in technique of many generations of athletes.

Morison has given something further on the inventions and cultural development in the football game at Harvard in the early nineteenth century:

Early in the century the primitive game of football was played informally in the "play-place," . . . By 1820 there was class football, for which every red-blooded freshman turned out the first evening of

---

[12] Linton, *op. cit.*, p. 304.
[13] Willard Waller, *The Sociology of Teaching*, p. 113. Copyright, 1932, by John Wiley and Sons, Inc.

the college years, to maintain the prowess of his class against the sophomores; and for weeks the battle continued, the ball being put in play
at the noon hour, and kept very much in play until the commons bell
tolled at twelve-thirty.[14]

The spontaneous growth of athletics was the most astounding phenomenon of student life to the old-timers in the first fifteen years of
Eliot's administration. . . . The old rough-and-tumble football games
between freshmen and sophomores were forbidden in 1860; "Boston
football," a new game, began to be played by class teams in 1871. . . .
A committee . . . proceeded to codify the rules that had grown up
more or less spontaneously in Boston schoolboy tests. These rules were
somewhat like those of English Rugby; but in the meantime Yale,
Columbia, and other colleges were developing a rudimentary soccer.
It was a toss-up which would become the American game until 1872,
when the Harvard University Football Club received a challenge from
the Football Club of McGill University to play a series of Rugby
matches; and it was agreed that the first should be under the Harvard
rules, and the second under McGill's modified English Rugby rules.
. . . Originally there were to be fifteen men on a side, but the number
was reduced to eleven men because four of the McGill men were unable
to leave Montreal. . . . Harvard contributed some "plays" unknown
to English Rugby, which enabled them to win the first match. . . . A
return match which the Harvard University Football Club played at
Montreal weaned Harvard from her peculiar Boston rules to the game
from which American football has developed.[15]

Morison goes on to say that in the Harvard-Yale football game of
1882 every Yale man was threatened with disqualification for foul
tackling:

This "fouling the backs" complained of was the beginning of interference; but Harvard had no right to "kick" because her initial victory over McGill had been won by springing new plays that were
neither forbidden nor anticipated by the Ruby rules.[16]

Football was a constant subject of discussion among alumni, students, and the Governing Boards; . . . a determined effort was made
to change the rules of play and eligibility. In 1906, freshmen, special
students and students in the graduate and professional schools were
first barred from varsity teams and crews; and the "new football" be-

[14] Reprinted by permission of the publishers from Samuel Eliot Morison, *Three
Centuries of Harvard, 1636–1936.* Cambridge, Mass.: Harvard University Press, 1936.
p. 206.
[15] *Ibid.,* p. 404–405.
[16] *Ibid.,* p. 406,

gan. . . . Percy D. Haughton as head coach built up a football machine that in the next twelve years of play gave us eight victories over Yale. . . .[17]

The growth of athletics tended to integrate college life in the Eliot era; participation in them, both as players and as managers, brought together men of the widest social origins, and victory over Yale in the four "major" sports of football, rowing, baseball, and track was something that the entire College prayed for.[18]

Thus football through a series of innovations and inventions in each particular college, and diffusion from college to college, became a great social institution in the college world. We see from its development and innovations at Harvard that down through the years it met a great need of the students for social and recreational life. It acquired form and meaning and performed an important integrative function in the college culture complex, bringing about an interaction of personalities not only in the student realm, but also on the faculty-administrative-governing board levels, in the local community, and in the outside culture.

Invention on the part of the students may, however, take the form of a new social technique, origination of a new group, or introduction of a new custom. Slosson in the early twentieth century writes concerning invention in the campus culture of Leland Stanford University, which took the form of the introduction of new customs:

The first students of Stanford . . . realized that the University was short on history by one or two hundred years, so they set themselves to inventing student customs and manufacturing traditions. . . . The sombrero and corduroys affected by the Senior men are picturesque, convenient, and indigenous. . . . The headgear of the Juniors, the Plug-uglies, shows an interesting development from the merely grotesque to the artistic and significant, reminding one of the evolution of imagery in primitive religions. . . . Year by year the stiff white hats are more elaborately painted in colors according to the taste, or, in the absence of taste, the caprice of the wearer; sometimes becoming veritable totem poles, epitomizing in symbol and legend his entire academic career, his fraternity, his athletic and scholastic triumphs, his adventures, and his ambitions.[19]

[17] *Ibid.*, p. 413–414.
[18] *Ibid.*, p. 415.
[19] From Edwin E. Slosson, *Great American Universities*. Copyright, 1910, by The Independent and The Macmillan Company and used with permission. p. 136.

Slosson further hoped that the Stanford Museum was not neglecting to acquire some specimens of these hats, for they would be useful material for the anthropologist as well as the college historian of the future.

Competitions between classes and groups on a college campus are often the setting for the invention of new social techniques. Competition between fraternity groups for political power may result in more democratic processes of voting. A novel social event, or a novel way of staging a social event, sometimes acquires permanent form and meaning and remains a custom to be handed down. The invention will be disregarded, however, unless it serves some function in the college culture complex. Thus culture exerts upon invention the influence of selection. The same things are invented again and again, and rejected again and again, until changes in the culture continuum have prepared a place for them. Invention, more than any other phenomenon on a campus, is a response arising to certain needs. To ascertain, therefore, which needs stimulate students to invent becomes important. Usually inventions come about through students who are discontented with the *status quo;* the dissatisfactions may be due to lack of prestige or subjection to inferior status. The inability of a neurotic student to cope with the cultural situation results in certain types of inventive, creative behavior. The inventor receives the highest degree of recognition and reward in a crisis situation in a college community, such as a student strike against the dismissal of a president whom they like very much. To be sure, this process of invention is often unconscious on the part of students; sometimes students add to the content of the culture without any realization of the unmet needs and largely without any feeling that they are doing so.

DIFFUSION

Another cultural process that brings about change in the mores of a student body is diffusion. An invention takes place on a campus, let us say in the form of a custom or a new group. Through visiting teams, conferences, and exchange of campus newspapers, the custom spreads and becomes diffused on other campuses. It is rarely ever reproduced in the exact form and never with the exact meaning. Again, the diffusion will depend upon the possibilities a student body sees in the new idea or invention on their campus. For example, a denominational college may accept the cheer of a large university without its "swear words." A custom at Vassar during the commencement ceremonies is the "Daisy Chain," in which the best-looking sophomore girls take part. By coming in contact with the custom or hearing about it, many colleges have adopted something similar. Diffusion of customs and ideas may be effected by a personality within the college culture, whether student, faculty member, or administrator. An Eastern personnel worker entering a Western university could not see the great difference which is supposed to exist between colleges of these two regions. Upon investigation she found that the early history of the Western college in question was closely associated with an Eastern group of professors, and through a diffusion of ideas the Eastern influence had made its imprint on the Western college culture.

Diffusion, like invention, on college campuses sometimes takes place without any realization on the part of members that they are contributing new ideas to the campus and effecting a change.

BORROWING

What customs and new ideas one college consciously borrows from another, or one group on a particular college campus borrows from another group, depend upon what each college as a whole or each group within a college *allows* to be borrowed. In the contact of two groups with different customs and traditions, the dominance of one over the other may be practical or psychological. Practical dominance will take place, depending upon the rewards the group or campus will achieve as a result of borrowing. If new elements are of high prestige in their culture, they are likely to adopt them. Practical dominance on a college campus may be illustrated by the reactions to the changes which President Lowell of Harvard advocated after the Eliot regime. One change was the tutor system, which caused much discontent among the students and alumni because, having been conditioned by the freedom of the Eliot era, they felt that this new system was a step backward. The practical dominance, however, achieved by students in obtaining honors at graduation because of the increased reading under tutors' direction made the system better liked and more possible for adoption in the Harvard culture.

Psychological dominance implies recognition of cultural inferiority on the part of a group which at the same time recognizes the superiority of some other group. As an example of psychological dominance, in an Eastern college there were two well-defined student groups—one specializing in art education, the other in elementary and secondary general education. The latter group recognized its cultural inferiority, and very often wished to be "like" or "up to" the other group and frequently tried to adopt its novelty and creativity.

This process of borrowing is usually adopted by those who are innovators. The innovator differs from the inventor in that he popularizes within his own group campus inventions that have previously been made in other groups. He introduces and promotes these new elements in the culture-matrix of the group to which he belongs. With the innovators, there are the followers who merely imitate, but who also help to bring about change in campus life. Tardé speaks of two kinds of imitation: (1) imitation from within to without and (2) imitation of the superior by the inferior.[20] The student has his own inner value-system, his own ideas, his old wants and old needs which are continually operating. He is led to copy from others everything that seems to him to be a new means of attaining his old ends or of satisfying his old wants, or of giving new expression to his old ideas; and while he copies he begins to adopt innovations which awaken in him *new* ideas and *new* goals. With regard to imitation of the superior, the thing that is most imitated is that which is in highest prestige or seems to be a move toward practicality on the campus. That is, the innovation may so well fit some need that to go on without it would not seem practical. Again students or personalities on the campus who are innovators may have such prestige that not to follow them would make other students seem inferior.

Blake's article on why college girls dress as they do presents rather forcibly the laws of imitation. This article suggests that perhaps campus sloppiness may be a relic from the days when many college girls dreamed of the idea of living on the Left Bank

[20] Gabriel Tardé, *Laws of Imitation*, p. 207.

in Paris and "going Bohemian." Today, in a more "domesticated" age, they can still feel like people-who-don't-care and can live in an atmosphere of delightful bohemianism. It's fun to look outwardly like an intellectual, like an artist, or like a pauper—declares the writer of this article—particularly when you're none of these things.[21]

To come back to the basic thesis—mores are "the ways of doing things to satisfy their needs"—these dress mores of social exhibitionism on a college campus, which are designed to startle those of the out-group, seem to be used to satisfy the old needs of security, of confidence in oneself, and the need for social recognition. The college girl not only has the instability of her adolescence but competes with hundreds of other girls. Blake further relates that college girls only exchange one "hideous" stereotype for another; blue serge was compulsory at their private preparatory school; but blue jeans are worn in college with glee.[22]

WHO CHANGES THE MORES?

It is important, then, for personnel workers to study who the innovators are, where their ideas come from, what is the extent of receptivity, what groups accept, whether all members of the group accept the new element of change, and what the elements are that are accepted. The way in which new elements disseminate is important to observe: to what categories—age group, sex, occupation, interest—are they disseminated? In this connection, two studies of significance for personnel workers may be cited.

Janney[23] endeavored to discover the social position that the imitators of fads occupy among their fellows, whether different types of fads are initiated by different persons, whether any differential classification is possible among those who do not initiate but follow fads, and what is the social position of those who are insensitive to fads.

A longitudinal observation and item analysis of sixty-seven clothing fads occurring among 279 undergraduate women seemed

21 Patricia Blake, "Why College Girls Dress That Way," *New York Times Magazine*, 95 : 23, April 7, 1946.
22 *Ibid.*, p. 23.
23 J. E. Janney, "Fad and Fashion Leadership Among Undergraduate Women," *Journal of Abnormal and Social Psychology*, 36 : 278, April 1941.

to indicate that fads do not occur in a random manner, and that those followed are originated by young women who are members of prestige-bearing cliques and are leaders in various types of activities, particularly choreography, design, decoration. Janney's observation further indicates that the cliques in which fads are tried out may show differences in types of fads—differences which may be congruent to the different types of social activity in which the clique engages. Also, the overwhelming majority of young women studied not only did not originate fads but were several weeks late in following any of them. Those young women who are insensitive to fads were found to be unskillful in other types of social situations also. Consistent "dowdiness" may be a symptom of unsocialization, but academic standing, intelligence, athletic participation, financial income, and health fail to differentiate any of the patterns reported in Janney's paper.

Newcomb in a study (1935–1939) of attitude formation at Bennington College found some results which are of importance in reviewing the role of invention, innovation, and imitation on a college campus.

Bennington College, founded in 1932, was an experiment, an innovation in the new educational movement of liberalism. Its faculty members were young, not more than two or three members over forty, and none over fifty, most of them selected for their capacity for working well in a community relationship as well as for their professional qualifications. The student body came from schools where they had had to face, with varying degrees of success, the problem of achieving independent personal status, and from homes in which they were well protected. They entered into a college community where they were given an unprecedented degree of personal freedom and responsibility, where there was much pressure to consider contemporary public issues, where there was a highly intelligent college faculty and students whom they were expected to imitate in order to develop less conservative thinking.

With regard to which group will accept new ideas, the extent of their receptivity, among which categories of individuals the new ideas are disseminated, the degree of awareness or unawareness of prestige characteristics and which types of personalities imitate and accept, and which do not, Newcomb found the following facts from his study of college community influence upon attitudes:

Those most susceptible were characterized by habits of conformity, with varying degrees of passivity or personal initiative. The more passive among them had fewer social skills and lower social ambitions. The more aggressive among them had greater social skills and ambitions. Attitude change was to them an aspect of the responsibility that goes with leadership. . . . Those who were little or not at all susceptible to community influences upon attitudes were characterized by negativism, by indifference, or by divided allegiance toward the community. Habits of negativism were in some cases of precollege standing, and in others represented a reaction to frustrated hopes of social success in college, following some measure of precollege success.[24]

Habits of indifference were in nearly every case traceable to feelings of inferiority accompanied either by a strong dependence upon parents, by engrossment with a very limited circle of friends, or by absorption in academic work.[25]

Many kinds of evidence conspire to suggest that each campus has its own brand of conservatism, of which freshmen have more and seniors less. . . . Whatever the content of the term 'conservatism', those who show it least on any given campus tend to make higher scores on intelligence tests, or to make better scholastic records, or both, than those who show it most.[26]

In short, faculty members of college communities tend to have most prestige and to be least conservative; freshmen tend both to have least prestige and to be most conservative. All this is tantamount to saying that the Bennington Community is not, after all, so very different from other college communities, except, perhaps, in degree. There is, however, one sort of difference of great importance. If, in most other colleges as in Bennington, the order both of nonconservatism and of status and influence is from faculty to upperclass students to freshmen, there is less awareness of the differences in degree of conservatism in the other colleges.[27]

To return to what has been mentioned as motives for imitation, namely, practicability or prestige, it would seem from Newcomb's

24 Theodore Newcomb, *Personality and Social Change,* p. 155. Copyright, 1943, by The Dryden Press, New York. Reprinted by permission of the author.
25 *Ibid.,* p. 156.
26 *Ibid.,* p. 171.
27 *Ibid.,* p. 172.

study that there is in most contemporary American colleges an under-awareness of the degree to which non-conservatism actually is characteristic of those having most prestige. This under-awareness affects student mores. Also, from Newcomb's analysis, we can observe how attitudes, personality, and the mores of home culture influence students; similarly, how the personalities and attitudes of teachers can transform the mores of a student body.

The power of tradition, inherent in the mores of college students, has exerted great social control. Tradition, in most colleges, has bequeathed certain symbols of sophistication to distinguish upperclassmen from freshmen, such as "wearing cords" by senior men, using canes, the privilege of certain paths on the campus, but non-conservatism has not been one of them in most colleges. Newcomb also mentions sophistication as a tradition in most colleges and proposes the following reason:

Perhaps, incidentally, one reason why nonconservatism is included among the marks of senior sophistication at Bennington is that the college, which first opened its doors during the depths of the economic depression of the 1930's, is too young to share in the contrary tradition.[28]

Newcomb more than once suggests that the unusual degree of liberalization which is found in the Bennington student body can be traced, originally at least, to faculty attitudes. Here again, one sees the motive behind imitation, viz., prestige, functioning in a marked way. The faculty are superior in the minds of students, so their attitudes are worthy of imitation; further proof is afforded from the fact that seniors are more non-conservative than freshmen, which can undoubtedly be explained by the fact that seniors have had more contact with their professors and have learned more about conditions causing social change. Further, according to Newcomb's study, those upperclassmen who participate most actively in discussions and activities tend to have most status and influence. This situation corroborates Tardé's two laws of imitation already mentioned, viz., imitation from within to without and imitation of superior by inferior. At the same time that students adopted as their inner ideas the non-conservative ideas of the faculty, they also made adaptation by expressing their ideas out-

[28] *Ibid.,* p. 174.

wardly in activities. This experience in turn gave them prestige in the eyes of their underclassmen.

It can be presumed from Newcomb's study that comparable adaptations can be made in most other contemporary American colleges if there is common awareness within the college communities of the significance of contemporary social trends. One might therefore conclude that greater emphasis in our colleges should be upon problems of contemporary social change. This emphasis should be brought about not only by formal class discussions but by ensuring that students are sufficiently conscious of the significance of these problems to want to express themselves overtly in activities. This expression is an important factor in changing mores. Overt expression of a constructive idea in an activity facilitates change.

Another type of change is labeled "compulsory." Compulsory changes of customs and mores on a college campus by administrative fiat frequently come about through a severe crisis or other precipitant. For example, all hazing practices may be abolished entirely by administrative dictum after a freshman has been accidentally killed or has developed a lingering illness because of the experiences he was subjected to in the hazing process. An overt change of behavior may occur because of administrative fiat or student pressure which will very soon change a whole ideology. At Swarthmore College student pressure against the snobbishness of fraternities and sororities brought about their abolition, and, consequently, a more democratic campus; changes in this college also illustrate how a disturbance in one element of culture brought about a profound change in the whole culture-matrix. There is a functional interrelation between culture factors, and the disturbance of any one element can have a profound effect on the total culture.

As to revival of certain elements in the college culture from time to time and change occurring according to patterns and periodicity of swings, Morgan states, concerning student religion,[29] that in the period 1877–1890 the primary objective was to secure personal commitment to the Christian life, and one's readiness to

[29] W. H. Morgan, *Student Religion During Fifty Years*, pp. 197–208. Copyright, 1935, by Association Press.

be a foreign missionary was deemed essential as evidence of conse-
cration. In the period 1890–1910 there was greater emphasis on
mass evangelism. Although the Y.M.C.A. continued to encourage
students to be active in the parish church of the college town, it
also developed its own program to reach more students on the
assumption that the college constituted a community and student
grouping was essential. The period 1910–1917 reflected the influence of a rising social-educational consciousness. An effort was
made to have alumni continue their social activities after college
and to become consecrated to social evangelism. This was much
more of a group approach.

During World War I (1917–1918), there was a return of emphasis on personal religion, a "swing-back" to the period of 1877–
1890. Renewed emphasis was given to recruiting workers for the
foreign-missionary program. Similarly, from 1919 to 1930 there
was a period of diversified educational approaches to social problems and issues in student life, and a "swing-back" to the period of
1890–1910. Emphasis was on the development of a program concerned with the prevailing complex conditions on the campus,
with an examination of the moral assumptions underlying student
behavior, with democratic processes for counseling students on
personal questions, and with a democratic approach to the changing of social attitudes.

In conclusion, the cultural processes of invention and discovery,
innovation and imitation, as well as diffusion and integration, continuously shape and reshape campus life. It is increasingly important that personnel workers and educators understand these cultural processes of change which affect student life on their campus.
Not only should they be aware of them but they should use these
forces consciously for constructive purposes.

It is only as new elements of change have *meaning* for a particular campus that they can be completely integrated into the pattern.
Sometimes a new personnel worker wants to change undesirable
customs too quickly. She has not lived in the college culture long
enough to *know the meaning* to the students of some of the cultural demonstrations on the campus. She has not lived there long
enough to have become a member of the "in-group." She may have

come from another section of the country, from another college which makes her unable to understand what the customs of this college mean. It would seem to her that the student needs of her former campus should be the needs of her present campus. Generally speaking, to be effective, the idea of a change in the mores should be shared by established members of a culture, and further, as the Bennington study indicates, if a change is to be effective on the total culture, administration, faculty, and students must all desire and be led to see that it is necessary. Also, the interpersonal bonds between these persons in a college community are by far the greatest force for altering attitudes.

Rather than issue an administrative fiat, social behavior should be studied from the point of view of personality, character, needs, and the underlying meaning that this particular sort of behavior implies. Growth and change, as explained earlier, are inherent in a college culture. Educators must therefore study the processes of change and what they mean on the campus.

Do the Mores Control Student Life on a College Campus?

Hollingshead believes that "The essence of social control is to be sought in the organization of a people."[30] This position assumes that "Society is composed of the interrelations among persons acting within the confines of the rules, regulations, practices, and beliefs common to their culture."[30] From this definition of social control and from the previous development of the scope of the mores, one can deduce that the essence of control on the campus lies in its mores. A college community is organized, as any other type of community, in a way peculiar to its needs; it is organized according to certain value-systems, and has certain folkways, usages, and customs. Interrelations develop within confines of the rules, regulations, and beliefs common to a college community's culture. Organization also implies structure and ways of living in a group. Therefore, organization reveals the mores.

If one understands the mores of the culture, one sees how they

[30] A. B. Hollingshead, "The Concept of Social Control," *American Sociological Review*, 6 : 220, April 1941.

exert a social control on student life on a campus. If the mores cover the totality of human interests, if they are the whole configuration, as authorities assert, then one can understand something of their scope as factors of control on a campus. The writer holds to the belief that the whole social control of a campus lies in the multifarious working of the mores.

Whither the Mores?

During the present period of unusual unrest and confusion after the second World War, a period of great social transition and reconstruction, it is important to reassess and re-evaluate the mores of the college world. The American college is witnessing the greatest influx of students to the campus that has ever taken place; it is experiencing a great heterogeneity of student clientele; it is offering these many different types of students the greatest challenge for the optimum development of their potentialities.

For some years an evaluation of the *educational process* has been taking place. Educators have recognized that certain social controls affect this process. There seems to be no better time in the history of the college than the present to provide an analysis of how the mores affect social control of student life on the campus. The college has entered a new age in its history: it is building a new culture which will be conditioned by the values and the moral commitments of the people within the college community today.

If the mores are ways of doing things to satisfy human needs, will the new heterogeneous student bodies have the same needs? Or, if they have the same needs, will the usual ways of doing things be satisfactory in meeting them? What sort of group relationships will evolve? What social ritual will they be interested in? What kind of inventions and diffusions will take place? Will established traditions endure? Will established mores become flexible enough to meet the needs of the new generations of students? If its mores are the *living* character of a group, it is obvious that the campus will undergo a change. The stage is now being set. What do educators, faculty, and students want the living character of the new college community to be? How will a new superstructure of mores be erected?

It would seem that *now*, when change on the American college campus is imperative, is a most appropriate time to analyze college mores: how they arise, how they function, and how they might contribute social control in the inevitable reconstruction of student life.

The following chapter gives an analysis of the campus as a culture-matrix and shows how the mores of a student body arise from, function in, and are a product of the various interactive elements of the culture of a college community.

Bibliography

Blake, Patricia. "Why College Girls Dress That Way." *New York Times Magazine*, 95 : 23, April 7, 1946.

Chapin, Francis Stuart. *Contemporary American Institutions*. New York: Harper and Brothers, 1935. 423 p.

Hollingshead, A. B. "The Concept of Social Control." *American Sociological Review*, 6 : 216–224, April 1941.

Janney, J. E. "Fad and Fashion Leadership Among Undergraduate Women." *Journal of Abnormal and Social Psychology*, 36 : 275–278, April 1941.

Linton, Ralph. *The Cultural Background of Personality*. New York: D. Appleton-Century Company, Inc., 1945. 157 p.

Linton, Ralph. *The Study of Man*. New York: D. Appleton-Century Company, Inc., 1936. 503 p.

MacIver, R. M. *Community, A Sociological Study*. New York: The Macmillan Company, 1928, 1931. 446 p.

MacIver, R. M. *Society, Its Structure and Changes*. New York: Ray Long and Richard R. Smith, Inc., 1931. 569 p.

MacIver, R. M. *Social Causation*. Boston: Ginn and Company, 1942. 414 p.

Malinowski, Bronislaw. *A Scientific Theory of Culture and Other Essays*. Chapel Hill: The University of North Carolina Press, 1944. 228 p.

Mead, G. H. *Mind, Self, and Society*. Chicago: The University of Chicago Press, 1934. 400 p.

Morgan, W. H. *Student Religion During Fifty Years. Programs and Policies of the Intercollegiate Y.M.C.A.* New York: Association Press, 1935. 233 p.

Morison, Samuel Eliot. *Three Centuries of Harvard, 1636–1936*. Cambridge: Harvard University Press, 1936. 512 p.

Newcomb, T. M. *Personality and Social Change*. New York: Dryden Press, 1943. 225 p.

Prescott, Daniel Alfred. *Emotion and the Educative Process*. Washington, D. C.: American Council on Education, 1938. 323 p.

Slosson, Edwin E. *Great American Universities*. New York: The Macmillan Company, 1910. 575 p.

Sumner, William G. *Folkways.* Boston: Ginn and Company, 1906. 692 p.

Tardé, Gabriel. *Laws of Imitation.* New York: Henry Holt and Company, 1903. 404 p.

Thomas, W. I. and Znaniecki, Florian. *The Polish Peasant in Europe and America.* Second Edition. New York: Knopf Company, 1927. 2 vols.

Waller, Willard. *The Sociology of Teaching.* New York: J. Wiley and Sons, Inc., 1932. 467 p.

Young, Kimball. *Social Psychology.* New York: F. S. Crofts and Company, Inc., 1946. 558 p.

II

THE COLLEGE AS A CULTURE-MATRIX

Roucek states that "While the most remote areas of the globe have been combed in the attempt to ferret out and place under the microscope hidden and practically forgotten culture patterns, the rich possibilities inherent in the compact contemporary American college and university have as yet been largely neglected."[1] The work of Waller, Strang, E. Hartshorne, Cowley, Angell, Warren, Lloyd-Jones, Price, Edwards, Artman, and Fisher, and a few others, in addition to several analyses of one particular group, the college fraternity, constitutes the major part of the material now available. Cowley and Waller have pointed out some especially interesting points which facilitate a study of the culture of the college: the college period is but four years long, the ancestors of each generation remain a part of the particular culture pattern as alumni, and the college community is a smaller and better defined group than most groups that are available for analysis.[2]

An understanding of the culture-matrix of the college in which one is serving leads definitely to a better understanding of "student ways of doing things" on that campus. An attempt is made here to show that an understanding of three interactive elements in a college culture complex is essential in working with the student mores of a campus: first, the culture which the student brings to the campus; second, the traditional and established culture of the college community; third, the material structure and physical equipment on a college campus.

[1] Joseph Roucek, *Sociological Foundations of Education,* p. 503. Copyright, 1942, by Thomas Y. Crowell Company.
[2] W. H. Cowley and Willard Waller, "A Study of Student Life," *Journal of Higher Education,* 6: 133, March 1935. Reprinted with permission of The Journal.

Since the traditional and established culture of the college community can arise through both the administration and the students, it is treated therefore from the point of view of administrative mores and student mores. In the established culture of the college community, the social heritage as revealed by traditions, folkways, and customs is first described as sources of social control of student life. A descriptive treatment of traditions is developed along the following lines: tradition which comes entirely or almost entirely from the outside; tradition which is in part from the outside and in part indigenous; and tradition which is almost entirely indigenous to a college community. Similarly, since mores in the traditional and established culture of the college indicate to a great extent the element of force, the second part of the section is devoted to a treatment of further sources of mores of control.

The Culture Which the Student Brings

The culture which the student brings presents first of all an important angle for study, for here are cultural norms of many different types. The rural students frequently fit their patterns close to rural life. The commuting students adjust to the pattern of their families. What is the composition pattern of the student body? Is it the grandfather-son-grandson pattern? Is there a pattern of the region from which the students come? If so, what political and religious influences did they bring with them? What are the interests in composition patterns which pull the campus together, or draw it apart? Sherif has shown that

. . . in the course of the life history of the individual and as a consequence of his contact with the social world around him, the social norms, customs, values, etc., become interiorized in him. These interiorized social norms enter as frames of reference among other factors in situations to which they are related, and thus dominate or modify the person's experience and subsequent behavior in concrete situations.[3]

This statement has meaning for the college culture and the college personnel staff. Because of the differing social norms of a

[3] Muzafer Sherif, *The Psychology of Social Norms,* p. 43–44. Copyright, 1936, by Harper and Brothers.

student group, acquired from family, home, and local groups, the college may expect crises in group-life which will periodically interrupt its traditional or habitual flow of life. Change in conditions may arise from the interaction of differing social norms. How to gain control after a disturbance is important to study. How was equilibrium established? Which individuals emerged as leaders?

A former student of a large cosmopolitan city college who later served as a personnel worker on its staff remarked to the writer: "The cultural factors in our college which make student life less enjoyable and thus affect academic work are extreme parental domination, apartment house living, traveling to and from college, a low socio-economic level, and the fact that a majority of the students are from a minority culture in society." Traveling to and from college in many cases requires a full hour or more; many of the students are not physically able to stand it. The size of the apartment in which they live looms large as a problem because of its lack of space for adequate study habits. Having little money to spend makes them very conscious of their use of it. The difficulty of a minority group in achieving prestige and status in a society is well known. There is nothing, however, in the college mores to bring home to a student that he represents a minority group. The personnel worker believed that students in this college should be led to develop more understanding in meeting the problems of a minority group in the outside culture. He felt the students representing minority groups in our culture should thoroughly understand their own and others' attitudes and know why people behave as they do. The composition of a student body thus plays an important role in conditioning college culture.

A personnel worker from another cosmopolitan college in a large city remarked: "As to the culture strains which the students bring with them, there are the mores of different races and nationalities, the socio-economic mores of the laborite class from which most of our students come. Outside pressures constantly try to exercise influence on the student body; consequently, the personnel staff constantly works at freeing students from the outside pressure of the community in which they live, from family culture and domination."

Another example of the influence of the culture which the students bring is drawn from a denominational college. The personnel worker from this college stated: "The young ministers of the campus, coming, in the main, from rural, conservative backgrounds, try to influence the campus. In the spring of 1946 quite a competition arose between them and the returned veterans for positions on the campus. The girls, many of whom were also from rural backgrounds, became interested and nominated the GI's for all positions while the ministerial students nominated their own delegates. The GI's won most of the posts." The worker went on to explain that it also was customary to have freshman initiation on this campus but the ministerial students urged freshmen not to enter into or carry out the commands of the initiating committee. They felt these were not democratic practices. Their interference caused quite a commotion on the campus. The personnel worker interviewed started discussion groups on some of these subjects and felt that, as a result, more tolerance resulted on both sides and better social intelligence developed among the rural ministerial group.

Another incident in this college which brings out more clearly the mores of the culture was the desire on the part of the rural ministerial students to observe days or periods of fasting in order to contribute to the World Student Service Fund. They petitioned the president with biblical reference in hand to give back to them the amount of their food tuition for a number of weeks in which they would fast; the money could then be handed over to the WSS Fund. The president, liberal in attitude, tried to speak to them from the standpoint of their health but finally convinced them in terms of their own religious scruples that they were violating the religious tenet of "letting not thy left hand know what thy right hand doeth." The college community would all know about the fasting. The president suggested that instead the students do part-time work on the campus until the amount of money they wished to raise was accumulated. The personnel worker spoke of how difficult it was to reach this group, saying that they "stick to themselves" much of the time and become "ingrown in their thinking."

These students, having been ministers and conscientious objectors during the war period, were, one might say, "on the spot among the GI's." However, the need for security, recognition, and response—essential needs of all young people—seems to be represented in this incident. These ministers apparently need to feel superior, they must gain prestige from fasting so that their contributions will be recognized and the particular ways of meeting their needs arising out of the mores of the family, church, and locality from which they come may also be recognized.

Many personnel workers, particularly those in small colleges whose students come from rural and small-town backgrounds, describe the strong home pattern that influences their students. In one such college for women, a vast majority of the students go home over week-ends; on closed week-ends parents come to visit their daughters. Rooms and roommates are a source of anxiety to parents. There is also the grandmother-mother-daughter pattern and much "homesickness." Mothers usually are quite concerned about living conditions, about food, about rules and regulations, and, in general, about having their daughters "looked after and supervised."

Jameson,[4] in his study at the University of Oregon concerning the adjustment problems encountered during the first year on the campus by 571 girls, found four problems to be outstanding: homesickness, parental precaution, parental domination, and incompatibility with parental views. Incompatibilities between the modes of behavior of the diversified types of parents on the one hand and the stratified educational institutional modes of behavior on the other nourished the root of maladjustment manifested by these university girls. This is an excellent example of two conflicting social units in the mores of the college culture. It would seem from Jameson's findings that the student not only brings himself into a new culture when he or she enters college, but also brings his parents.

To suggest here some things that are done to meet this problem in a large city college may be of some value. At this particular college the student council traditionally entertains high school seniors and their parents. Pride in parents and at the same time a

4 Samuel Haig Jameson, "Adjustment Problems of University Girls Because of Parental Patterns," *Sociology and Social Research*, 24 : 262–271, January–February 1940.

certain independence from parents are manifest on this campus and have come about through an educational process. During the school year an eight-session parent institute is held for the parents of freshman students, the purpose being to orient the parents to the life of the campus. When they see all the activities that go on throughout the campus they are more understanding and willing to sacrifice the time of their sons and daughters in order to have them participate in these activities rather than perform duties at home or carry a part-time working job. The parents ask questions and forums are held. A well-developed freshman orientation program is also carried on with the incoming students.

It must be remembered, however, that it is not altogether a matter of parental influence and domination which the student brings to college. The student brings himself—his own value-system, developed from the experiences and influences of all the groups with which he has come in contact. Out of it he has set up certain ideals—certain aspirations concerning what he wants to be. He may be seeking, through a college education, a higher social status and an opportunity to escape from his social class.

Warner, Havighurst, and Loeb have stressed this fact:

The college dean or college president needs to understand the part that social status and social mobility play in the lives of his students. He may be dealing with students who come from middle- and upper-class families and are assured of maintaining their status. Or he may be dealing with the lower-class students who are working to rise in the social scale. Or he may have both types of student on his campus. Especially in the guidance and advisory program of the college should these matters be considered. No student can be helped by a counselor if he is thought of merely as a combination of abilities. His social past and his social goals must come in for consideration. The college administrator should have a clear picture of where his institution fits into the social system, what social groups it serves, and how it can serve these groups in promoting democracy and social solidarity.[5]

Students should have some of this understanding, too, so that a readjustment of the mores on the campus will be intelligently and consciously studied for the greatest opportunities for democratic social life.

[5] W. L. Warner, R. J. Havighurst, and Martin B. Loeb, *Who Shall Be Educated?* p. 168–169. Copyright, 1944, by Harper and Brothers.

Every personnel worker, teacher, and educator should look out, as did the teacher in *Who Shall Be Educated?*,[6] at the student body and study the sociological characteristics of each one—how students who have different sociological backgrounds and training act, how they intermingle, what they strive for, and how they achieve happiness—or sometimes unhappiness—on the college campus.

IMPLICATIONS FOR PERSONNEL WORKERS
AND EDUCATORS

In this discussion of the culture which the student brings to college, it should be clear that a knowledge of the composition pattern of student bodies is essential to an understanding of the mores. The geographical districts from which students come, the ancestor patterns, family culture, parental domination, socio-economic level, minority cultures represented, racial patterns, and other mores of the culture from which they come are all factors in understanding a student body and in creating the best adjustments for each student. The basic needs of young people for response, recognition, and security are evident in the "ways of doing things" and are often evident in a manner peculiar to the family and community cultural patterns which have become a part of them.

One must work *with* student culture to improve it. The culture which students bring conditions their "ways of doing things" and exerts a strong and undirected control on student life unless a personnel staff is cognizant of it and constantly works with it. Crises arise in student life because of the influence of "family in-grown ways of thinking" interiorized in students. How does one deal with them? The crises in the college with the rural ministerial students was handled through group discussion and resulted in the development of more social intelligence. By understanding the student value-systems, their ends and goals, it is possible to select "learning" experiences through which they can achieve these goals. Basically, culture is a learned and a socially acquired behavior. Changes in educational and social programs, as well as changes in curricular and administrative areas, may have to take place. Also, one should be particularly alert to observe behavior on the college campus and study what particular culture

6 *Ibid.*, p. 1.

mores are operating. It is important to study how the entire student body functions in an interrelated pattern, representing, as it does, many cultural patterns.

As to the parental patterns, the writer has found in interviews with numerous personnel workers that the expectancies of parents dominate many mores on the campus. In this struggle for the direction, the molding, and the control of behavior patterns or mores of youth, it is perhaps imperative for the college to define the province of the family and the educational institution. If one gave greater attention to parental-institutional compatibilities and adjustments, young people might be spared the hazards of parent versus college objectives. After analyses of these family cultural problems of their students, personnel workers and educators should create the necessary setting for social nearness and mutual help between the student, the parent, and the college. An educational process and program may be necessary to meet this problem —more attention to the problem in orientation programs, and wherever possible on the campus, the holding of parent institutes, as has been mentioned earlier in this chapter. It is only as parents understand themselves and what the college is trying to do that improvement can take place.

One should not have the impression that family values and beliefs must be overthrown. They cannot be. But it is important for the student to learn to rethink his values, reconstruct them, broaden them as he lives through his college experience.

Traditional and Established Culture of the College

As to the traditional and established culture of the college community, it is well known that sanctions and compulsions influence every student who comes to a campus. Students are taught what the college culture regards as important. Very often the social heritage of the groups and subgroups on a campus determines what the incoming students' college life will be.

THE MORES OF CONTROL IN THE SOCIAL HERITAGE

Social heritage includes the traditions, folkways, customs, and mores which have prevailed in a particular institution. To distinguish these forms of social heritage, standard definitions are presented. Tradition has been defined as an *inherited* culture, attitude, or the like; sometimes as a long-established convention. Two terms are associated with tradition, viz., long-established and accepted from the past. A *folkway* is any way of thinking, feeling, behaving, or achieving an end common to members of a social group; it may be a social habit or a culture pattern. It can be contemporary or rooted in the past. A *custom* is a form or course of action characteristically repeated under like circumstances. Customs are the accepted ways in which people do things together in personal contacts. The *mores* are customs, folkways, or traditions imbued with an ethical significance. They are the folkways, traditions, and customs that are considered *regulators* of behavior, not merely ways of behaving. A tradition or folkway may mean so much to an administration or faculty or to students that they believe it must be handed down as a form of social control and adopted by new students. When there is this element of force operating upon the societal welfare, the term mores may be applied.

TRADITIONS

Traditions, as well as folkways and customs, satisfy needs of students and have a genetic connection with the college culture. Because they have been deemed necessary on a college campus and involve the college societal welfare, they may be classified, as stated above, under mores.

Impressed by the baneful influence of student traditions, President Marion L. Burton of the University of Michigan dubbed them "the tyrants of every campus." At the other extreme, convinced of their power for good, President David Starr Jordan of Stanford pronounced them "the greatest instruments of culture in college." President Arthur T. Hadley of Yale remarked: "At Yale the value of education is due to college life even more than to college instruction."[7] As a further reference to the influence of traditions and folkways at Yale, Hawes writes that folkways, meaning old social customs long continued, makes the Yale system of social control the fundamental principle of all morals and man-

[7] W. H. Cowley and Willard Waller, "A Study of Student Life," *Journal of Higher Education*, 6 : 132, March 1935.

ners.[8] At Yale not only were there customs like unto the laws of the Medes and Persians, but the college and students were proud of these customs, advertised them, and capitalized them as part of the plan to attract new students. Yale even went so far as to make the customs do much of the educational and nearly all of the disciplinary work of the institution.

Tradition which clusters around the college campus may be divided, according to Waller, into three classes: "Tradition which comes entirely, or almost entirely, from the outside; tradition which is in part from outside the school and in part indigenous; and tradition which is almost entirely indigenous."[9]

The tradition of the first class, which comes entirely or almost entirely from the outside, refers to the whole educational culture complex, which had its origin in Western Europe and has become diffused into the American culture. Harvard, Yale, The College of William and Mary, and many of the earlier colleges were at their beginning entirely carried on under the plan of the European system. Tradition from that time on has governed pretty much what is taught, the manner in which it is taught, who shall teach, and the requirements for teaching. In these institutions, tradition has also largely determined which students should go to college.

An example of the mingled tradition which is in part from outside the college and in part indigenous in the college may be observed in the traditions which govern teachers. There is a teacher morality, as well as a student morality, and it regulates the teacher's relation to his students and to other teachers. There is the traditional attitude toward the student on the part of teachers, requiring that a certain social distance be kept between them. There is also the ceremoniousness toward the administration of the college; the discrimination between the established teachers and the new, between the professorial rank and those subordinate to it.

Furthermore, the tradition that is in part from the outside and in part from within refers in many instances to the traditions and mores arising from the cultural and historical development of a

[8] James A. Hawes, *Twenty Years Among the Twenty Year Olds*, p. 148.
[9] Willard Waller, *Sociology of Teaching*, p. 108. Copyright, 1932, by John Wiley and Sons, Inc.

college. If a personnel worker were to study the origin of various clubs and groups on a campus, he or she would find some that were coeval with the founding of the college, having a genetic connection with the purposes of the college and very often remaining the same in standards, ideals, and established norms throughout the years. Price relates how the story of the development of student life at Stanford is largely the story of two presidential regimes.[10] Pervasive traditions inherent in the ideas of the founders and the administrators who carried out the trust greatly influenced the emotional tone and quality of student life at that institution. One of the most powerful traditions which govern the foster children of Stanford is the feeling of clan or family. Price believes that this flowed originally from the dramatic story of the inception and founding of the institution, which its administrators have wisely used in promoting a feeling of belonging and kinship on the Stanford Farm. "To encourage students in intellectual growth, individual responsibility, and dependence on personal worth, David Starr Jordan gave to Stanford students a motto: 'The Winds of Freedom Blow.' Students were encouraged to think independently, to act independently, and to wear what they pleased, as long as their behavior exemplified 'conduct becoming a gentleman.' "[11] In the course of the years "The Winds of Freedom Blow" suffered several different interpretations and misinterpretations in student traditions.[12]

Later in Stanford student life came the development of social control by students: their self-direction and responsibility with faculty guidance, then the Leadership Institute, then the reorganization in Women's Residence Plan. Administrative leaders gifted with imagination, versatility, sound judgment, and courage were shown to be important factors in the development of a colorful cultural situation toward socially useful ends. Price further relates that "The genetic history though complex and time consuming has revealed the interrelatedness of behavior and the situation and a consistent intent and concern on the part of the Stanford

[10] Louise Price, *Creative Group Work on the Campus*, p. 195. Copyright, 1941, by Bureau of Publications, Teachers College, Columbia University.
[11] *Ibid.*, p. 211.
[12] *Ibid.*, p. 80–82.

administrators for the achievement of democracy in student life."[13]

Other examples of the mingled tradition that is in part absorbed from the general culture and in part produced by the particular institution are the occasions where the history of the college is intertwined with customs and traditions related to the general culture out of which the institution developed or for which its philosophy stands. Customs in the springtime at Vassar College bring to the campus a history of the past. Founder's Day, on May 4th, is a day when both students and faculty forsake work to honor the birthday of Matthew Vassar, out of whose prosperous Poughkeepsie brewery flowed the ale that brought in the funds that created Vassar. On the traditional Tree Day held each year the first year students select their class tree; the senior frolic on odd years is celebrated by a hoop-rolling contest, and on even years by a dance around a maypole. There is also the traditional Class Day ceremony, the "Daisy Chain," when sophomores ceremoniously wind a laurel rope decorated with daisies around the senior tree.

"The Masque of the Yellow Moon," a customary event at a junior college in the West, is another example of mingled tradition. Its origin goes back to Indian times. It is an occasion on which all the schools of the town as well as the junior college join with the town and community in dramatizing some historic event, some "legend of the West," some happening of Indian days.

In a Southern state college for women, where the cultural background of students is that of the small town, a personnel record form has asked consistently the same question, viz., "What do you want to do after graduation?" For fifteen years it has received the same answer: "Have a home and family." At this college many students go home over week-ends; consequently there is a strong tie with parents. The grandmother-mother-daughter pattern is quite common on this campus. An interesting custom enhances the "desire for marriage" pattern. One gate on the campus is called "Old Maids' Gate." The custom declares that if girls walk in forwards, they will be "old maids," but if they walk in backwards they will be married. This custom of walking in backwards has been done by girls for years and is still practiced.

The custom of "continually keeping vigil on their health" is

[13] Price, *op. cit.*, p. 261–262.

evident in a Western denominational college of strong religious faith. The students here, because of their conditioning in the religious culture of their faith, believe that "their bodies belong to God." Therefore, they are careful of what they eat and usually confine their eating to the three meals a day. There is little eating or drinking between meals; the "coke" drinking custom and eating "hang-out" do not exist there.

Another significant example of a mingled tradition is the Ham and Egg Show and Folk Festival of a Negro state college in the South. The traditional event was started by a county agent who felt the community should be educated, and also the students, as to the products on which they could capitalize to support themselves. All the near-by towns on this day bring produce to the campus. Charts are displayed showing how much the various districts produced. People of national importance make speeches. County agents, both Negro and white, are judges. For the folk festival the folklore of the Negro in the particular rural sections is reproduced, their original culture is revived, and dancing is participated in by parents, children, and students. Ham and eggs are placed in the auditorium so that all people, including students, can see and admire them. The spirit of independence and pride in being able to produce enough for themselves are emphasized.

As to traditions in the oldest girls' school west of the Mississippi, the campus itself has historical significance to the town—the first hanging in the county took place under the arch which connects two of its buildings! An alumna, more than eighty years of age, who has given liberally to the college both financially and in service, lives in a suite of one of the dormitories. She actively promotes the traditions, and still edits an alumni bulletin. The students used to make a good deal of fuss over her. A few years ago, however, she became ill and was away from the college for several years. During that time the girls who had known her graduated and now the new girls attach much less importance to her customs and conversation.

A tradition that has grown up on this campus is called "Grey Lady Walking." It seems that the college girls in the early years of the college wore uniforms and sunbonnets. One of the girls at that time was in love and planned to elope. She left the table at mealtime one day and was never seen again. Now, whenever there is a lull or moment of silence in the dining room, girls will say, "The grey lady is walking." The result of this tradition is that students very frequently create the hush. Other equally naïve customs are perpetuated or created from time to time in this college. This situation on the campus is thought to have a disintegrative effect, and the leaders are eager to establish a more constructive social maturity.

The third class of traditions—traditions almost entirely indigenous—is found at its best among students. They may have been originated by the faculty, and then imposed upon the students, but once accepted by students, they may be passed on by students to other student groups.

There usually are two types of student traditions on every college campus—the specific and the pervasive. Specific traditions are concrete, unitary acts obvious to everyone and in general participated in by the student body as a whole, for example, college songs, cheers, rally bonfires, and "pep" meetings. Other flourishing specific traditions have to do with wearing apparel or personal adornment, the derbies, striped ties, green carnations, "sloppy-Jo's."

But Cowley particularly emphasizes that a study of college mores must not be "limited to such superficial expressions as college songs, cheers, or rally bonfires. Instead, they must be recognized as kinds of social energy which determine the intellectual, social, and moral tones of every college and university campus."[14] They include the subtle, pervasive traditions, more difficult to define, such as attitudes, dispositions, moods, which express themselves through a variety of acts and set the character of a college community. These traditions are manifested on many campuses; they are the "underneath the surface" customs which are not verbalized but tacitly understood among students. Examples of some of these customs are: being dubbed "apple-polisher" if a student makes friends with the faculty, the "C grade" tradition,[15] not dat-

14 W. H. Cowley, "Challenge to Physical Education," *Journal of Higher Education,* 16 :175, April 1945.

15 From *Higher Education and Society: A Symposium,* by Arthur B. Adams and Others. Copyright, 1936, by the University of Oklahoma Press. All rights reserved. p. 40–41.

ing certain kinds of girls because they are non-sorority or belong
to a particular sorority.

These examples illustrate pervasive traditions; they pertain to
faculty-student relationships, the quality of academic work, the
class and caste structure, the honor code, the restraints on drinking,
the quality of sportsmanship on a campus. In general, these set the
tone and spirit of the college.

COLLEGE SPIRIT

Of particular significance as a pervasive tradition is what is
termed "college spirit." The college is marked off from the world
that surrounds it by the spirit which pervades it. Feeling makes
the college a social unit. The college world is well known by its
demonstrations of feeling before a football game, after a game, and
on other public occasions. This sort of college spirit is readily
recognized. There is also a pervasive college spirit that is not so
obvious and is not to be confused with the "rah, rah" of the
athletic field. It is concerned with how each student governs himself, with that power within which blends with his independence
and confidence toward his self-sufficiency in the college community.

A personnel director of a small college has spoken quite often
to the writer of the "spirit of honesty" which prevails on her campus. When she first came to the college the director was concerned
over the lack of keys for the dormitory rooms. A student committee informed of her anxiety appeared at her office and reported
"that they never use the keys to their rooms; there need be no concern over it as dishonesty never occurs on this campus." This was
proved as time went on. The personnel director has also been able
to use the mores of honesty in many constructive ways when from
time to time disturbing situations have arisen among the student
body.

At one large Southern university there is the spirit of the "unwritten constitution" and the campus code of gentlemanly conduct. Bradshaw relates that

. . . the spirit and practice of student self-government at Carolina has
been developing gradually during more than a hundred years. Every
advance has come not through a grant of legal power from above but
as a result of moral power effectively expressed by the students them-

selves. Hence it is that this student body has rested its government on an unwritten constitution.[16]

On further inquiry into the student government of this university one finds that the administration and faculty have not occupied a passive position during its growth. Individual faculty members have always counseled with student leaders and have inspired much that is recorded in the story of growth. The student council combines the legislative, executive, and judicial functions of student government; it administers all cases arising under the honor system and campus code. The honor system covers all cases of cheating and lying. The campus code, in short, is a code of gentlemanly conduct. What that constitutes is the judgment of the students as to what is acceptable in the campus mores.

At an old Southern college for women, where the discipline of the college has evolved from a long history of self-government that goes back genetically to the faiths and the beliefs of a former president and faculty, there has developed an almost indescribable "spirit of the campus." In a conversation with a student concerning it, she began by saying thoughtfully that she did not believe she could express adequately the spirit of her campus. She spoke quite often of how the students govern themselves and help others to govern themselves. There are no punitive measures; each girl explains any of her actions which do not seem to correspond to the spirit of the campus. If some girl consistently violates the spirit of the campus it is mentioned to the Judiciary Committee composed of faculty and students, with students predominating. The girl is asked to clarify her actions. If some girl has to leave the campus, the student body feels it is because she did not "feel the responsibility," "she didn't understand," or "she couldn't control herself." It is the dynamics of this type of "spirit of the college" in which students "feel the responsibility" for conduct that the personnel worker needs to know and nurture for growth on a campus.

A dean from a Midwestern campus spoke of the social cleavages of her campus, but ended by saying that "there are cleavages which create rivalry but not bitterness for there is always the spirit of ——— College." Upon being asked to explain what the spirit was,

---

[16] Francis Bradshaw, *Contemporary Student Government at the University of North Carolina,* Foreword. Chapel Hill, The University of North Carolina, 1938.

she answered: "It is, I believe, a spirit of friendliness. Of course, students have their differences but underneath them all is this spirit of friendliness and extreme loyalty to one another."

A different type of pervasive characteristic exists among students in a college of a large cosmopolitan city. There they are said by their dean to have inferiority complexes and to be resentful of their economic deprivations. The students on the whole are from the lower socio-economic class of the city but they have high academic records. According to a personnel worker on this campus there is, despite the resentments of various kinds, genuine college spirit on the campus. "They are social-minded, interested in national events and all social movements. They are tolerant, serious, and willing to work on themselves."

In a large state college for women in the South a state law required until one year ago that a "blue or white uniform" be worn by all girls on the campus. This state requirement was democratic in intent; it made it economically possible for more girls of lower socio-economic status to attend college, and it prevented the girls of a higher socio-economic level from "splurging" on expensive clothes. Economic equality and democratic standards are in the institutional mores of this college. The personnel worker interviewed felt, however, that this uniformity of dress had a constructive effect on each student. It gave rise to a pervasive tradition of great importance, one which shows up in many different aspects of campus life, namely, that "a girl makes her own position on the campus without money and family influence." "She is as she is." Since all girls dress alike, a girl must show herself outstanding in other ways if she wishes to win a position on the campus; "personality must step out of uniformity."

A dean from a small denominational college located along the Mississippi gave as a pervasive characteristic of the student body their "loyalty to the old river" and "the hilltop." An honor organization on the campus is called "Hilltop." The hilltop is a symbol to them of "spiritual uplift." When the morale of the student body is low or some difficult situation has to be encountered, reference to the symbolism of the hilltop is often found beneficial and constructive.

Recently an independent spirit at a Western university has been symbolized by a sorority and a fraternity. These groups a few years ago gained the greatest prestige on the campus because they defied national regulations concerning selection of new members and invited to their membership anyone displaying a rare individualism. Their choice might have been the wealthiest man or woman, the poorest man or woman, or an outstanding student of a minority group. The criterion was one of individualism, an independence of spirit.

On the campus of a strong small denominational liberal arts college, the personnel worker, a former student of the college, spoke constantly of the prevailing spirit of "tolerance": "The students always feel they are being given a chance of being tried out on this campus."

A personnel worker from a strong denominational college of the Far West spoke of college spirit on her campus as emanating from the president. Further, there is a strong religious belief on the campus and students build their lives around it.

Another personnel worker from a Negro state college in the South spoke of the "development of the individual" as the spirit of the college.

A novelty in the way of arousing college spirit, which is called "Oscar P," was started by a former elderly dean and is carried on at an agricultural college in the Southwest where two secret clubs exist, each consisting of ten members. The twenty people chosen are not known until the yearbook comes out. When college morale is low, signs are put up at nights reading "Where's Oscar P?" When the veterans returned lately to the campus, they were welcomed by these signs.

A dean from a junior college in Arizona related as the most pervasive tradition of the student body in this college the friendliness which students have for each other and for the faculty; "apple polishing" is not heard of there. There is the spirit of "give and take" which is quite real; there is the spirit of "face values" and not artificial standards; there is the spirit of "naturalness."

College spirit, such as has been described, very often is a carefully nurtured growth rather than a spontaneous creation by those who identify themselves with some belief or action. It is rather a love, a pride, a belief, a quality which puts into the consciousness of students something which they turn back to the institution and which also persists in their character and personality as members of a self-governing campus community and later as members of society.

FOLKWAYS AND CUSTOMS

The indigenous folkways which exist in college student life can be illustrated by examples cited in Crawford's study concerning one university's "student spending and recreation."[17] At that university students tend to think of recreation in terms of a "date," which in turn ordinarily involves some kind of refreshment. One of the commonest kinds of dates, known as "joeing date," usually occurs at the university commons or at some restaurant near the campus either between classes or during hours ordinarily set aside for study.

Sometimes students at this university "dutch treat" on dates. Rather than not go to the commons or stay home in the evening because the man with whom she ordinarily has dates is "broke" or has not received his allowance from home, a girl may prefer to pay for her own recreation and refreshment. Although this practice is usually most common among students who "go steady," the most casual acquaintances may drop in the commons for a "coke" and pay for their drinks individually. Movie dates are quite common and couples usually walk to and from the movies.

Walking dates, which are most popular in the spring and fall, usually involve the purchase of a "coke" or ice cream. They most often occur in the middle of the week when there is nothing else to do or when the man student is too "broke" to buy tickets to any form of amusement.

The churches of the town, according to this study, provide carefully planned social and religious programs for the students. These include a variety of evening meetings and parties. Men and women students who meet for the first time on these occasions often become accustomed to attending them together.

In 1940–1941, dates at the dormitories of this university were more popular than they were before recreation rooms were pro-

[17] Mary M. Crawford, *Student Folkways and Spending at Indiana University, 1940–1941*, p. 148–169. Copyright, 1943, by The Columbia University Press.

vided. In some of these rooms are ping-pong tables and shuffle-boards, as well as radios and record players. Most of the picnics and outings that students attend are planned by some one of the campus clubs. Ordinarily the place chosen for the picnic is within walking distance of the campus.

Often after a football game, the fraternities and sororities, as well as the dormitories, have coffee hours or buffet suppers to which a man can take his date. Fraternity men and non-fraternity men spend more on recreation and refreshments than do the sorority and non-sorority women. This is probably because they not only spend more for themselves but also more in entertaining co-eds. The smaller difference between the expenditures of non-fraternity men and non-sorority women suggests that non-sorority women pay for relatively more of their own recreation and refreshments than do the sorority, since, in general, fraternity men do not date non-sorority women. In general, non-sorority women are more likely to "dutch treat" than sorority women, because the sororities tend to frown on the practice and because the sorority members usually feel that their escorts can afford to pay their expenses.

Similarly, the amounts spent by students who earn part of their own expenses suggest that if a student has to earn a large proportion of his own expenses and economize more than the student who earns less, he will not economize noticeably on recreation, refreshments, and tobacco.

Student spending is thus conditioned by the usages and the traditions generally accepted and adhered to by the members of individual groups on the campus and by the student body as a whole. Crawford writes:

Some of these student folkways are found among students on all campuses, some in a single college community. Some are associated with traditions of long standing, others "pop-up" in impulsive and unpremeditated fashion in response to particular situations. . . . Campus folkways may be responsible either for additional spending or in some instances for economies on the part of students. The obligation of a fraternity man to send flowers to the girl to whom he has given his pin and to her sorority sisters often costs him a considerable sum. On the other hand the wearing of senior "cords" reduces the clothing expenditure of the men in that class. While the economic status of the student is undoubtedly the major determinant of the amount he spends in college, the folkways of campus living have an important influence on how he spends that portion of his funds which is not required to meet certain uniform costs.[18]

Folkways, as typified on this one college campus, reproduce themselves in one form or another on all campuses. Similar examples of other specialized folkways follow:

1. Backing of the college athletic teams, rallies, and other rites surrounding this phase of campus life. Adherence to the folkways surrounding intercollegiate athletics is one of the strongest of all phases of American college life.

2. Wearing of the general type of clothing that tradition has prescribed, such as green caps for freshmen. The student who violates clothing traditions has a sad fate.

3. Living up to "no-tattling code." It is usually the height of violation of campus mores to inform the teacher.

4. Maintaining distance between student and instructors is a patterned condition in many colleges.

5. Participation in the activities which have prestige in the eyes of a majority of the students, such as attendance or non-attendance at assembly exercises, being a member or not of a sorority or fraternity.

6. Knowing the accepted social standards, as when to "date" and when not to, having or not having an automobile, dancing at campus or at off-campus "hangouts."

Fashions, fads, affectations, poses, and all kinds of popular delusions are also included in the mores. According to Sumner, "They have characteral qualities and characteral effect. However frivolous or foolish they may appear to people of another age, they have the forms of attempts to live well, to satisfy some interest, or to win some good."[19]

Thus, on each campus, in ways peculiar to its past and present culture, arise many folkways and customs which are obvious to any visitor. They often have been generated throughout years of history, and acceptance of a student is dependent to a considerable extent upon his unquestioning adherence to these group customs.

[18] Crawford, *op. cit.*, p. 228.
[19] William G. Sumner, *Folkways*, p. 57. Copyright, 1906, by Ginn and Company.

IMPLICATIONS FOR PERSONNEL WORKERS
AND EDUCATORS

Customs, habits, and traditions, whether they come from the established culture outside the college, or in part from outside and in part from within the college, or entirely within the college— all have cultural and social heritage power which is hard to break and many of them do not prove constructive. All, whether constructive or destructive, exert a social control over the life of students. A personnel worker should be interested in the traditions and customs of his college community as they affect student behavior, and from time to time should think through and assess their values in his dealings with students, faculty, and administrators. But, first of all, he must know what they are, why they exist, how they originated, what purpose they serve, and whether they should be continued or discontinued.

First, as to knowing what they are—many exist, as one can see from illustrations of this chapter, in very overt forms, as customs related to certain special days, as founders' day, home-coming affairs, and football games. On the other hand, the pervasive characteristics which have even greater control of student life are often in covert form. The prevailing spirit of the college, codes of honor, beliefs, and social systems among students are often hard to penetrate. One should know these pervasive hidden controls which students exert among themselves in the social life on the campus. Thought should be given to ways in which they can be carefully nurtured in so far as they lead to constructive social control on the campus.

Second, why do traditions and customs exist? Some of them exist, if one will analyze the illustrations which have been given, to satisfy or continue a pattern in the culture from which the students come, such as the Old Maids' Gate on the Southern campus. Some exist to immortalize the culture of the institution, as those of the Yale system and the Founders' Day customs of Vassar and many other colleges. Others, such as "The Masque of the Yellow Moon" at the junior college noted, continue because they vitalize and bring to mind the culture and history of the community in which the college is located. Others exist to satisfy the faith, codes, and beliefs of the founders and of those who still support the institution, for example, the customs evident in strong denominational colleges. Still others exist to educate the college and the community to their responsibilities to the society in which they live, for example, the traditional events of some of the Negro state colleges of the South. All exist to perpetuate a system of social relationships, as attested by the university in the Crawford study, where not even a change in economic resources of the students could alter the pattern.

Third, how do traditions and folkways originate? Again, observing the illustrations mentioned as well as examples from other colleges, one can discern as some of the sources the presidents or founders of the college, an outstanding faculty member, and the students themselves. Many of them originate in spontaneous informal student groups, or from outside sources, such as people who can envision what certain traditional events can mean in the life of the community. Many traditions, too, have come about from invention, imitation of other colleges, and diffusion from college to college, particularly those near by.

Fourth, what purposes are traditions and customs serving? Essentially, one can say they are meeting the basic needs of students —the social needs, the need for stability, for response, and for recognition. They give the student a sense of "belonging," of having an experience in common with his peers, and of satisfying the "we" feeling. Again, the mores cement a student body in common feeling, they create morale, they furnish social control and stability on the campus. Also, traditions serve to arouse the spirit of rivalry and competition—the patterns in our American culture on which colleges also thrive. One college must have what other colleges have. Colleges must transmit and hand down a social heritage to younger generations so they will still enjoy prestige and status.

Fifth, should traditions, folkways, and customs be continued? Certainly those traditions and customs which give a pervasive constructive tone to a college student body should be continued. The pervading spirit of a college campus, as the examples illustrate, has a definitely uplifting effect and creates good morale. From careful observation and study and by keeping records of student sayings and behavior patterns one may discover what are their underlying codes of honor or beliefs. If the pervasive spirit is *not* constructive, then by discussions of values, by drawing on interests of students for campus activities, by cooperation of the faculty, by use of all-college convocations, leadership classes, students may be brought to develop a sense of responsibility and a better pervasive philosophy for campus life. Certainly, traditions and customs which work for better understanding, better integration of all groups on the campus, greater morale and satisfaction in meeting the needs of all students should not be abandoned.

Sixth, can traditions and customs be done away with? Changed interests of the students very often eliminate them. Contacts with groups of other colleges which may have more constructive customs sometimes change them. Leaders with strong personalities have been successful in changing them. Administrative fiat is used in some instances where in a crisis the good of the whole student body may be at stake. Usually, however, it is not satisfactory for the administration to change by fiat destructive mores. In conferences with deans one hears of state laws and administrative ultimatums against hazing and other undesirable customs, but generally they end their remarks by saying that "they slip in anyway." Substitution of another custom may have some effect, but if it is not carefully thought through, the second custom may become as undesirable as the first. At a college in the Southwest, "beating the drum" continuously on a campus for a week before a game with a rival college was a substitute made by faculty members for writing on the streets and campus paths of the college. In time the noise of the drum, although it kept students on their own campus, became undesirable to both college and town residents, especially as it affected the health and social development of the students.

This discussion on social heritage ought not to be concluded without reminding each administrative officer or personnel worker that it is also necessary to assess himself. He should analyze how customs peculiar to his background and experience have influenced and continue to influence his ways of thinking. In fact, lack of this ability to analyze himself may be his greatest hindrance in working on a campus with young people of many different backgrounds, customs, and cultural strains.

Further Mores of Control in an Established
Institutional Culture

In addition to the power of social heritage which includes the traditions, folkways, and customs already discussed, various other forms of controls arise and become established in a college's institutional culture.

REGULATIVE AND SUGGESTIVE CONTROL

Warren speaks of social control on the campus as being regulative or suggestive.[20] Regulative control has to do with specific rulings and powers of the administrative authorities, such as courses of study, residence requirements, attendance, scholastic requirements, point system of extracurricular control.

To observe further examples of regulative control, one has only to examine college catalogues, handbooks, and courses of study and note the innumerable rules which govern student life from an institutional standpoint. Administrative rules pertaining particularly to the social conduct of students occupy space in the handbooks and in many of the catalogues. If one were to look into the origin of these regulations one would find numerous influences and pressures at work in the institutional culture of the college. A large number of control patterns from the past are transmitted by faculty and administrators from generation to generation and become administrative mores thereafter maintained through indoctrination. In the catalogues for at least twenty years—those from 1920 to 1940—issued by a liberal arts college one reads, "Students must meet the requirements of *good morals* and *good citizenship.*" One also can read in the same catalogues under "Student Organizations" a regulation concerning certain literary societies:

Two societies, purely literary in their character, nearly coeval with the college, have been maintained in continuous operation throughout most of its history. There are two similar societies for young women, the——founded 1896, and the——founded 1921. Not the least of the

---

[20] Roland L. Warren, "A Sociological Analysis of Student Activities," *Educational Forum*, 5 : 443–445, May 1941.

advantages of college residence is the special training secured in these societies. For many years the work and worth of these societies have been recognized in the following regulation: "No student will be graduated from the college who fails to meet reasonable financial obligations to these societies."

This regulation has been transmitted from year to year and generation to generation. A vast culture complex going back to the origin and development of these societies may account for this regulation. This particular college is one of the oldest in the country, being granted a charter in the late 1700's. It is located in a Scotch-Irish center in Pennsylvania where during the Colonial era many of the influential men of the state lived, men who later became eminent in the nation. Many of the founders and pro- moters of the college were active in establishing the government of the United States. The students of this college were from its inception interested in the events of the times. Faculty came to the college to make it the place of their life's work. Practically none of the faculty thought of leaving to teach elsewhere. Also through the crises of the years the college has held steady to its first objective, the liberal arts and cultural studies. According to a history of the college written by a former president, in 1786 eleven students of the college met with "an earnest desire to im- prove in Science and Literature" and perfected the organization known as——Literary Society. Three years later ten students united in a similar manner to form the——Society. Through the years the work of both societies has been to discuss the topics and problems of the times. There was friendly rivalry between them and they engaged in an annual debate. This continued for many years but was finally displaced by intercollegiate debating. With the growth of fraternities, interest in literary societies declined. However, even today on this campus, as elsewhere, they serve a number of students. Because of their historical and cultural back- ground and the famous people in the history of our country who belonged to them, these societies lived through the years as or- ganizations for cultural development and had prestige, not only in the eyes of students, but particularly in the eyes of the faculty. The mores of students at this college were tied up for many years with the institutional control of these two societies. In the 1946 catalogue, however, the regulation does not appear; changes in curricula and other changes have been made. This may be accounted for by a period of change in the whole college, the death of a president who served for many years, and the short terms of several successors. The staff personnel has undergone change; many new members have appeared recently on the faculty staff. There has ensued a period of confusion due to changes in administration and the war. Also, the needs of students have changed. As on other campuses new mores seem to be emerging.

A regulative control is represented at a Western university, where a personnel worker remarked that the students love the natural beauty around their university but little is done in the curricula to develop the artistic. It is still dominated by a "man viewpoint," as the various colleges for men attest. However, a former personnel worker has asserted that the "man viewpoint" lies in the mores of the college culture. Price[21] has written a genetic history of student life on this campus which explains the culture from which this point of view arose. According to Price, it seems that in the early days of this college the *man*, not his clothes or possessions, was emphasized by the president and the founders. Many of the students who came to this college in the early days had little money and few clothes. To make them comfortable, the "rough" tradition which looked with aversion upon men with "too good clothes" was encouraged by the president. During the twenties a distortion of the rough tradition grew in student life, partly as the result of the administration's holding inflexible one factor—the number of women students. The limitation of women students to five hundred meant that men outnumbered women five or six to one. This control, more or less dominated by a "man viewpoint," led to important changes in the social mores of the campus. The women were of superior ability intellectually, and, as the enrollment of men grew, there was increasing friction between the sexes in their social relations. The fact that the women were intellectually able, dressed well, and frequently were well traveled, increased the discomfiture of many men. Because of the preponderance of men on the campus, the women had ample opportunities for dating. The reaction of the average man to the keenness of the com-

[21] Louise Price, *op. cit.*, pp. 212–217.

petition for feminine favors expressed itself through various avenues, which included an increasing number of dirty "cords" and "whiskers." Thus some men defied their situation and covered their feelings of inadequacy. This situation brought in its wake the tradition of the "import." Many of the men scorned their own college women as "snobs" and "grinds." By the late twenties there was much criticism and bad feeling. Parents complained and also alumni whose daughters were ineligible because of high admissions requirements. An improvement rested in a change of administrative policy regarding the admission of more women. The depression came along and approximately three hundred fewer men registered; desirable women were turned down. Plans were then made at a meeting of the board of trustees for a coordinate college for women. The restriction to five hundred women had been maintained because the founders thought of an institution of approximately one thousand students. Because the founders wanted equal representation of the sexes, the number of women was limited. The review of the founders' grants, charts, etc., disclosed a paper in which the founders released the trustees of any promises made by them if and when any such requests were deemed by the unanimous vote of the board of trustees to interfere with the welfare of the institution. In 1933 the limitation gave way to a percentage basis of women.

The above brief chapter in the genetic history of student life relates the regulative influence which the "man viewpoint" of this college exercised. The second influence bearing on this "man viewpoint" revolved around the fact that the founder of this college was trained in law, experienced as a Civil War-time governor and as a senator from his state, a builder of railroads, and a philanthropist who had the practical man's belief in the pragmatic, and at the same time in science. This point of view underlies the curriculum even today, which naturally includes more of what have been fields for men.

Some colleges, particularly denominational liberal arts colleges, still have in their institutional culture the control by administrative officers of the social conduct of students with regard to smoking, drinking, and dancing. The "no dancing" clause seems to have been eliminated first. Many colleges have now made provisions for smoking rooms. "No drinking" still remains, even though there is drinking off the campus and in many cases close to the university or college. At one college where students are not permitted to smoke on the campus, they smoke just at the edge of the campus, thus abiding by the regulation.

In a strong denominational college of the West the regulation of "no drinking, no smoking, no dancing" has been rigidly followed in the college because of the influence of the church which sponsors the college. The students, with their past conditioning in the religious culture of this faith, believe thoroughly that "their bodies belong to God"[22] and continually keep vigil on their health. Bible as a study is required of every student. The faculty consists of members of the religious faith of the church involved; most of them are strong personalities and consciously or unconsciously influence the student body with their religious philosophy. The student association in this college does not have the authority for discipline of the students; the discipline is handled through an administrative committee. A recent catalogue states:

It was the purpose of the founders to provide educational facilities with a denominational stamp and according to the denominational blueprint. These principles call for a rural setting, instruction by Christian Teachers in the arts and sciences of living and service, a strong industrial arts program, and the part-time employment of all students in vocational activities on the campus.

In a Southern state college for women, there are nine different dormitories, in which some rooms are equipped better than others. Because the state pays for the rooms, the administration wishes that no discrimination be shown, so rooms are assigned in order of the excellence of grades received. If the rooms in the junior dormitory are being assigned, a list of junior girls is posted in order of rating of grades. The girl receiving the highest grades gets the first choice of room desired for herself and a roommate.

Similar regulative controls are found everywhere, but a great deal of control is also exercised indirectly by the faculty through suggestive controls. The power of a faculty adviser is seldom fully defined. The fact that without any clearly defined authority the adviser is still held responsible to the administration for the major

22 See pages 38–39 of this study.

activities of his group indicates the importance of suggestive control. It is well known that a good adviser needs no written and definitely defined authority. The rapport which he establishes with the group is a stronger basis for control over the group than any regulative power could be.

Students, like faculty, exert regulative and suggestive control over new members. Suggestive control is exercised by students in various ways. Sometimes this control may be understood through mechanisms of group living among students. Sumner distinguished between the "we" group and the "others" group or the "in-group" and the "out-group."[23] Every "we group" or "in-group" develops its own folkways, mores, customs, and traditions, and these produce a sense of oneness within the group and what might be called a "group ego." This phenomenon he calls "ethnocentrism." An ethnocentric practice is implicit in the "college spirit" on a campus. However, other ethnocentric practices are of the regulative type, as illustrated when sophomores make freshmen "toe the mark," know the college cheers, and sing the college songs. "Groups with strong ethnocentric drives," writes Cowley, "not only preen themselves upon their own superiority, but they crack down upon any member of the group who questions that superiority or who is indifferent to the ceremonies which express group unity."[24] This is illustrated on the campus by the pressure brought to bear for attendance at rallies, by requirement of freshman attendance at all football games, and by carrying off the players on their shoulders at the end of the game.

INDOCTRINATION, ASSIMILATION,
    CULTURALLY TRANSMITTED ATTITUDES

Cowley and Waller[25] have shown that a large number of control patterns from the past shape the behavior of college students. There is a whole set of interactions and processes of social control by means of which behavior norms are established and en-

23 W. G. Sumner, op. cit., p. 12.
24 From Higher Education and Society: A Symposium, by Arthur B. Adams and Others. Copyright, 1936, by The University of Oklahoma Press. All rights reserved. p. 33.
25 W. H. Cowley and Willard Waller, "A Study of Student Life," Journal of Higher Education, 6 : 136, March 1935.

forced. One student generation transmits these patterns to the next, and they are unreflectively accepted and obeyed. This constitutes control through indoctrination. It was found, in a perusal of certain liberal arts college handbooks covering a period of twenty years, that the freshman regulations were the same each year, but that the penalties for offenses might vary with each class.

The mores of the honor system and honor codes are also brought about by control through indoctrination. Along with the mores of indoctrination are the mores of assimilation, such as initiation and hazing practices and "hell-weeks." Also there are the mores due to coercions and selective mechanisms of activity groups, such as fraternities, athletic teams, and campus publications, which exert their control by not electing certain members, or express their control by molding members to their model, or will elect members only on the basis of the schools from which they come.

An interesting contrast in the usual mores of the dominance of underclassmen by upperclassmen is a custom in a Texas college called "Fish Day," when freshmen tell seniors what to do and what to wear.

On many campuses, culturally transmitted attitudes, as mentioned before in this study, prescribe that members of elite fraternities may invite to their dances only the members of a small number of elite sororities. No less important are those unverbalized codes of a student body, the existence of which the new students are only half aware of but which derive great power from the fact that they work unobserved. "College spirit," already described, is an excellent example of this form of control.[26] There is also a great amount of unverbalized control in the expectancy that students will know "the proper thing to do." Hand advocates helping the student in this respect:

> In addition to becoming acquainted with other students, the new student should be helped to learn the social amenities of the campus so that he may avoid the embarrassment of unwittingly doing the wrong thing. If coking at the College Union is the thing to do, he must discover it. If one doesn't take a girl to Blank's Restaurant, he should find this out before it is too late.[27]

[26] See pages 41–45 of this study.

[27] By permission from *Campus Activities*, by Harold C. Hand, Copyrighted, 1938, by McGraw-Hill Book Co., Inc. p. 63.

CEREMONY AND RITUAL

A control which is somewhat different from the above patterns, but which is widely used on all campuses to establish certain mores, is the ceremony and the ritual. The ceremonies have value, or are thought to have value, in the mobilization of individual attitudes with reference to group objectives. The ordinary "pep" meeting, probably the commonest in college, is one of the best examples. A crisis situation looms; the group must be organized and whipped into line. The team is thought of as the defender of the group in the crisis. It is necessary that the team know that the student body to a man is with them, or else the members of the team will not be able to put forth their best efforts. Organized cheering is a minor culture complex subsidiary and one of the ceremonies connected with athletic sports.

In their psychological aspects ceremonies exert a compulsive force in human behavior and personality. Analysis of ceremonies reveals some of the psychological mechanisms upon which they depend for their effectiveness. There are, first, numerous identification mechanisms which act upon the individual by casting him in a particular role for which he receives group approval, or by causing the individual to wish to play such a role because of the public praise connected with it. In all college ceremonies are numerous collective representations, insistently repeated and brought to the attention of the individual in many different guises. According to Park and Burgess,

Collective representations are the concepts which embody the objectives of group activity. . . . Every society and every social group has, or tends to have, its own symbols and its own language. The language and other symbolic devices by which a society carries on its collective existence are collective representations.[28]

These collective representations have emotional meaning but no intellectual content. Some are objectified in such symbols as college colors, banners, and trophies. Many of them, tinged with a highly emotional tone, are carried over into after-years. The writer recalls a sorority woman who remarked how the five points

[28] R. E. Park and E. W. Burgess, *Introduction to the Science of Sociology*, p. 166–167. Copyright, 1924, by The University of Chicago Press.

on her sorority pin representing high ideals had been a guide throughout her life.

Ritual, in general, tends to be dramatic in character and instrumental in developing group unity. Secret fraternalism represents one of the major patterns of American civilization. The very fact of secrecy provides a bond of union which seems to have a strong appeal to certain individuals. Gist, in writing of culture patterning in secret society ceremonials,[29] has given much evidence on the functioning of these ceremonials, and the roles and culture patterns involved. According to Gist, the dramas are invariably moralistic in tone, being designed to convey the dogmas and doctrines which characterize the ideological framework of the clubs. For the themes of ceremonial dramas, the Bible seems to be the most common source of ideas. One of the most characteristic aspects of the ceremonial patterns is the dramatic role of the novitiate. "Ordinarily this role is such as to impress upon the candidate certain doctrines or principles which the society seeks to impart and to heighten the person's awareness of his own status of subordination as a newcomer from the outside."[30] Then there is the ceremonial journey "in search of light, truth, or protection." These ceremonial ordeals function partly as a device for testing the candidate's suitability for full membership in the order and partly as an instrument for indoctrinating the novice with the accepted dogmas of fraternalism. The candidate is given a test of loyalty or fortitude, or is subjected to some humiliating or disconcerting experience. The secret societies also make use of the ceremonial oath to further the cohesiveness of the group by guaranteeing the loyalty and support of the members. Frequently it is accompanied by prayer, by chanting, or by special lighting effects to add impressiveness to the situation. The candidate is conducted to the altar in the center of the room to receive the obligation. Frequently he is required to perform some symbolic act, such as kissing an open Bible. Here one can see the control culture patterns of religious organizations dovetailing the pattern of secret societies.

[29] Noel P. Gist, "Cultural Patterning in Secret Society Ceremonials," *Social Forces*, 14 : 497–505, May 1936.
[30] *Ibid.*, p. 499.

The entering novice promises in proper ceremonial fashion to render assistance to fellow members who may be in distress; to observe the principles of honesty in his financial dealings with other members; to obey the orders of his superior officers; to obey all signs. Usually a certain in-group morality is evident in these promises, that is, the definitions of conduct are restricted to relations between members of the club rather than to relations between members and non-members.

Lest the ritualistic dramas themselves be inadequate as instruments of indoctrination, the ritual is supplemented by what is known in fraternal parlance as lectures, which are explanatory and hortatory in nature; explanatory in that they are presumed to explain for the candidate the moral lesson of the ritual-drama, and hortatory in that they exhort him as to the way he, as a member, shall be expected to act. It is in these lectures also that the general, social, political, economic, patriotic, religious, and racial creeds of the various organizations are expounded.

The installation and founding services, the opening and closing ceremonies, the ceremonial balloting, all tend to conform to a common pattern or design. "The significant point is, however," according to Gist, "the fact that these cultural patterns do exist, that they may be described with some degree of accuracy, and that in their totality they constitute an institutional framework which functions as a social matrix to determine certain outlines of human thought and conduct."[31]

Waller has also given an excellent description of the social dynamics of ceremonies. He writes that it is interesting to observe by what common patterns mass emotions of loyalty, affection, and support are produced and sustained. It is in ceremonies that the full emotional impact of the group with its traditions, myths, "collective representations," and sense of unity is brought home to its members. Assemblies, pep-rallies, commencements, convocations, although often arousing quite different emotions, nevertheless have a tremendous effect on the group consciousness of the student body.[32]

A description of a ceremony given by a personnel worker from

[31] *Ibid.*, p. 505.
[32] Willard Waller, *op. cit.*, p. 120–130.

a junior college of liberal arts in the Southwest offers an excellent example of the emotional effect and control that a ceremony can exercise on the lives of students as well as faculty. It concerns a class day ceremony in which the tradition of the "Ivy Chain" is presented. The senior girls form a procession with ivy stretched from shoulder to shoulder; ivy orations are given and the president of the senior class cuts the ivy between each girl and says some personal remark to each one. The ceremony is accompanied by much demonstration of affection and genuine tears. There is an unusually close spirit on the campus, as each one knows the others personally. This commencement ceremony is used as a form of control on the campus in that no undergraduate is allowed to leave the campus in the spring until she has witnessed the "Ivy Chain." It is thought that the emotional content of this ceremony will carry over to undergraduates and hold them as students in this college. Thus, these ceremonies give rise to problems, both emotional and administrative.

It is evident enough that the mores of dominance operate on college campuses. "From the first day as a Freshman to the last ceremony of Commencement he is being fashioned by pressures which he understands but little, but which he knows to be vital."[33]

STUDENT GOVERNMENT

One might take this last statement, "the student is being fashioned by pressures which he understands but little, but which he knows to be vital," and discuss an organization on the campus which has long been neglected in most colleges as an instrument for bringing about an intelligent understanding, greater social maturity, and patterns of cooperation—viz., the student council. Cannot a student through this instrument from his first day as a freshman to the last ceremony of commencement be fashioned by *responsibilities* of which he *has an intelligent understanding and which from constructive learning experiences he knows to be vital* instead of by pressures which he understands but little, but knows, mainly by authority, to be vital?

Thirty personnel workers in colleges throughout the country reported, with two exceptions, concerning the strength of their stu-

[33] W. H. Cowley and Willard Waller, *op. cit.*, p. 141–142.

dent councils and student governments that "They are not strong." A summary of the factors mentioned for their failure in effective functioning falls into the following items:

First, not enough time is spent to develop them to their fullest capacity for functioning.

Second, too much time is spent on delivering penalties for violations of rules and regulations.

Third, there is an unwillingness to govern themselves which may lie in the mores of the culture.

Fourth, student problems are too much "aired"—there is too much responsibility given to students in handling severe cases of personality maladjustment.

Fifth, there is need for a more constructive program.

Sixth, students are willing to legislate but are not willing to assume responsibility for students' actions.

Seventh, the students do not see the need for it.

Eighth, it offers possibility for great leadership but fails to develop it.

Inquiry into the composition of the student government associations brought out many different types of representation and selection: representatives sometimes selected by an administrative committee, representatives selected by the student body with a faculty advisory board, representatives chosen from classes with other strong functioning groups on the campus not being represented, men's and women's student governments functioning separately, and occasionally representatives from all the organizations on the campus.

According to McKown, there are in the main two plans for the election of members: (1) election by the school as a whole or (2) election by organized groups.[34] The latter plan, in his estimation, does not seem as desirable as the first. When student council members are selected from organized groups, not all the students are represented because not all belong to them. Further, more petty policies are likely to develop as well as loyalty to the group instead of loyalty to the school. It is also felt there should be proper education of the student body as to what constitutes good leadership qualities before an election takes place. Perhaps some of those

[34] H. C. McKown, *The Student Council*, p. 50.

students who organize and lead the informal, spontaneous groups and cliques on the campus are the ones who have the qualities to lead in government of the student body. Proper representation and types of leaders are important, both for the council and for the committees appointed to accomplish a task.

The first factor for failure of student government was that not enough time is spent to develop the association to its fullest capacity for functioning. When five years were taken out of the lives of young men and many young women to fight for the survival of democracy as a way of life, would it not seem worth while to give the necessary amount of time for developing the mores of democracy on our campuses? The student government is the most important activity and technique for this purpose. It is an activity in which students can really function. To achieve one's fullest capacity for functioning is a goal of youth in any endeavor. It is surely an ideal, then, for personnel workers to set up for every area of student life.

That "too much time has been spent on delivering penalties for violations of rules and regulations" has surely been true on many campuses. Students at one college, according to a personnel worker, very often feel that the "sin is in attitude rather than deed" and that "more emphasis should be made on understanding than on penalties." Here is a statement from *students* revealing the desire for more constructive mores on their campus. This also suggests, as the personnel worker herself felt, that much work of the student council should be a matter of guidance and education. Students in a leadership capacity on a college campus should themselves be sufficiently well informed on personality problems that they may understand themselves and each other, may understand attitudes, maladjustment difficulties, ethical considerations, and principles of mental hygiene.

The third factor in failure to function that is possibly due to "the mores of the culture" was noted in particular by Negro personnel workers in the South. The feeling on the part of the Negro in the South is very understandable—with a social heritage of slavery, submission, and even today the denial of the right to vote —these mores of the culture are powerful determinants of an attitude of apathy. However, it is to be expected that college students should be equipped through their campus experience to go back to their home communities and educate their people to a role of democratic citizenship and their obligation to work for it.

"The mores of the culture" may also be a factor in many of the small rural colleges and therefore the reason why students in these colleges do not see the need for student government. The background of students in these rural areas has been that of simple lives built around a rural and family pattern. The pattern of government in the villages from which they come is very simple. It is on campuses with students such as these that personnel workers must see that experience in student government is vital.

"The mores of the outside culture" function in some particular way on each college campus, whether they be in the form of rural patterns, economic deprivations, or racial issues. It is only as personnel directors and faculty see and work with or against these mores, and only as they keep the pattern of the total American culture in mind, viz., a democracy, that any form of student government can exist on their campuses.

As to the need for a more constructive program in their meetings—herein lies the fault of many student organizations. They spend too much time on the disciplinary function, which should probably be turned over to a particular committee or court, and do not spend enough time as deliberative, legislative bodies, working on problems of the campus which, by the technique of discussion, can lead to desirable action.

Finally, as to the assumption of responsibility, one may raise the question: Are students on the college campuses today being given responsibility or are they so hemmed in by advisers, by regulations, by fear of the administration, that they feel there is no need to develop responsibility? The most important areas of responsibility are sometimes taken away from them. In some colleges, ways of using, budgeting, and collecting activities money, or allotting to groups money from an activities fee required by the administration is discussed all year long. This may be *one* function for a committee to work on, but what are the social problems of the campus, the responsibility for which they should be assuming? What are the social mores they would like to discuss and see develop on their campus? Do personnel workers, faculty, and administrators give students the responsibility for social conduct on the campus and train them likewise in civic responsibility for their college community? Do students know that it is *their* community to build? Can the student be "fashioned" by responsibilities and guided participation in his college culture—a culture which he understands and which he knows to be vital?

If student mores on the campus are "ways of doing things" to satisfy their needs, it is through a strong student organization of government that the needs of students can be made known and discussed, and constructive social mores be built on the campus.

IMPLICATIONS FOR PERSONNEL WORKERS AND EDUCATORS

From the preceding discussion and from an analysis of one's own college community it can be observed that various forms of control operate on a campus and bring about mores which enter strongly into the traditional and established culture of the institution. Along with the customs, folkways, and traditions are the ceremonies and the ritual. It seems appropriate that organizations on a college campus should adopt for control on special occasions these devices which throughout human history have been powerful stimulants to emotion. The use of music, processionals, symbols, repetition of ceremonial words, and the use of large numbers of people performing in simultaneous action—all have proved valuable in emotional transfer. An emotional fusion of individuals takes place and creates cohesion in the organization. These occasions closely resemble those *rites de passage* common in primitive life. Coyle states that "The ability of ritual to carry two levels of drama simultaneously by its multiple systems of meaning makes it a particularly suitable instrument for developing group unity. . . . More than that, its dual meaning often provides an attraction for various types of mind."[35] For the simple in mind, there is the drama of action reinforced by the strong emotional appeals of music and uniform action; for those more profound mentally, there is the drama of the allegorical or philosophical meaning which gives depth to the experience.

[35] Grace Coyle, *Social Process in Organized Groups,* p. 155. Copyright, 1930, by Rinehart & Company, Inc.

Ritual and ceremonies have their value in the creation of group cohesion and esprit de corps, and the enhancement of group emotions, but one should not overlook their dangers. First, their emotional content often leads to unconscious rather than conscious attitudes; second, they often submerge individuality to group interests and pressures; third, they have a tendency to bind group expression within certain traditional limits which often hinders their adaptability to changing conditions; fourth, they are sometimes used for exploitation and compulsion.

The wholesome effects of group unity, intelligent emotion through programs of action, and dynamic rather than static control may, however, offset the limitations stated and make of the ceremony and corresponding ritual an uplifting, inspirational force in student mores.

In analyzing the regulative and suggestive forms of control, personnel workers and educators must look to the objectives and philosophy that first led to the establishing of certain regulations, to the early history and development of various forms of control, to the faculty stability established by traditional status throughout the years, all of which may account for the persistence of a form of control in a college. Student handbooks, administrative guides, college catalogues of the past, contain year after year unchanged statements of administrative and student regulations. These administrative regulations, as well as strong methods of indoctrinations by students, coercions, selective controls, hazing initiations, and such, still appear in print today when the aim of education in this democracy of ours is to replace this strict obedience to authority *per se* with controls from within. To be sure, on any campus there must be government, authority, control, discipline; the question is whether this control should be exercised authoritatively by administration and faculty on students, by upperclass students upon lowerclass students, or cooperatively, through policies formed by administration and students working together and by students working with other students. Is not the real aim of campus government that of supplying desirable learning experiences to new students by older students and by the administration so that an increasing self-direction will result? On a college campus there are "in-group" and "out-group" pressures, "group egos" in the form of ethnocentrism which exert authority on the individual. It is what the assimilation and integration of these pressures do to the individual, how he is molded by them, what responsibility he takes in acquiring self-control and self-direction in spite of these pressures, that makes for his success or failure.

When a strong student government organization is built on the campus, one that grows out of the needs of students and possesses power, authority, and responsibility, the loyalty of the in-group can be supplemented by a loyalty to the student body as a whole. More desirable mores of control can then arise, built on a pattern of cooperation not only of students with students but of students with faculty and administration, and built on the use of democratic practices, and responsibility for action.

What can a personnel staff do to bring about a strong student government and democratic mores of control? For one thing, they can build on the particular "mores of the culture" already opera-tive in the student body and put them in the framework of the "mores of control" of our total American culture. They can start with a foundation principle of our democracy, the consent of the governed, and upon that principle build the purposes and plans of a democratic student government, even though the need may have to be originated and developed through a process of educa-tion. The dynamics of the process might be as follows: first, to start with gaining the cooperation and sympathy of the adminis-tration and faculty; second, to interest a small group of student leaders in the plan; third, to proceed with the help of student leaders to educate the many small groups on the campus, each rep-resenting little democracies in themselves; fourth, to educate the entire student body through representatives and committees; fifth, to continue developing leadership, with each leader feeling a responsibility to understand and be guided by the thinking of his group, and with all members of the student body feeling a responsibility to participate in their government.

It can be seen from this process that leadership is necessary in establishing a strong student government. For this purpose, an in-service training program may be needed on the campus. In the leadership classes, some of the topics might include the qualities of leadership, the selection of leaders, types of leaders, a study of successful followership, an understanding of students' duties, ways of improving programs, a study of group dynamics, development of student cooperation in government, and the psychology of college students.

In such a developmental process, instead of faculty and student domination in the various forms of control, a college community can build *mutual* faculty and student *participation* and *cooperation* in its institutional mores of control.

Physical and Material Culture

Another element of culture that should be mentioned is the physical and material culture of the college environment. The drama, struggle, and mores of student life on each college campus are not only tied up with its cultural and historical development, but also with its geographical location, architectural design, and many material objects and symbols. The mores of student life growing out of the cultural and historical development of a college have been treated in a former section of this chapter under tradition which arises in part from the outside and in part from within the college.

The location of a college very often entangles its diversified student clientele in the problems of the larger society peculiar to that geographical region and brings about revolutionary mores on their part. A college in Pennsylvania, situated close to the Southern line and enrolling a large number of Southern students during the Civil War, was the scene of many student rebellions against the help offered to runaway slaves. At the same time, a Southern general passing through this college town ordered that its buildings be saved from conflagration because it was his alma mater.

Each college has its own cultural mores peculiar to its physical and geographical location. Even the most ardent believer in standardization would not assert that college life among the lakes of Wisconsin is identical with that in a Princeton dormitory or upon a Southern campus. Slosson at the beginning of the twentieth century traveled from campus to campus over various parts of the United States and has given a vivid description of how the physical culture and geographical location of a college affect the mores of a student body.[36] In the universities of the West he found that the young men with a loping Western gait and garbed in corduroys and sombreros did not remind him in the least of the college students he had known in the East. The rough redwood buildings did not look at all like the Colonial Club of Cambridge, or the Nassau Club of Princeton. There was at Stanford University an indescribable air of peace, of spaciousness, of leisure, of freedom, an air of the frontier and the farm, altogether symbolic of the larger region. He detected in students of the West more literary and artistic originality, which showed itself in their annuals, magazines, parades, and dramatics. Drama was a major interest. The University of California had a Greek theater, the largest of its kind in the world, located in a wooded, semicircular dell reached by a steep and winding path.

Slosson also observed a curious difference between Eastern and Western colleges with regard to the influence of the alumni. In the West the alumni were always urging their alma mater forward into untried paths. In the East, on the contrary, the alumni seemed to be, as a whole, a conservative, even a reactionary influence, opposing almost any change, wise or unwise. Eastern alumni were inclined to regard their alma mater as a relic of happy schooldays and as such to wish its physical and material environment kept intact and unaltered, so that when they returned they might find it as they remembered it. In 1888 over two thousand Yale alumni signed a petition remonstrating against the removal of an old fence that was in the way of one of the new buildings; they celebrated twenty years later the anniversary of "the fight that failed."[37]

In dealing with the Eastern universities it is impossible, according to Slosson, to ignore history. All the walls at the University of Pennsylvnia are literally covered with it. The buildings are veritable genealogical museums. Paintings, bas-reliefs, inscriptions, relics, manuscripts, and similar memorabilia catch the atten-

[36] From Edwin E. Slosson, *Great American Universities*. Copyright, 1910, by the Independent and The Macmillan Company and used with permission. p. 111, 137, 158–159, 362–363, 442, 522.
[37] *Ibid.*, p. 72.

tion of the visitor wherever he goes. The arrangement of dormitory groups about the courtyards, Slosson found, gave the effect of a cloister, a design which is traditionally regarded as conducive to idealistic thinking. The University of Pennsylvania had a widely diversified student body. There were representatives in the university of all the Old World groups which had been drawn upon to work in Pennsylvania's mines and factories. The son of the capitalist and the son of his humblest laborer might be found in the same classroom. Some of the students were poor and had parents who could not read. Others were well-to-do and well-groomed young men, who had automobiles to carry them from their luxurious fraternity houses to their classrooms a few blocks away. Then again there were the street cars which brought pale-faced, stoop-shouldered young men who snatched at learning and hurried away with it to unknown parts of the city. There was a noticeable atmosphere of informality and congeniality about the place. Princeton had the democracy of the club while Pennsylvania had the democracy of the street car. Slosson found at Columbia University that the first thing the visitor saw as he approached was the great gilded statue of Alma Mater; an old, old book is spread open upon her lap, but her eyes are not directed upon it. She is looking straight before her into the heart of the big buzzing city to the southward, while her open-handed gesture suggests that she regards knowledge not as something to be hoarded and hidden, but as something to be scattered as freely as possible to the world. After analyzing the issues in the student periodical, "The Columbia Spectator," over a period of ten years, one can say that the philosophic symbolism of the statute is represented today in the mores of the students. Their main interests are on the social problems of the society in which they live, seeking which lines of action to follow, and conducting campus opinion polls on national and international issues.

Such differences as existed in the character of these universities at the beginning of the century arose, according to Slosson, more from their history, culture, and physical environment than from any difference in their aims. Thus Harvard and Yale were coupled together because for more than two centuries they had been chief contributors to the intellectual life of the nation. Princeton and

Stanford might be conveniently classed together, notwithstanding their difference in age and the distance between them. Both were small institutions, admirable in architecture, and because they were situated in the country, had distinctive forms of student life. Princeton, like Yale, in the early twentieth century was much concerned over the question of how to develop the graduate and professional training demanded by modern conditions without destroying the unity of the college, which had been its chief pride.

This treatment by Slosson of physical and material culture assumes value today in a study of student mores. The climate, environmental setting, cultural facilities, accessibility to other places of culture, geographical location, all structure student "ways of doing things." According to a personnel worker in a junior college in a Midwestern state, an unfortunate situation exists there because the college is located on the third floor of the high school building. The impact of this physical housing situation is to make the students feel that they are still part of the high school. They continue to attend the high school dances and their social mores as college students remain the same as in their high school student life. It will always be of value for a personnel worker in a college community to study its physical environment, the parts of it particularly endeared to students, about which constructive mores can be built, and the particular line of development the environment can foster. Artistic development has been particularly indigenous to the Western universities. There may be especially fine environmental settings for religious meditation and spiritual development; there may be, as at Columbia, a center where the culture of the environment is conducive to a study of social and economic problems of society. There is always some particular phase of development in ways of student life that can be worked on. In one instance a skiing clubhouse belonging to a college is used for week-end parties of faculty and students, in which codes of good sportsmanship, character, and social building are particularly stressed. A retreat of student groups to near-by lakes, mountains, or the construction and use of a building on the campus, such as the Greek theater at the University of California, may develop the particular abilities and interests of a student body, and lead to mores indigenous to certain institutional material-physical culture.

In addition to the campus cultural and historical development, its regional location and the wider physical environment, its material equipment and architectural design also affect the mores of a student body. This subject will be covered more in detail in a later chapter under the title of social structuring.[38] The very setting of the buildings, their groupings, their compactness, or their spatiality affect student social life. Social cleavages exist on campuses where clubs, such as fraternities and sororities, have exclusive types of houses. These clubs are often rated in prestige according to what novel things architectural design could create for each house. Similarly, a dormitory housing many students will tend to have a social-cultural pattern different from that of small cottages housing a small number of girls. Residence halls with common rooms for recreational and social life, with a kitchenette and library on each floor, will likewise develop different social-cultural patterns from those of residence halls without these physical facilities. The location of student "gathering places," such as a Student Union building, also tends to affect social patterns.

Finally, many material objects and symbols work their way into the sentiments and mores of students. Morgan, in writing about Dickinson College, observes that President Durbin's final touch to the college building program in the early nineteenth century

was a system of trap-doors from every section of East College to the roof. This was a needed exit in case of fire, for which, fortunately, it has never been used. It was, however, useful to many student generations for all sorts of college pranks and especially as a way of escape when hard pressed by faculty pursuers.[39]

President Durbin's bell, obtained in Philadelphia, from which city its predecessor had been "waggoned" in 1810, was also the focus of college pranks for many years. The bell was rung so often that President Collins, on suggestion of the faculty, secured an "iron door and casement for the bell room." This added zest to

[38] See pages 130–133 of this study.
[39] J. H. Morgan, *Dickinson College*, p. 269. Copyright, 1933, by Dickinson College, Carlisle, Pa.

the game, and some of the most daring escapades for fifty years concerned the bell.

The bell, for example, inspired a rollicking drinking song, which was sung by saints and sinners alike for years:

> I wish I had a barrel of rum
> And sugar three hundred pounds,
> The college bell to mix it in,
> The clapper to stir it around;
> I'd drink to the health of Dickinson
> With the boys who are far and near,
> For I'm a rambling rake of poverty
> And the son of a gambolier.[40]

This incident in the history of one college shows how physical and material apparatus is used both destructively and constructively in the life of a student body. Had the social needs of the students at that college been more adequately met, perhaps the destructive influences would not have been so rampant. On the other hand, the bell afforded a sentiment, an attachment, a camaraderie in song for the campus life for many years.

Sometimes, throughout the years, a bit of campus property may become in contests an object of rivalry between colleges. Two years ago in a certain college a commotion arose when the college dining-room bell was confiscated by a visiting football team which had been defeated. It had long been the custom in this particular college to celebrate football victories by ringing the college dining-room bell, therefore to have it grabbed by a defeated visiting team was unpardonable. The entire college—president, faculty, students, and townspeople as well—were mightily disturbed until midnight, when the state police returned the bell. The old custom connected with the bell was near the hearts of the people of this college community. The entire system of "victory" mores which had existed on this campus for many years was threatened.

One has only to peruse college handbooks and yearbooks to see many evidences of how much objects and symbols of material culture on the college campus mean to students. References are made to "flirtation walk," "lovers' lane," the "old tower," the "cloistered walls," the ancient "ivy" on the chapel wall, the "hanging lanterns,"

40 *Ibid.*, p. 270.

the "dim gray chamber," "the cluster of trees," the "gateways" donated by the various classes, certain endeared old buildings as "Old West," "Old South," "Literary Hall," etc. Very frequently traditions spring from these material cultural objects, such as the Senior Tree Planting Ceremony, Vespers beneath the Ivied Walls, Easter Sunrise Ceremony in The Old Tower. Certain buildings may be set aside for particular ceremonies and reverence. A uniquely designed chapel on a college campus may affect the religious mores of youth.

The personnel worker would do well to study how these material cultural objects create a sentiment, a style, and a structuring of desirable student mores.

IMPLICATIONS FOR PERSONNEL WORKERS
AND EDUCATORS

Problems of the larger society peculiar to a geographical location appear very often on the horizon of student life and many of the schisms and student battles on the campus occur because of them. Personnel workers and educators should know something of the social problems common to the adult society in the environment in which the college is located. They should analyze also the type of college in which they are working, whether it has mainly a resident or a commuting student body. Then, they should ask themselves what are the limitations which the physical environment presents and how best to work with them. Also, on what parts of the physical environment can one capitalize for more constructive social mores? What kinds of relationships, social patterns, and character structure are being created by physical factors? In short, physical environment like cultural environment, as discussed earlier, is a conditioning factor in the lives of students, very often creating a character structure which leads to "ways of doing things" peculiar to the specific geographical location. Also, objects of material culture work their way into the sentiments of students and should be noted for their values.

Summary

It is hoped, first of all, that personnel workers and educators will become "culture-conscious" in whatever college they are. It is important that they see the relationship of cultural factors to the social behavior displayed on their campus. It would seem desirable for them to study the history and culture of the college for a better understanding of the mores in order ultimately to modify them in educationally desirable directions.

Personnel workers and educators must likewise see how three elements of culture, namely, the culture which the student brings, the traditional and established culture of the college, and the physical culture, interplay in the mores of student life. They must see the interdependence of these three elements and study how they can be drawn together in successful interaction. Incompatibility between parental, institutional, and societal domination leads to maladjustment in student life. Culture as manifested in physical objects should be reassessed by weighing the limitations as well as the potentialities it has for desirable social patterns.

Traditions and customs on a college campus represent a cultural and social heritage. This heritage is usually thought of as something static and persistent, something handed down from one student generation to the next. Traditions and customs on a campus which make up this cultural heritage are not ordinarily thought of as "ways of doing things" which each generation must interpret and reintegrate in terms of its own needs and interests. In the present age when educators and specialists in guidance are emphasizing the development of the college into an educational and cultural center for the community, it is a most appropriate time to reinterpret traditions and other legislative controls in terms of student needs. Curriculum is being adapted to the growth needs of students. International-mindedness is becoming an objective in college training. Campus activities are being carried into the work-world. The postwar world is becoming more of an organized world, a world of racial equality and a world of equal economic privileges and opportunities. In line with such change, all traditions, customs, and other traditional mores of control should be reassessed on every college campus by students as well as by the administration.

Furthermore, it is as personnel workers and educators are conscious of the cultural factors in the college environment and can work constructively with the total college community that mores can be built which will exert an effective social control on the campus.

Bibliography

GENERAL

Benedict, Ruth. *Patterns of Culture.* Boston: Houghton Mifflin Company, 1934. 290 p.

Boas, Franz. *Anthropology and Modern Life.* New York: W. W. Norton and Company, Inc., 1932. 255 p.

Cowley, W. H. and Waller, W. "A Study of Student Life." *Journal of Higher Education,* 6 : 132–142, March 1935.

Linton, Ralph. *The Cultural Background of Personality.* New York: D. Appleton-Century Company, Inc., 1945. 157 p.

Linton, Ralph. *The Study of Man.* New York: D. Appleton-Century Company, Inc., 1936. 503 p.

Lynd, Robert S. *Knowledge for What?* Princeton: Princeton University Press, 1939. 268 p.

Plant, James S. *Personality and the Cultural Pattern.* New York: The Commonwealth Fund, 1937. 432 p.

Roucek, J. S. *Sociological Foundations of Education.* New York: Thomas Y. Crowell Company, 1942. 771 p.

Todd, John E. *Social Norms and the Behavior of College Students.* New York: Bureau of Publications, Teachers College, Columbia University, 1941. 190 p.

Ware, Caroline. *The Cultural Approach to History.* New York: Columbia University Press, 1940. 359 p.

SPECIAL BIBLIOGRAPHY

The Culture Which the Student Brings

Day, D. D. "Rural Attitudes of Mississippi College Students." *Sociology and Social Research,* 25 : 342–350, March 1941.

Hale, Lincoln B. and Hartshorne, H. *From School to College.* New Haven: Yale University Press, 1939. 446 p.

Jameson, Samuel H. "Adjustment Problems of University Girls Because of Parental Patterns." *Sociology and Social Research,* 24 : 262–271, January–February 1940.

Katz, Daniel, Allport, F. H., and Jenness, M. B. *Students' Attitudes.* Syracuse, New York: The Craftsman Press, Inc., 1931. 408 p.

Moffett, M. L. *Social Background and Activities of Teachers College Students.* New York: Bureau of Publications, Teachers College, Columbia University, 1929. 133 p.

Sherif, Muzafer. *The Psychology of Social Norms.* New York: Harper and Brothers, 1936. 209 p.

Strang, Ruth. *Behavior and Background of Students in College and Secondary School.* New York: Harper and Brothers, 1937. 515 p.

Warner, W. L., Havighurst, R. J., and Loeb, Martin B. *Who Shall Be Educated?* New York: Harper and Brothers, 1944. 190 p.

Williamson, E. G. and Darley, J. G. "The Measurement of Social Attitudes of College Students; I. Standardization of Tests and Results of a Survey." *Journal of Social Psychology,* 8 : 219–229, May 1937.

Williamson, E. G. and Darley, J. G. "The Measurement of Social Attitudes of College Students; II. Validation of Two Aptitude Tests." *Journal of Social Psychology,* 8 : 231–242, May 1937.

Young, Kimball. *Social Attitudes.* New York: Henry Holt and Company, 1931. 382 p.

Young, Kimball. *Social Psychology.* New York: F. S. Crofts and Company, Inc., 1946. 558 p.

Traditional and Established Culture
of the College Campus

Bradshaw, Francis. *Contemporary Student Government at The University of North Carolina.* Chapel Hill: The University of North Carolina, 1938. Foreword.

Cowley, W. H. and Waller, W. "A Study of Student Life." *Journal of Higher Education,* 6 : 132–142, March 1935.

Cowley, W. H. "Challenge to Physical Education." *Journal of Higher Education,* 16 : 175–178, April 1945.

Cowley, W. H. "Significance of Student Traditions." Chapter I in *Higher Education and Society: A Symposium.* Norman: University of Oklahoma Press, 1936.

Coyle, Grace. *Social Process in Organized Groups.* New York: Richard R. Smith, Inc., 1930. 245 p.

Crawford, Mary M. *Student Folkways and Spending at Indiana University, 1940–1941.* New York: Columbia University Press, 1943. 271 p.

Gist, Noel P. "Culture Patterning in Secret Society Ceremonials." *Social Forces,* 14 : 497–505, May 1936.

Hand, Harold. *Campus Activities.* New York: McGraw-Hill Book Company, Inc., 1938. 357 p.

Harriman, Philip. "The Student-Faculty Congress." *Journal of Higher Education,* 8 : 413–417, November 1937.

Hawes, James A. *Twenty Years Among the Twenty Year Olds.* New York: E. P. Dutton and Company, Inc., 1929. 259 p.

Hosman, E. M. "Convocations in Urban Universities." *School and Society,* 47 : 316–318, March 5, 1938.

Lloyd-Jones, Esther. *Social Competence and College Students.* Washington, D. C.: American Council on Education, 1940. 89 p.

McKown, Harry C. *The Student Council.* New York: McGraw-Hill Book Company, Inc., 1944. 352 p.

Park, R. E. and Burgess, E. W. *Introduction to the Science of Sociology.* Chicago: Chicago University Press, 1924. 1040 p.

Price, Louise. *Creative Group Work on the Campus.* New York: Bureau of Publications, Teachers College, Columbia University, 1941. 437 p.

Sumner, William G. *Folkways.* Boston: Ginn and Company, 1906. 692 p.

Waller, Willard. *Sociology of Teaching.* New York: J. Wiley and Sons, Inc., 1932. 467 p.

Warren, Roland L. "A Sociological Analysis of Student Activities." *Educational Forum,* 5 : 442–457, May 1941.

Physical and Material Culture

Morgan, J. H. *Dickinson College.* Carlisle, Pa.: Dickinson College, 1933. 460 p.

Seeley, Evelyn. "Geography, Youth and Idealism in the Colleges." *Literary Digest,* 119 : 17, April 13, 1935.

Slosson, Edwin E. *Great American Universities.* New York: The Macmillan Company, 1910. 575 p.

III

THE CULTURE OF THE WIDER COMMUNITY

An analysis of the college as a culture-matrix has been presented in the preceding chapter, together with the development of three interactive elements of culture on a college campus—the culture which the student brings, the established and traditional culture of the college, and the physical and material culture of the environment. At this point a fourth interactive element in the culture-matrix of a campus should be added—the culture of the wider community. Since this phase also deals with a number of influences, it has been thought wise to devote a separate chapter to it.

The purpose of this chapter, then, is to describe how the culture of the wider community intermeshes with that of the college campus. It shows also how social conditions of society at large have reflections in the mores of a college campus. It presents four influences in the culture of the wider community which intermesh with that of the college and create a particular kind of mores: first, the influence of alumni; second, the influence of the local community in which the college is located; third, the influence of certain national organizations which have local representation on the campus; and fourth, the influence of society at large.

Influence of the Alumni

In 1929 the Aims and Policies Committee of the American Alumni Council stated that it believed that the period of organization of the college alumni associations was nearly over, and that before entering upon a new era it would be well to take stock of their accomplishments to date. A study was therefore begun by

79

sending a questionnaire of 135 questions to all alumni secretaries of the colleges and universities in the United States and Canada. According to J. G. Olmstead, at that time president of the American Alumni Association, the conclusions of the study showed that "The purpose of practically all alumni associations, stated in whatever way they may be in their constitutions, is to promote the welfare of their Alma Mater. Incidental to that, they may try to forward their own material prosperity, educational development, and social enjoyment."[1]

One section of the questionnaire was devoted to undergraduate relations. In general the questions centered around the relations the alumni associations have with undergraduates, the ways in which the local alumni clubs cooperate with the admissions office in finding and selecting students; and whether the alumni association conducts athletic contests, debates, oratorical contests, and gives financial grants and scholarships to interest high school students indirectly in the college. In reply to this particular section of the questionnaire, sent to members and non-members of the American Alumni Council, 131 alumni groups gave statements regarding their efforts to strengthen the relationship between graduates and undergraduates. These efforts bear out in one way or another what has been stated above as the main purpose of alumni associations. Some of the replies were as follows:

An alumnus sits as a non-voting member of the student senate; the alumni secretary works in close touch with the dramatic association, glee club, and any organization road tours.

The Alumnae are invited to the annual prom, to the student recitals and speaking programs, to Moving-Up Day, May Day, Founders' Day, college lectures, and other occasions, and, of course, to all Commencement affairs.

The alumni office aids in management of Union building, which is closely connected with the student council and woman's governing association. The secretary also works closely with senior class, takes part in Freshman Week, Initiation Ceremony, and organizes the Second Generation Club.

The Council has a committee on undergraduate life that meets at

[1] J. G. Olmstead, *Alumni Achievement*, p. 5. Copyright, 1931, by The American Alumni Council.

dinner with representative undergraduates to discuss problems of campus life, periodically during the college year.

The alumni loan fund is in constant use by seniors; alumni prominent in various lines of work speak to and advise students interested in their vocational future; alumni present athletic trophies.

Vocational teas, at which prominent alumnae speak to students on various professions. We always give a tea for foreign students.

Freshman banquet the night of registration; after that continuous contacts from the standpoint of vocational guidance, employment, and financial assistance.[2]

Besides the purely social gatherings which the alumni arranged for the undergraduates, their vocational counsel, and their cooperation in finding employment, the alumni also controlled in various ways the selection of students. Some of the reports on this subject are as follows:

Our local clubs are including high school seniors in their interest and have entertained several groups this fall. They are planning cooperation with our admissions office.

One club sends lists of prospective students, and another offers a high school prize.

The alumni award several high school scholarships, medals, trophies, etc., for special accomplishments.

We have about twenty regional scholarship committees who raise money and select students from their localities to whom scholarships shall be given.

The college allocates to larger local clubs the privilege of selecting from one to three outstanding local boys for scholarships valued at about $400 a year. The local clubs hold competitions and obtain valuable newspaper publicity. Some locals hold high school track meets or award trophies.[3]

The above statements show a desire on the part of a large proportion of alumni to keep in touch with the college, and to do something for it. On the other hand, there are the college administrators who also want things done for the college. Olmstead states:

[2] *Ibid.*, p. 106–107.
[3] *Ibid.*, p. 109–110.

The past five years has seen a very decided effort on the part of colleges to secure the cooperation of their alumni along three lines. The most general is that of interesting high school students in the college. The second is asking the alumni to pass critical judgment on applicants. This usually means one or more interviews and the filling out of an extended factual and reaction blank. The third is asking the alumni to furnish funds for scholarships.
. . . The alumni are being asked to furnish funds which they themselves will assign, usually by selecting someone from their town or their class, depending upon the group that has raised the fund. They are also being asked to furnish funds which the college at its discretion may assign to worthy students.[4]

One can see from these reports that the relationship between alumni and college has been interdependent; the college has depended on the alumni, and the alumni on the college. Olmstead's report was written during a depression period, and the likelihood of the presence of some undesirable alumni influences on the campus may be understood by the pressure of that particular period for students, for publicity, and for financial aid. There is no doubt that the alumni of various colleges contribute in a constructive way to student life. However, these reports serve to call to attention the influence that some of these alumni relationships have on the mores of a student body.

To have alumni attend a student senate, even as non-voting members, and work with other student organizations may lead to pressure to have things continue unchanged on a campus, that is, to meet the needs of alumni instead of students. When alumni take part in organizing the "Second Generation Club," entertaining daughters of alumnae, and having charge of the selection of students, there may be an increased emphasis on social stratification on the campus and an inbreeding of the student body. Undesirable admissions techniques may result from having alumni choose students for the college. The influence of alumni is particularly marked in this respect where they contribute greatly to the support of the college in the form of endowments or by various kinds of financial contributions. By these means alumni are able, in many cases, to dictate policies. Noteworthy attempts to dictate policies are usually made in relation to athletics, a spectacular

4 *Ibid.*, p. 109,

aspect of student life. The influence of alumni, for example, operates definitely in a New England college where they contribute
greatly to its financial support. According to a former student,
in the selective process of the admissions program of this college
the son of an alumnus will always be given preference. The
grandfather-father-son pattern thus exists and the customs and
folkways are transmitted to the present student body through
direct social inheritance. The mores of the alumni are closely
identified with the money and the college spirit they represent.
All colleges attempt to cultivate their alumni through such familiar devices as class reunions, "gab fests," football occasions,
alumni journals, and anniversaries.

Another molding influence of alumni on students would seem
to stem from vocational teas and addresses at which students decide to follow the careers of alumni. The fact that the alumni
secretary takes part in Freshman Week or Initiation Ceremony,
and that alumni are especially invited to such traditional events in
student life as Moving-Up Day, May Day, and Founders' Day
would seem to indicate their desire to "hold fast" to their "college-
day" memories. The alumna, eighty years old, who lives on a
present-day campus in a college referred to earlier in this study
and tries to extend the customs and traditions of her day—which
upon analysis are filled with superstition and fictitious episodes—
presents a serious problem to a personnel worker. It is this "holding fast" to the college-day memories and the values of undergraduate days that exerts a problematic influence on the campus
and interferes with the college mores of the present. But the average alumnus is loathe to see his college campus change and to have
new ways of doing things replace the old. The veterans on first
returning to the campus of a New England college, according to an
alumnus, wanted to do away with the old traditions and customs,
but after some months on the campus expressed a desire to have
them back. They had heard their families so often talk about
them and, if they no longer exist, they will feel that they have
missed the great events in college life. As Cowley and Waller have
expressed it: "The ancestors of each generation do not die and
pass out of the picture. On the contrary, they are very much alive
and vocal and must be reckoned with in the persons of alumni

who return at frequent intervals to beat their 'tom-toms' lest the old tradition fail."[5]

A good example of alumni wanting the old mores of their undergraduate life to remain on their campus is the upheavals which were brought about on the Yale and Harvard campuses when new house plans were developed. The alumni fought the new plans vigorously because they recognized that student life would be changed into a pattern different from that which they had experienced. If one were to make a study of scholarships granted by alumni to their alma maters, one would without a doubt find many traces of their undergraduate mores. These regressive tendencies that alumni exert thus help to maintain the rigidity of the mores in a college culture complex. Waller speaks of this regression:

It is the unadjusted and the failures in life who are in general most enthusiastic about keeping up their school connections; if they have adjusted themselves to adult life their interests and desires will have moved on irrevocably from their school-day memories.[6]

Besides the particular influences mentioned here, alumni also exert their influence on a student body through various national organizations on a campus, particularly fraternities and sororities. Rivalry between alumni groups on campuses in connection with fraternity housing often creates a financial burden on a student body. Fraternity men and women spend much more time and thought upon this phase of college life than should be allotted to it.

Occasionally, as mentioned in the previous chapter, alumni operate to keep a college administration and student body from meeting the social problems and societal influences of the times in a reasonable way. According to several personnel workers interviewed, it is the alumni active in the college's denominational church organizations, who keep the regulation "no dancing, no cardplaying, no smoking" in the college mores. As a result students may not smoke on the campus but they smoke at the outskirts and visit outside places where smoking and dancing are allowed.

[5] W. H. Cowley and Willard Waller, "A Study of Student Life," *Journal of Higher Education*, 6 : 133, March 1935.

[6] Willard Waller, *Sociology of Teaching*, p. 84. Copyright, 1932, by John Wiley & Sons, Inc.

Besides the regressive tendencies of alumni which make them want to keep the college as it was "in their days," there are many alumni influences which have a broadening effect. There are many instances where cooperation, intelligent attention, and financial contributions and endowments have been given by alumni for educational equipment and enterprises, for the enlargement and improvement of faculty and curricula, and for fellowships and scholarships.

IMPLICATIONS FOR PERSONNEL WORKERS AND EDUCATORS

The alumni can be an influence for good and for strength to a college and student body if they have broad vision, work with the philosophy of the institution, and keep alert to the needs of its present student body. This is a matter of interaction between the college and the alumni association—the college educating the alumni concerning the needs of students, and the alumni informing the college of the educational deficiencies they have discovered since graduation. Perhaps through this interactive process of education, student life may move forward with less pressure and with more cooperation from those who have gone before.

Influence of the Local Community

The influence of the local community in which the college is located plays a role in the creation of student mores in a college culture. College students who work in town stores and hotels may be exploited as to working hours and wages. Eating places and amusement centers may or may not have high standards. The town may commercialize college souvenirs. Churches, lodges, and other organizations may drain the college students' talents and energies. On the other hand, the college may not use enough of these opportunities in giving students experiences in a community's life. This may result in a debilitating isolation of the college from its most immediate wider environment.

The town may become socially a leech to the college men, as happened between Boston and Harvard in the late nineteenth century. Morison writes:

. . . When the supply of eligible young men in Boston was decreased by the westward movement, the Boston mamas suddenly became aware that Harvard contained many appetizing young gentlemen from New York, Philadelphia, and elsewhere. One met them in the summer at Newport or Beverly or Bar Harbor; naturally one invited them to Mr. Papanti's or Mr. Foster's "Friday evenings" when they entered college, to the "Saturday evening sociables" sophomore year and to coming-out balls thereafter. What was more natural than to ask your brother's college friends to your coming-out dance? This was very nice for the right young men, and pleasant for the girls; but it cut a deep chasm in the college.[7]

These boys formed a masculine contingent of Boston society and the necessity fell upon them to determine which of their college friends were most socially presentable. This social cleavage widened the chasm between the Yard and the Gold Coast. Here we have differences of position in the local community determining important differences in the college student body. The young man's status as the friend of a brother of a Boston feminine elite, or as a graduate of a certain preparatory school, or as a son of wealthy parents determined his position in Harvard as well as in Boston.

On occasion, the doctrines of a college and the community come sharply into conflict. In one small college town a petition was started to abolish beer-drinking places. The ministers, various associations, and people of the town petitioned the president and deans of the college to sign the petition. The president knowing that parents of many of his students allowed beverages within their homes and accompanied their sons and daughters to various places where drinks were served, refused to sign the petition. Straightway, the town put on a campaign to reform the social mores of the college.

In another instance, a small denominational university of about one thousand students located in a small town is subject to a church domination symbolized peculiarly by the location of the four churches of the town on the four corners of the town square. Retired ministers of the denominational faith of the university live in the town. Many times there is a clash between "town and

[7] Reprinted by permission of the publishers from Samuel Eliot Morison, *Three Centuries of Harvard, 1636-1936*. Cambridge, Mass.: Harvard University Press, 1936. p. 420.

gown" if those representing the "gown" do not conform to the Christian ethics of the "town." Activities are not scheduled in the college on certain days of the year because these days have special Christian significance to the town.

An instance is recalled where freshmen in another college were to gather wood for bonfires. No wood was available on the college campus nor were the students able to buy wood, so they resorted to the next possible step, that of stealing the wood from the local community. This did not coincide with the community's standard of honor, so straightway a short term in jail was used to correct the mores of these college youths.

In one college town in the Midwest a great medical center in many respects overshadows and rules the college mores.

A Negro college in the South presents an example of how the social mores of the college have been tied up with a town environment resulting in various types of social regulations. The environment in question is a congested undesirable Negro district located between the college and the downtown section. Sometimes students visit undesirable places in this neighborhood. Because of the necessity of passing through this section to reach the downtown section, girls are not permitted to leave the campus on Saturday and Sunday nights. On other nights and during the day, they must go in groups. This situation has inevitably led to new social regulations and procedures in the college.

The examples presented in the preceding pages show that the folkways and mores of the campus may come into conflict with the culture patterns of the local community. On the other hand, the college may not exert a good influence on the town. College youth very often reject even the social elite of the town; girls of the town are invited to college dances only when the preferred girls from their homes or other colleges cannot come. College men may make it a custom not to buy corsages or souvenirs for the town girls, although they may supply these for their own college girls or for girls from an outside college. According to a personnel worker in an Eastern state, the town in which her college is located is quite conservative while the college, a denominational institution, is more liberal. The college requires a liberal and well-trained minister in the church of its denomination which most of the students attend. Many times conflict arises between college officials and townspeople who belong to the same denomination. Townspeople occasionally come to the campus for lecture series or Christmas services, but the college does not extend its influence too well into the community because of the basic incompatibility and an unwillingness on the part of the college to work educationally with the community.

One might say, however, that the influences of gown and town are interactive. Canby points out that the college town has a character and a personality unlike other towns; its imprint of small-town respectability, convention, and common sense is deeper upon American education than has ever been guessed.[8] In his own alma mater, Yale in the early twentieth century, Canby relates that the campus and the college buildings dominated New Haven's architecture like the temple and citadel of a Greek city-state, a difficult relationship since there was always some doubt in the minds of the town folk whether the college was an asset or a parasite. The college was sometimes a credit to the town but also an embarrassment. The nature of the community was conditioned by the college, of which it was the irritable but fostering mother. Yale, relates Canby, was privileged socially, not only in the hand-picked sons of the cultivated and well-to-do that came as students, but in the close contacts between the faculty and the aristocracy of the college town. But it was limited and conditioned also by the life of a small-town community, which no matter how good its traditions, how genuine its culture, was a little priggish, and very much inbred.

Canby notes that there were subtle jealousies between town and gown which could not be assigned to differences in income. New Haven was irritated by its own deferences to an institution that did not live for profits. The town derived a goodly share of its income from the expenditures of the college and its students, and this, too, it resented, feeling that it was committed to an approval of what the college was doing. Hence, there was more interpenetration than appeared on the surface. The college taught the town to discuss ideas; the college and the town blended in the adult life of the community, for the habit of the undergraduate fraternity

[8] Henry S. Canby, *Alma Mater*, p. 3. Copyright, 1936, by Farrar and Rinehart, Inc.

persisted in dozens of little clubs of talkers which flourished throughout the town because their members had learned club-ability. The influence of gown upon town and of town upon gown was indecisive and yet interactive. The undergraduates by and large belonged to the faction of the gown, but had themselves come in a vast majority from other small towns, and so were in ideas and attitudes toward learning far closer to the Philistines of the streets than to the Israelites of the campus faculty. The studentry was a faction within the college body, which constantly practiced direct warfare or passive resistance against its superiors, usually with the sneaking sympathy of both parents and town. Hence there was a split in the college itself, so that in his days, relates Canby, not a duality but a trinity—town, gown, and sweater— would have best described the community.

A present-day event of an unusual nature is built upon an inter-action between students and faculty of one college and the people of the local community in which it is located. This is the Ham and Eggs Show and Folk Festival which is held on the campus of a Negro state college in the South the first week in March each year. This is an event planned for the express purpose of educating the community and also the students who go back into the rural com-munities. A description of this event was given in the previous chapter.[9] Furthermore, in this college the main purpose of the extracurricular activities is the best development of the individual. The activities are correlated with home activities. Students are made mindful of their needs and the health viewpoint is empha-sized, such problems being considered as using health measures in their own community, earning a living, and beautifying the home community. The students practice teaching in the rural areas; fre-quently a home economics division is established in her own com-munity by a graduating teacher. In the college's effort for integra-tive education, the needs of one public school in the community are assumed by the college. In this school, not only personal and social needs are considered but physical needs, such as illustrative materials and equipment.

An event related by a dean of girls in a high school of a Mid-western state shows how the institutional or administrative mores

[9] See page 39 of this study.

of a school affected faculty and community mores and finally how the student mores intermeshed with those of the institution and society. The superintendent of this particular school system who had held the position for some thirty years was quite authoritarian in his relationships with the teachers. It was in the teachers' contract that they could not appear before the school board. Much friction existed in the school, and many members of the faculty left each year. The school buildings were crowded, so a bond issue was proposed to start a building program. The superintendent made a speech at a Rotary Club on the postwar building program. One of the former faculty wrote a letter to the newspaper praising the superintendent for his postwar building program, but asked, "What is being done today? Children are displeased, teachers' salaries are too low, and good teachers are leaving." Her letter was followed by innumerable letters from town citizens. A school board election was to be held within a month. The election of new school board members flamed into a vital issue. The townspeople organized a citizens' league to represent the people versus the superintendent. They also selected a good candidate for the board of school directors. The bank group, which was tied up with the business group and interested only in having the bonds issued by their bank, chose a lawyer of an outstanding firm for their candidate on the school board. The lawyer was interested in the business end of the building program. The election was bought and the law firm won.

After the election, editorials by a prominent school official and criticisms by the people of the recent election were run in the newspaper. After a certain amount of criticism, the students entered the scene. The president of the student council and a committee had attended a student council convention, accompanied by the head of the town youth center. When they returned the committee set to work to draw up a satisfactory plan of guidance and student activities to meet their needs. They studied guidance manuals in the library in order to map the kind of administrative plan they wanted. They asked to present the plan to the school board. The school board, beset with newspaper criticism of the politics that had been used to get the lawyer on the board, realized that they must take some step to allay the criticism. They allowed the student committee to present their plan, offered some helpful suggestions, and the superintendent was instructed by the board to let the students proceed as they wanted.

The students then met the faculty members in groups of three, presented their plan, and each time asked for suggestions. Helpful suggestions for clarifying the plan were given. After the faculty had all been reached, the students asked permission to visit the classrooms on a certain day in order to educate the students of the school in the matter. The teachers were to help them, if students were too unruly in their behavior. The plan was explained to the students. It called for the appointment of two deans, a dean of girls and a dean of boys, the extension of extracurricular activities, the establishment of a debating club, a lighter teaching load, and more pay for teachers. After the students had been informed of the plan, they were asked to take home a copy of the plan, tell their parents about it, and have them telephone a school board member to tell him whether they were or were not in favor of it. Almost all telephoned in the affirmative. A complete reorganization of the school was thus effected.

The dynamics of this situation should be of interest to a personnel staff. The old authoritarian mores were shaken when new outside contacts, personified in the citizens' league, became powerful. The citizen mores met the arm of politics symbolized in the mores of the business group. However, the powerful drives of youth in this institution, directed by a person with vision, actually overthrew authoritarian and special-interest groups.

If they can be brought to see the problem clearly, to understand all the facts, students very often through their own efforts can build a superstructure of constructive mores upon those which for a long time have been disintegrative to the stability of an institution. This incident also shows that interaction between a school and a local community can bring about the needed strength for building new and constructive "ways of doing things."

IMPLICATIONS FOR PERSONNEL WORKERS AND EDUCATORS

The American college is molded and conditioned by the nature and practices of the town in which it is located and, vice versa, the town is conditioned by the college. This conditioning has had exploitive and also constructive effects in the structuring of student mores. These patterns in the main affect the social, economic, and religious realms of student life. The town may be a social and economic leech on the college and create a caste and class structure on the campus. The college may induce a destructive caste and class in the social and economic life of the town, which, in turn, reacts again on the campus. The religious mores of the town may come in conflict with the social behavior of the students; this may lead to open warfare.

The small town has long been too provincial and restrictive in its influence upon college students. The college has too long been a "cloister" for youth. New civic patterns must be built in the mores of college youth, and it would seem appropriate for the college, representing as it does an educative force, to take the lead. This new town-college influence should be interactive. Much is written today of the "School and Community." The columns on this subject in *Readers Guide* exceed in number what is written on any other subject. Although "College and Community" is also mentioned and a few colleges are working on the angle of "work experiences" in the community, too many colleges are neglecting to use the community as a laboratory in which their students may lead, work, and exercise civic responsibility.

The college is not doing enough to educate the town; adult education has too long been neglected. Use of college facilities and student leaders has often been denied the town. Many colleges draw a large part of their student clientele from the neighboring community districts and the students return to work in these same communities. One of the examples given previously in this section shows how a Southern state college interacted with the community in which it was located to meet both the needs of the community and of the students. The last example given shows how a total interaction of administration, faculty, town, and students was able to build a superstructure of new mores.

It would appear that if the town is to become less provincial in its influence upon students, and the students less cloistered, there must be more chance for social control by the constructive interaction of town and students.

Influence of National Organizations

As to the influence on student mores of certain national organizations which have local representation on the campus, the case of the influence of national sorority and fraternity organizations comes to mind. The desire of alumni in national fraternities to compete with each other has brought about large and expensive houses with financial burdens too great for the current undergraduate body to bear. This resulted, particularly after 1929, in the college taking over the fraternities and refusing to let them expand without presenting careful plans and obtaining the consent of the administration of the college. Many national organizations establish philanthropic centers, such as clinics, girls' and boys' camps, to which the local chapters are expected to contribute financially and whose cause is expected to be fostered on each campus. Although this has some advantages, very often it seriously drains a student's energy and time. Recently, the necessity of doubling up in living conditions in a strong denominational liberal arts college of the Middle West put girls of different sororities and independents or non-sorority girls together. The housemother of this particular group remarked on the friendliness which existed. This arrangement, leading to what seems more democratic mores in college social life, is being opposed, according to a personnel worker, by a national sorority association which desires that its own members have a separate house and live together. It is this kind of "return to the old ways of doing things" that is being criticized on many campuses.

Many constructive plans are being made, however, by the fraternity-sorority world of today, such as plans for fraternity counselors and more inclusive patterns of selection. In an article[10] from one of the national sororities in our college world, the challenging question is posed: "How may the fraternity more effectively live up to its responsibilities?" The following lines of attack are proposed: first, by squarely facing its unforgivable sin, its *methods of selecting* members, rushing. The article develops the

[10] Edith Crabtree, "Mutual Suspicion Blocks Full Attainment," *Themis of Zeta Tau Alpha*, 43 : 97, March 1945.

thesis that if this problem were really faced, most others would become insignificant. "We believe in the right of social organizing. We give everyone else the same right. But we lay ourselves open to just criticism if we disrupt the whole campus in the exercise of our right." Second, chapters should be established only with the knowledge and the approval of the administration. Third, fraternity officers and all those having campus contacts must really know the campus, its attitudes, its objectives, its traditions, and its mores. Suggestions which visiting officers may make must be in accord with the needs and conditions of the specific campus. Fourth, the fraternity should keep the administrative officers in charge of student life, usually the dean of women and the dean of men, informed about the fraternity in its chapter relations. Fifth, fraternity officers should keep in touch with educational trends and changes. Opportunities for doing this are legion. Sixth, the fraternity should keep its alumni up to date. Nothing is more disastrous than for an alumna, no matter how loyal, to attempt to counsel students from the platform of "When I was in college."

National overhead organizations also exert an influence on student religious groups on the campus. Very frequently national conferences of these organizations bring about changed mores on a campus. Students attending these conferences become imbued with new ideas of service, and organization, and return to their alma mater ready to reform its organization and thinking. Sometimes this change does not meet with the established mores of the administration and faculty. It frequently interferes with the established mores a certain denomination has developed in a particular college culture. The Y.M.C.A. and Y.W.C.A. are the oldest and most persistent of voluntary student associations. Some of the most creative movements in the religious mores of college students have come out of the religious insights and pioneering of these Christian associations. They dramatize the essential unity of the church and carry forward a non-sectarian campus religious ministry, drawing Christian and non-Christian students together in a wide variety of campus, community, national, and world services.

A parallel and almost identical program has developed among Catholic students with the formation of college Catholic clubs, called the Newman Foundation. These clubs are joined together in the National Association of College Catholic Clubs. In 1923 the Jewish students formed the Hillel Foundation. Denominational organizations also exist on many campuses—the Wesley Foundation, the Lutheran Student Association, the Southern Baptists—mainly to keep the student close to the church in which he has been brought up.

In 1944 the United Student Christian Council was created by the National Intercollegiate Christian Council and by the National Committee on University Work. Through this organization, denominational groups as well as Y.M.C.A.'s and Y.W.C.A.'s are now members of the World's Student Christian Federation, which binds together Christian students of all nations and races.

Other national organizations, voluntarily and otherwise, have entered the college campus and have been a constructive influence, although not all of their potentialities have been developed. The National Youth Administration, for example, penetrated the colleges in the early 1930's. It was a national organization of particular value on a college campus, permitting a group of students to remain in college and enjoy a certain mobility on the campus which would otherwise not have been possible. Although the N.Y.A. exerted a constructive influence, it also had grave faults. It often lacked real planning and purpose; work projects were chosen on a haphazard basis; little attention was given to relating the work to the student's abilities and aptitudes. Students were made to fit the job instead of the job fitting the students. There was careless supervision of the work; it also created a bad morale on the part of the student body as they felt anything they did was to be paid for. However, in this organization there is a possibility for building work patterns into the mores of student life. A social control might be effected which would lead to a program of work assigned with a guidance and educational point of view, and mores of better and wiser spending would result. It is hoped that more real work experiences, such as at Antioch, will be in the picture of the mores of the campus.

Another national association which has brought about constructive mores, according to a personnel worker of a Negro state college in the South, is The National Association for the Advancement of Colored People. About three fourths of the students in this particular college belong to this association. They hold regular meetings and keep in close touch with national Negro problems. They take many of the national problems as local issues; they frequently raise money for certain drives; the past year students wrote a play for the national association.

IMPLICATIONS FOR PERSONNEL WORKERS
AND EDUCATORS

The national fraternity-sorority system has for many years been discussed as to its advantages and disadvantages. Some campuses have disbanded fraternity organizations because of pressure from the student body for more democratic mores. Recently because of large college enrollments the national organizations have permitted the local chapters to open their doors and take care of more students. However, the national organizations on many campuses even in the enrollment crises have reverted to "their old ways of doing things." The following is a frequent remark from the sorority world: "By taking in more people the organization would be unwieldy; the old traditions, ways of governing would be changed."

Others are making a desperate attempt to revise their thinking, habits, and traditions. If, as one national sorority has outlined, the national organizations are really interested in making the selective mechanisms more democratic, if they are willing to cooperate with the administration and with the rest of the student body in building constructive mores, and if they are willing to educate their own alumni concerning their regressive tendencies, then they may furnish a structure and an organization that would be acceptable on a democratic campus.

The two national religious organizations, the Y.M.C.A. and the Y.W.C.A., have long been the center on the American college campus for the development of religious and moral life, offering opportunities also for student growth and leadership. In some colleges they have not extended too satisfactorily their influence and cooperation into the community in which the college is located. Perhaps a greater interaction could be effected. The national racial and denominational student groups on the college campus have a worth-while purpose, but too often they create segmental patterns which do not work together in a unity of purpose, in interracial equality, or in the development of *interfaith* fellowship and cooperation. The World's Student Christian Federation, with its unity of program for all races and all nations, seems to be meeting this need at the present time.

In this crisis of war disillusionments and of injustices suffered by racial minorities, college youth need to go on religious pilgrimages—to ponder religious values, to find a satisfying philosophy of life, and to take part in building a better world. The religious mores of the college world should be reassessed and faith-provoking values brought to the fore. Most colleges are falling short of their possibilities in both the curricular and the extra-curricular religious program. Pulpit, classroom, organized groups, national overhead organizations, campus programs, and counseling services should all be integrated in creating a total religious program to meet the personal, social, and religious needs of students today. In this way can one build a pervasive religious quality into the mores of the campus.

It would seem that in the postwar world, with more young people in the colleges, these national organizations could give the student broader perspectives and visions on the social problems of the day. As to the importance of national overhead organizations, Chapin writes:

Local face to face groups are supplanted by, become linked with, and are dominated through national overhead organizations. This is not only the era of trusts, business consolidations, and chain stores; it is also the age of hierarchies of social groups with centralized guidance and remote controls. . . . These social changes are reflected in extra-curricular activities. Thornhill and Landis have shown that the average amount of extra-curricular activities of the classes of 1900 and 1910 in Wesleyan University shows a marked increase. The average number of points for 1900 seniors was 24.6 as compared with 42.7 for 1910 seniors.

Of 533 campus organizations in existence at University of Minnesota from 1887 to year 1924–1925, there were 300 in existence in 1925. . . . An examination of the sorts of organization that ceased to function as compared with the kind that were active in 1925 shows a high mortality among music, literary societies, publications, oratory, debate, and dramatics and a low mortality among sororities, fraternities, honor societies, religious organizations, and student government.

It is evident that the sort of organization which survived is the sort of organization for which there were national ties, strong traditions, and in some cases centralized control. In other words, it seems that the remote social controls of derivative groups, such as national organizations, supply a source of strength in our modern complex social order that extends even to extra-curricular activities.[11]

Influence of Society at Large

The influences of the culture of the wider community on the mores of a college campus have been discussed in relation to alumni, the local community, and national organizations. In the culture of the wider community there is, lastly, the influence of society at large on the college mores. There are innumerable evidences to show that societal influences have always been felt, many times with conflict, and will undoubtedly continue to be felt on the campus.

Allen mentions the fight against Bolshevism in the colleges in the 1920's and how college graduates called for the dismissal of professors suspected of radicalism. A cloud of suspicion hung in the air and intolerance became an American virtue.[12] He also speaks of other societal influences:

As year followed year of prosperity, the new diffusion of wealth brought marked results. There had been a great boom in higher education immediately after the war, and the boom continued, although at a somewhat slackened pace, until college trustees were beside themselves wondering how to find room for the swarming applicants. There was an epidemic of outlines of knowledge and books of etiquette for those who had got rich quick and wanted to get cultured quick and become socially at ease. . . . Business was regarded with new veneration . . . college alumni, gathered at their annual banquets, fervently applauded banker trustees who spoke of education as one of the greatest American industries and compared the president and the dean to business executives. The colleges organized business courses and cheerfully granted credit to candidates for degrees in the Arts and Sciences for their work in advertising, copywriting, marketing methods, elementary stenography, and drug-store practice.

---

11 F. Stuart Chapin, "Research Studies of Extracurricular Activities and Their Significance in Reflecting Social Changes," *The Journal of Educational Sociology,* 4 : 492, April 1931.

12 Frederick Lewis Allen, *Only Yesterday, An Informal History of the Nineteen Twenties,* p. 58–59. Copyright, 1931, by Harper and Brothers.

. . . The Harvard Business School established annual advertising awards, conferring academic éclat upon well-phrased sales arguments for commercial products.[13]

Allen shows how the diffusion of wealth and the veneration of business in the 1920's had its reverberations on the college campus. Angell, in the latter years of the same decade, writes concerning the changes in standards of entertainment which also were reflected on the campus. He relates how this change was more fully achieved in the American life of the twenties than ever before because of the modern means of communication, new inventions such as motion pictures, and the high per-capita wealth of the country. He writes:

The amount of interest among students in entertainments is perhaps not, however, as significant as the kind of entertainments they generally choose. Those types which appeal primarily to the higher powers of the mind, such as good drama, symphony concerts, and the more thoughtful lectures have a comparatively small following, while those which, like athletic contests and frivolous or sensual moving pictures, appeal to the grosser emotions and require little critical appreciation are very popular. The underlying cause for this state of affairs is the contemporary preoccupation with the immediately stimulating rather than with the vital aspects of life. Undergraduates, brought up in this current of externalism and superficiality, have never had the opportunity of developing refined sensibilities.[14]

In addition to the automobile we must reckon as contributing causes of the change in standards of female conduct the highly sexed motion picture, the weakening of religious control, and contact with the looser moral code; but more deep-seated than any of these is that movement generally called the emancipation of women. Old restraints are off; the modern girl refuses to be chaperoned; she wishes to see life on equal terms with her brothers. Parents are almost helpless in the face of their daughters' determination to live their lives in their own way.[15]

Writing of a later decade in America, the nineteen-thirties, Allen points out:

Among the hatless and waistcoatless young men of the college campuses, with their tweed coats and flannel slacks, and among the col-

[13] *Ibid.,* p. 175–178.

[14] Robert C. Angell, *The Campus,* p. 148–149. Copyright, 1928, by Appleton-Century-Crofts, Inc.

[15] *Ibid.,* p. 169.

lege girls in their sweaters and tweed skirts and ankle socks, there was
little of the rebellious talk about sex and marriage that had characterized the 1920's, little of the buzz of excitement that had accompanied the discussion of Freud and Havelock Ellis and Dora Russell.
. . . As the editors of *Fortune* said in their account of the college
youth of 1936: "As for sex, it is, of course, still with us. But the campus takes it more casually than it did ten years ago. Sex is no longer
news. And the fact that it is no longer news is news" . . . . The undergraduates and their contemporaries were on the whole less scorn-
ful of their parents and of parental ideas, less likely to feel that family
life was a mockery than the young people of ten years before.[16] There
were signs here and there of a reaction against drinking among the
boys and girls of college age; observers . . . were amazed at the vol-
ume of their consumption of coca-cola and milk.[17]

To quote the *Fortune* editors again, "The present-day college generation is fatalistic. . . . The investigator is struck by the dominant
and pervasive color of a generation that will not stick its neck out.
. . . Security is the summum bonum of the present college generation." This sort of caution was not confined to the campuses—one
saw it in business men.[18]

Dr. Ruthven, president of University of Michigan, writes in
1931 concerning the reflections on the campus of the social conditions of that day:

In general terms, the college will always reflect the homes from
which it draws its students, and clear thinking requires that the school
be not credited with 'evils' which in reality represent unfortunate
social conditions against which it must strive.[19]

Cowley and Waller likewise affirm how the campus parallels the
social order of the outside culture:

All social organizations, of course, have admissions barriers of one
sort or another. The analysis of these selective patterns reveals how
the control culture of the college intermeshes with that of American
society. The social hierarchy of the campus parallels that of the world
outside.[20]

[16] Frederick Lewis Allen, *Since Yesterday—The Nineteen-Thirties in America,* p.
133–135. Copyright, 1940, by Harper and Brothers.

[17] *Ibid.,* p. 143.

[18] *Ibid.,* p. 160.

[19] A. G. Ruthven, "Evils of Our Colleges," *Michigan Education Journal,* 9 : 775,
November 1931.

[20] W. H. Cowley and Willard Waller, "A Study of Student Life," *Journal of Higher
Education,* 6 : 137, March 1935.

Widener treats of the college as a victim of a pecuniary culture. He states:

The American colleges and universities which have become increasingly active trade rivals for tuitions and endowments, are really the victims of certain pervasive influences, inevitably arising out of a new urban-industrial world order. With changing times and folkways, the central cultural institutions of religion, the older professions, and liberal education have been seized upon and altered by ideas and practices which are entirely foreign to their avowed ethical codes and traditions. Among the more obvious of these altered cultural tendencies, whose influences center about the university, are the following: An increasing public desire for competent professional services, higher prices for these services, limited admittance to certain types of professional training in order to keep up the level of professional incomes or of professional standards, money-minded colleges and churches. . . . In short, a pecuniary purpose has invaded and fused with modern culture in practically all of its social phases.[21]

More and more, therefore, the collegiate bodies are likely to be made painfully aware of the invasions of their older, established cultural order by pecuniary forces. More than one notable institution now fears taxation of its properties. In many states, the various collegiate factions already carry on varying strife through attempts to influence the legislature and the board of regents, the private colleges against the state institutions, and the smaller state institutions against the big state university, which in turn "accredits" them all. Back of this rivalry is the new economic order, a far more complicated and slippery reality than the "banker capitalism" described by Dr. John Commons.[22]

The Proceedings of the 1937 Annual Meeting of Deans of Women record that the establishment of cooperatives on the college campuses paralleled the consumers' cooperation movement:

During the last two years, due to the recent depression, to the visit of the fighting Japanese pacifist, Kagawa, and to other causes, consumers' cooperation has come prominently to the fore in the United States. . . . The committee has found that 150 cooperatives have been reported on more than 100 campuses with some 70,000 students as members. . . . In California alone, there are 30 or more student cooperatives with some 35,000 members. . . . It is the committee's im-

21 H. W. Widener, "The College in a Pecuniary Culture," *Educational Record,* 17 : 180, April 1936.
22 *Ibid.,* p. 186–187.

pression that genuine cooperation operated on strictly Rochdale principles is found chiefly on the campuses in California.[23]

An analysis of these excerpts shows that each strain or stress in the wider culture of the outside, such as war, depression, or period of prosperity, seems to leave its imprint on the college campus. The diffusion of wealth and veneration for business in the outside culture of the 1920's was paralleled by a large enrollment of college students in the business courses and a display of greater spending of money on the campus. The interest of the students in new and more exciting entertainment on the campus was coincident with improved means of communication, the invention of the motion pictures, and the use of the automobile.

Rivalry, political movements, and "big business" techniques intermesh in the control culture of the campus, as they have in outside society. At the same time that consumers' organizations came to the fore in this country, college students instituted their own cooperative associations to meet their needs. The lack of security in society at large during the depression was paralleled in the same period by a sense of fatalism on the part of students. Refusals on the part of college girls to be chaperoned and the desire for stronger independence from parents were coincident with the "Emancipation of Women" in the 20's. Thus the social, economic, moral, religious, and cultural patterns of student life parallel or intermesh with those of adult society.

IMPLICATIONS FOR PERSONNEL WORKERS
AND EDUCATORS

The social behavior on the college campuses therefore represents, to a large degree, social conditions and behavior of society at large. It is in working with and thinking through with students these social conditions in the larger society that constructive change can be brought about on the campus.

The tendency has been to tighten old regulations and rules to meet current social conditions and evils. Not enough time and thought, however, have been spent on how to meet adequately,

[23] National Education Association, Department of Superintendence, Washington, D. C.: The Association, 1937, p. 71.

interpret, and control on the campus these social conditions of society, and thus to structure more desirable student mores.

To summarize, the influences of four groups in the culture of the wider community, viz., the alumni, the local town community, certain national organizations, and society at large—all have had an impact on student life. Sometimes this impact has been constructive, sometimes destructive. These influences at times have been interdependent with the college, at times they have been conditioning factors, and at still other times they have been interactive. It is only in successful interaction that more desirable mores can be built.

Bibliography

Albrecht, Arthur E. "A Student Venture in Cooperative Living." *Journal of Educational Sociology*, 10 : 262–268, January 1937.

Allen, Frederick Lewis. *Only Yesterday; An Informal History of the Nineteen Twenties*. New York: Harper and Brothers, 1931. 370 p.

Allen, Frederick Lewis. *Since Yesterday; The Nineteen-Thirties in America*. New York: Harper and Brothers, 1940. 362 p.

American Student Union. "The Student Movement Comes of Age." Fourth Annual Convention. New York: American Student Union, 1938.

Anderson, Grace M. "Practical Experiments in Student Government." *Social Education*, 2 : 627–629, December 1938.

Angell, Robert C. *The Campus*. New York: D. Appleton-Century Company, Inc., 1928. 239 p.

Angell, Robert C. "The Influence of the Economic Depression on Student Life at the University of Michigan." *School and Society*, 34 : 649–657, November 14, 1931.

Brown, Clara M. "A Social Activities Survey." *Journal of Higher Education*, 8 : 257–264, May 1937.

Canby, Henry Seidel. *Alma Mater*. New York: Farrar and Rinehart, Inc., 1936. 259 p.

Chapin, Francis Stuart. "Research Studies of Extra-Curricular Activities and Their Significance in Reflecting Social Changes." *Journal of Educational Sociology*, 4 : 491–498, April 1931.

Chapin, Francis Stuart. "The Child's Enlarging Social Horizon." *The Annals of the American Academy of Political and Social Science*, 151 : 11–19, September 1930.

Cowley, W. H. and Waller, Willard. "A Study of Student Life." *Journal of Higher Education*, 6 : 132–142, March 1935.

Crabtree, Edith. "Mutual Suspicion Blocks Full Attainment." *Themis of Zeta Tau Alpha*, 43 : 97, March 1945.

Crosser, P. K. "Social Change and School Adaptability." *School and Society*, 55 : 184–187, February 14, 1942.

Davis, J. N. "Student Morale." *Report of the Seventeenth Annual Meeting of the American College Personnel Association*, 1940, pp. 97–106.

Edwards, N. "Historic Relationship of Colleges to Community and the Society in Which They Have Flourished." *Institute for Administrative Officers of Higher Institutions. Proceedings*, 1945, p. 40–49.

Edwards, R. H., Artman, J. N., Fisher, Galen M. *Undergraduates, A Study of Morale in Twenty-three American Colleges and Universities*. New York: Doubleday, Doran, and Company, Inc., 1928. 366 p.

Ewer, Bernard C. *College Study and College Life*. Boston: Richard G. Badger Company, 1917. 228 p.

Gauss, Christian. *Life in College*. New York: Charles Scribner's Sons, 1927, 1930. 272 p.

Gavit, John Palmer. *College*. New York: Harcourt, Brace and Company, 1925. 342 p.

Hooper, Charles. "The Perils of Coeducation and Cigarettes." *School and Society*, 34 : 322, September 5, 1931.

Hull, J. D. "Adjustment to the Air Age." *School and Society*, 56 : 73–75, July 25, 1942.

Marks, Percy. *Which Way Parnassus?* New York: Harcourt, Brace and Company, 1926. 246 p.

McGlade, Madge I. "The Different Types of Successful Cooperative Houses." *Proceedings of the Twenty-First Annual Meeting of the National Association of Deans of Women of the National Education Association*, p. 71, 97–101. Washington, D. C.: The Association, 1937.

Morison, Samuel Eliot. *Three Centuries of Harvard, 1636–1936*. Cambridge: Harvard University Press, 1936. 512 p.

Neely, Wayne C. "Family Attitudes of Denominational College and University Students, 1929 and 1936." *American Sociological Reviw*, 5 : 512–523, August 1940.

Ogburn, W. F. *Social Change*. New York: B. W. Huebsch, Inc., 1923. 365 p.

Olmstead, John Griffith. *Alumni Achievement*. Ithaca, N. Y.: American Alumni Council, 1931. 147 p.

Parsons, P. A. "A State University Reaches Out." *Educational Record*, 12 : 450–459, October 1931.

Proface, Dom. *College Men, Their Making and Unmaking*. New York: P. J. Kenedy and Sons, 1935. 314 p.

Proface, Dom. "Results of the Survey of Social Life at Dartmouth College." *School and Society*, 43 : 664–665, May 16, 1936.

Roethlisberger, F. J. and Dickson, W. J. *Management and the Worker*. Cambridge: Harvard University Press, 1939. 615 p.

Ruthven, A. G. "Evils of Our Colleges." *Michigan Education Journal,* 9 : 774–775, November 1931.

Seeley, Evelyn. "Student Trends at Swarthmore and Princeton." *Literary Digest,* 119 : 22–23, April 20, 1935.

"The Students Speak Out. Symposium from Twenty-Two Colleges," New York: New Republic, Inc., 1929.

Tuttle, H. S. "The Campus and Social Ideals." *Journal of Educational Research,* 30 : 177–182, November 1936.

Van Wagenen, Beulah Clark. *Extra-Curricular Activities in the Colleges of the United Lutheran Church in America.* New York: Bureau of Publications, Teachers College, Columbia University, 1929. 156 p.

Waller, Willard. *Sociology of Teaching.* New York: J. Wiley and Sons, Inc., 1932. 467 p.

Watts, R. J. "Development of University Residence Halls and the Effect Thereof on Fraternities and Sororities." *Association of University and College Business Officers, Twenty-fourth Annual Meeting,* 1934.

Wechsler, James. *Revolt on the Campus.* New York: Covici, Friede Publishers, 1935. 458 p.

Widener, H. W. "The College in a Pecuniary Culture." *Educational Record,* 17 : 180–198, April 1936.

Woolery, W. K. "New Revolt." *School and Society,* 33 : 506–507, April 11, 1931.

IV

SOCIAL STRUCTURING: STATUS, ROLE, AND PRESTIGE IN COLLEGE SOCIETY

T HE purpose of this chapter is to give a description of the college as a social system in and through which students, faculty,'and other members of the college world live according to a set of social interrelationships. It aims to show how the pattern of these interrelationships will be different for each campus, according to type of college and culturally patterned behavior expected. It describes academic and student structure, how each member of a college community usually occupies a particular position in the social system and maintains a certain type of behavior expected of him because of that position; and, in addition, it relates how a student's position in the social group system determines to a large extent his participation in the culture of the campus, that is, the experiences he will have in college.

It further points out how status, role, and prestige operate on a campus; how social stratification, discriminations, social cleavages, and selective mechanisms of various types structure relationships within the social system. It describes, too, how social structuring is to some extent influenced by material equipment. Finally, it attempts to show how social relationships, thus structured, produce a set of mores peculiar to that college.

The college community is not merely an aggregate of individuals or of groups within a certain territorial limit; rather, it consists of individuals and groups organized according to a system of relationships. It is then a social system, made up of patterns according to which the attitudes and behavior of its members are organized. According to Linton, a social system "represents a particular arrangement of statuses and roles which exist apart from the individuals who occupy the statuses and express the roles in overt behavior."[1] Prestige and esteem, selective mechanisms, and social stratification operate in a college social system and structure the mores of a student body.

Colleges differ in the degree to which these patterns of social relationships are conscious and verbalized. The members of one college may be able to tell the behavior prescribed by their college, while members of another college can give only vague ideas about theirs. In some colleges there may be a rigid vertical hierarchy from the president down to the student with well-defined status and role for those on each level of the hierarchy; in others, there may be more of a horizontal arrangement, with actual friendships and close associations between faculty and students. In one college the alumni may dominate certain groups or perhaps the entire college. In another, the alumni may exert no influence at all. In one college, the town may create cultural interests and social life for the student; in another, the townspeople may be as leeches upon the college as seen, for example, in the habitual recruiting of the college men for their social affairs. Morison, it will be recalled, writes that Boston was a social leech of Harvard College in the latter part of the nineteenth century because the supply of eligible men in the town was decreased by the Westward movement.[2]

The college as a social system has both structural and functional aspects, that is, what it *is* and what it *does*. Every part exists in an interdependent relation to every other part. As Linton relates:

> The structure, that is, the system of organization, of a society is itself a matter of culture. Although for purposes of description we can turn to spatial analogies and plot such a system in terms of positions, such positions cannot be defined adequately except in terms of the behavior expected of their occupants.[3]

The positions in a college community, like any other community, can be divided according to age, sex, occupation, optional relationships, based on congeniality and common interests, and com-

[1] Ralph Linton, *The Study of Man*, p. 253. Copyright, 1936, by Appleton-Century-Crofts, Inc.

[2] Reprinted by permission of the publishers from Samuel Eliot Morison, *Three Centuries of Harvard, 1636–1936*. Cambridge, Mass.: Harvard University Press, 1936. p. 420–421.

[3] Ralph Linton, *The Cultural Background of Personality*, p. 20. Copyright, 1945, by Appleton-Century-Crofts, Inc.

munality of territory. According to Linton, however, such classi-
ifications cannot be defined adequately, except in terms of the
culturally patterned behavior expected of their occupants. When
it comes to such positions as freshman and faculty adviser, we find
it impossible to define them except in terms of what the occupants
of these two positions are expected to do for each other. Each of
the systems of social classification existing on a campus ascribes
certain culture patterns to the individual on the basis of his position in the system. In each college community there is the academic structure as well as the student structure. The faculty and
administrative folkways and mores in the academic structure interact and influence the folkways and mores of the student world.

Academic Structuring

The struggle for a place in the academic structure is institutional, departmental, and personal. There are inter- and intra-
institutional pressures. Inter-institutional pressures may arise
between colleges for students, faculty members, prestige, and equal
status. The system of offering scholarships, fellowships, and
other aids promotes competition and rivalry. In the intra-institutional structure, techniques and approaches are sometimes
inherited and transmitted to new members of the college academic
community. Departments take on this *status quo* stereotype of
conditioning which develops conformity of an inbred type. There
is an institutional fixation af authority in some colleges upon the
president, the deans, and the department heads. Because of this
fixation of authority, occasionally the administrative heads do not
show genuine leadership or effect rapport in their face-to-face contacts with members of the college community and of the departments. Much of the teacher's welfare, irrespective of his competence, depends on administrative and institutional policy and how
he fits into the scheme of things. Institutional ideologies deemed
desirable in the maintenance of traditional standards give rise to
a process of faculty in-group selection and promotion.

As to the departmental structure, Wilson states, "A number of
administrative units divide labor within the larger university organization but the most important for the ordinary academic man

is the department."[4] Very often the department creates staff tensions within the university. Departments compete for preferment, power, and general importance. Each department is fighting for students, time, and courses, since the larger the department, the more influential it is in the institutional structure. Rivalry exists between the various departments, particularly in securing students for their classes. Appeals are made by them either to the administrative organization which decides upon required portions of the curriculum or to the students themselves who decide upon elective courses. Rivalry also exists, according to Wilson, between departments in securing administrative favor in the apportionment of funds for maintenance and expansion or in the effort to enhance their academic prestige in the institution as a whole. Also, the interests and activities of the members of a department are narrowed to problems wholly related to the development of the subject of that department.

As to personal strains and stresses, Wilson further states that "Each lower member of the staff normally considers himself in line for the rank just above his own, and there is a constant pressure by departments upon the central administration for the promotion of their own younger men."[5] The criterion for advancement in many colleges is not teaching ability but rather the number of publications a faculty member has to his credit. There are universities, also, where faculty members are rarely advanced within a reasonable length of time unless they get bids from elsewhere. As Wilson puts it, "When this policy becomes generally known to the local group it plays havoc with morale and the building of institutional rapport and loyalty."[6] There are fights waged personally by the professors for promotion and administrative power. Marks comments, "Strings are pulled, boots licked, hands kissed, coalitions secretly formed, lobbying practiced with skill and cunning, tales carried to superiors for the 'good of the college' and general hypocrisy and mud-slinging indulged in with hysterical abandon."[7]

[4] From Logan Wilson, *The Academic Man.* Copyright, 1942, by Oxford University Press, New York. p. 83.

[5] *Ibid.,* p. 69.

[6] *Ibid.,* p. 70.

[7] Percy Marks, *Which Way Parnassus,* p. 93. Copyright, 1926, by Harcourt, Brace and Company, Inc.

Professors lose personal touch with fellow workers and students; they surround their desks with dictaphones, office assistants, and metal file cases. The click of the typewriter and the whir of the Hollerith machines become a substitute for leisurely talk and the personal contact. Members of a faculty club sometimes can produce more vicious scandal-mongering per hour than almost any other organization. Often the faculty wives, according to Marks, are willing aids in the gossiping, the wire-pulling, and the mud-slinging politics in general. However, it must be noted that these practices may not be true in all college communities.

STATUS IN THE ACADEMIC STRUCTURE

Many of the perplexities in the academic profession center about the matter of status. Academic organization is ideally expressed in the free association of equals, yet everywhere there is a hierarchical arrangement. Differences between the administration and the staff are supposed to be functional, yet more frequently they turn out to be scalar. Between the formal and informal organization are found many incompatibilities and imponderables. The effect of a capitalistic economy upon the university structure is evident. Immediate results are seen in course standardizations, departmental administrative systems, hierarchical gradations of staff, and lay board controls. The academic man has a certain status within the social system of his university and profession, but as a human being he has a broader socio-economic status or position in the larger society. He is a participant in an open-class society in which occupation is the most important single factor in determining class position. In this respect, income may be regarded as one symbol of status. However, these symbols of status may differ from one college community to another.

Status therefore, with others as well as faculty, is determined by all sorts of reciprocal relations, so that one's *self* is the net *result* of these relations. The acting out of status is seen dynamically in the functional aspects of organization. Professional organizations exist primarily for the protection and advancement of in-group status. They realize that only through the solidarity of organization can status be protected in a society where equilibrium is maintained through the counterbalance of pressure groups.

As to social status, some of the professions have attempted to enhance it by showing exclusiveness and class bias. The academic profession in the main has been one of those affording a particularly wide avenue for social advancement. Important in the academic structure is professional status, as evidenced in the written or unwritten code of ethics.

What is the code of the academic group? What is the relation of teacher to his profession, to his students, to his colleagues, and to his institution and administration, and to the non-academic world?

Sumner insists that the mores differentiate, as well as standardize, behavior, for status lies in them. Status, he says, pertains only to that part of one's role which has a standard definition in the mores or in law. A status is never peculiar to the individual; it is historic. The differential behavior which lies in status is particularly evident in certain institutional offices of the college community. Such offices in the college world are identified by their customary historic roles, are very often not rationalized, but are included in the mores of the academic structure. Students develop stereotyped ways of responding to these faculty roles and transmit these ways from one generation of students to another.

Further, with regard to these roles in the academic structure, in many colleges there is a regular hierarchy in order of precedence, that is, trustees, president of the college, college dean, dean of men and dean of women, professors of full status, associate professors, assistant professors, instructors, assistant instructors, staff assistants. There are as well-defined statuses for administrative officers as there are for the faculty. There are also series of prestige recognitions in this administrative hierarchy.

First of all, there is the status of the trustees in whom rest the control and educational policies of the college. They are chosen usually because they are men of wealth. Their legal position in the university is the same as that of a business corporation board. The actual patterns of control, whether autocratic, democratic, or bureaucratic, differ from one institution to another, depending upon size, historical development, financial resources, and a number of other factors.

Second, there is the president, who occupies a status which involves duties more diverse, complex, and far-flung than those of any other employee. He must be an educator, an administrator, a diplomat. The president is generally in an aloof position as the highest executive and is plainly regarded by the faculty as one apart.

Third, the deanships, represented usually by college dean, dean of women, and dean of men, vary widely in power and importance according to the capacities of the office-holder and the traditions of the college. "With some persons, the office becomes a mere clearing house; with others, it becomes a positive source of university policy."[8] Deans are the most important liaison officers between the staff and the president.

Fourth, the department heads have an administrative status. They are the liaison officers between the department and the next administrative unit. Much of their authority, according to Wilson, lies in the decisions and recommendations for appointments, promotions, assignment of courses, and teaching loads. Whether departmental power is democratic in practice depends often upon the aims of the executive head of the department. In order to be satisfactory to his colleagues he must justify the institutional fixation of authority upon him.

The classification of the faculty in order of their precedence gives each member a status with a differential degree of security and prestige. The staff member has probably been an in-group member, a previous student who has been cooperative; he has been accessible without the financial expenditure necessary in securing an outsider. His previous student and apprentice role has set a permanent stamp upon him as he mounts the first rung of the occupational ladder. As to the instructor, his tenure is brief, his remuneration lowest, the criteria for his advancement vague, and his future full of doubt. The assistant professors have intermediate statuses, and like the instructors are debarred in some colleges from participation in the inner circle composed of associate and full professors; the main solace of the assistant professor seems to be that he has at least a foothold in the hierarchy. As to the full professor, his adjustment to organization is complete and his status

8 From Logan Wilson, *The Academic Man*. Copyright, 1942, by Oxford University Press, New York. p. 87–88.

is secure. The only pressure upon him is the desire to sustain or enhance his established reputation.

As to relationships and recognitions in faculty mores, there are the differences in academic relationship between student and faculty when the student has achieved a higher status. In some colleges, there are differences in social relationships in this administrative hierarchy. It would be proper for an assistant instructor to date a girl graduate student or senior undergraduate student but a professor would probably not do so. It may be proper for an undergraduate assistant to date a woman instructor or a woman assistant instructor but probably not the dean of women. Seniors would feel free to visit professors' homes but freshmen would only do so if specially invited, and then would probably expect to be instructed by a senior as to how to act.

The role the student plays in his relationships with these prestige administrative positions would in itself afford an interesting study. A knowledge of student expectancies of what is proper for each position in this hierarchical series of administration would be valuable. The relationship of each age-group of students with the various administrative series and the consequent role development and expectancy would likewise be interesting to study.

Considering intellectual status, there are, according to some authorities,[9] the scholar-teachers, the scholars, the teachers, the researchers, the idealists, and, of more recent date, the teacher-counselors.[10] The scholars usually want to learn; they do not want to teach. Their prestige is independent of their students. The scholar-teachers are rare and exert a great influence on students. Their interest in knowledge is commensurate with their interest in humanity. To the teachers, their students matter above all else. They usually are the men whom the undergraduates call human. Also, there are the idealists; they too often hitch their wagon to an earlier or later century and are concerned only with the fallacies of their own; they have complete faith in the mores of another age and produce characters who would be eccentric within the mores of the present. The teacher-counselors are the personalized

[9] Percy Marks, *Which Way Parnassus?*, p. 70.
Henry S. Canby, *Alma Mater*, p. 109 ff.
[10] Esther Lloyd-Jones and Margaret Smith, *A Student Personnel Program for Higher Education*, p. 105.

teachers who see the student's life as a whole, his social, moral, emotional, and physical as well as his intellectual life. They personalize and integrate education.

How does this academic structuring with its institutional, departmental, and personal ideologies, its assortment of staff statuses and roles, affect the mores of student life on a college campus? In the first place, the faculty have the same needs as the students. The specific contributions which faculty members can make in the lives of students depend upon how well their own needs for security, response, and social status are being recognized in the academic structure. The teacher's security in professional status, in salary, and in tenure has its effect on the attitudes he has toward his students. Whether the intellectual status of the faculty membership is that of scholars, researchers, teachers, idealists, or teacher-counselors must be reckoned with if constructive student mores are to be built by college teaching. The subject must be made plain to students; it must be made a part of their lives, and its significance to them as human beings must be made evident. The faith of the faculty in the mores of another age must be reconstructed for the present age. Teachers as a whole must see the whole life of students.

To what kind of faculty member is the institution of the college giving prestige? Are mores of good critical thinking on the part of students being developed by faculty members? Are students being exploited in the over-valuation of research and the under-valuation of teaching?

What kinds of scholarships, fellowships, and other aids are being offered by the administration and the faculty to students and for what purposes? What kinds of pressures are being generated upon student recipients? If awards are to be made exclusively on the basis of scholastic marks, may not the grind tend to stereotype the student body? This type of competition is more likely to foster mores of opportunism than independent thought on the part of students. Certainly imagination and the joy of learning might be stifled. Similarly, the institutional inheritance of academic techniques and approaches may ultimately have a narrowing and stifling effect upon individual initiative.

Rivalry between departments may cause schisms and social cleavages among students. They may be torn between loyalties to various professors. Lack of integration of different departments builds tightly compartmentalized units in the education of the students. If integration is not effected throughout the curricular world, one can expect confused thinking on the part of students. In all conferences with personnel workers, mention was made that the key to cementing relationships in many difficult situations on the campus lay in the power of the president or the mediation of some other strong personality. The lack of a democratic administrative personality on a campus or the presence of an overly-aggressive, dominative administrator very often led to disintegrations of various kinds. The Lewin and Lippitt experiments with young children under autocratic and democratic leadership substantiate the above situation for college campuses.[11]

The educational culture which the institution develops has its influence on student ways of doing things. Through the classroom the codes, beliefs, ideologies of a faculty diffuse to the student body. As was shown in the study of the Bennington Community,[12] students imitate those with highest prestige—the faculty on a college campus.

To promote a democracy in a college community, it would seem that greater emphasis should be placed on institutional flexibility rather than rigidity and vertical hierarchy. Status should be reappraised more in terms of democratic conceptions than of traditional power.

Student Structuring

The social classifications among students according to age, sex, occupational interest, optional relationships based on congeniality and common interests, and common residence present a structuring in terms of positions for which culturally patterned behavior is expected of their occupants. For example, each social fraternity acquires or is ascribed a certain position, or prestige, in a particular college community. Because of this position, the rest of the

[11] Kurt Lewin and Ronald Lippitt, "An Experimental Approach to the Study of Autocracy and Democracy: A Preliminary Note," *Sociometry,* 1 : 292–300, January–April 1938.

[12] See pages 18–21 of this study.

student body expect certain patterned behavior on the part of the members of the group in question.

From the above classifications, it is clear that a college student's participation in the culture of his campus is not a matter of chance. It is mainly determined by the training he has received in anticipation of his occupying this position and by the particular cultural demands which his campus makes upon him because of his place in it. A campus expects different behavior from underclassmen and upperclassmen, from dormitory residents and off-campus residents, and one cannot understand the behavior of any particular individual or group without knowing what these expectations are. College societies perpetuate themselves by teaching the students of each generation the culture patterns which belong with the positions in the social system which they are expected to occupy. The new recruits to a campus learn how to behave as freshmen and by so doing perpetuate these positions and with them the social system as a whole.

It is to be remembered also that no two colleges have identical cultures or cultural demands. Each college tends to develop its own set of transmitted culture patterns and expectancies and thus establishes for its members certain unique obligations. The cultural demands and social structuring of a student body in a large college would be different from that in a small one. A cosmopolitan college differs from a rural one; a dormitory-resident college from a college to which students commute; a liberal arts college from a state teachers college; a college specializing in art from one specializing in physical education; a wealthy college from a middle-class college. Also, there are differences in colleges with respect to policies and aims, types of students, educational methods, levels of accomplishments, composition of faculty, types of leadership, and available facilities.

AGE-SEX AND SOCIAL GROUP SYSTEM

The individual's position in the age-sex system and social group system does more than almost any other classification to determine his participation in the culture of the campus. Waller[13] describes

[13] Willard Waller, "The Rating and Dating Complex," *American Sociological Review*, 2 : 727–734, October 1937.

the complex social system on the campus of a large state-supported school, where about half of the male students live in fraternities among which there is great competition. A feature of this campus is the unbalanced sex ratio, for there are about six boys to every girl. Competition for dates among both men and women is extremely keen. Waller relates that there are certain men who are at the top of the social scramble, and may be placed in a hypothetical class A. There are also certain coeds who are near the top of the scale of dating desirability, and they also are in class A. The tendency is for class A men to date principally class A women. Waller relates further how students on this campus are extremely conscious of these social distinctions and of their own position in the social hierarchy. Young men are desirable dates according to their rating on the scale of campus values. In order to have class A rating they must belong to one of the better fraternities, be prominent in activities, have a good supply of spending money, be well dressed, "smooth" in manners and appearance, have a "good line," dance well, and have access to an automobile. Members of leading fraternities are especially desirable dates; those who belong to fraternities with less prestige are correspondingly less desirable.

The requirements of girls are that they have good clothes, a smooth line, and ability to dance well, and are popular as a date. The most important of these factors is the last, for the girl's prestige depends more on dating than on anything else. Therefore, the clever coed contrives to give the impression of being much sought after, even if she is not. Coeds who wish campus prestige must never be available for last-minute dates; they must avoid being seen too often with the same boy, in order that others may not be frightened away or discouraged; they must be seen when they go out, and therefore must go to the popular and expensive meeting places; finally, they must have many partners at the dances. They do not drink in groups or frequent the beer parlors. Above all, the coed who wishes to retain class A standing must consistently date class A men.

The coed has a descending cycle of popularity. The new girl starts out with a great wave of popularity; during her freshman year she has many dates. Slowly her prestige declines, and is expedited by such "mistakes," from the point of view of campus prestige, as "going steady" with one boy, especially if he is a senior who will not return the following year, by indiscretions, and by being too readily available for dates. This competitive process involves a number of fundamental antagonisms between the men and the women.

The men, who are warned repeatedly against coeds, are always afraid the girls are going to "gold-dig" them. The coeds wonder to what degree they are discussed and are constantly afraid of being placed on the black-list of the fraternities. They wonder to what extent they can take any man seriously. Status in the one-sex group depends upon avoiding exploitation by the opposite sex.

Non-fraternity men are practically excluded from dating. Many girls elect not to date rather than take the dates available to them. Every boy whom a girl dates is discussed and criticized by the other members of her group. This rigid control often keeps a girl from dating at all.

The accommodations and rationalizations worked out by one group of girls who were toward the bottom of the scale of campus desirability are typical. Four of these girls were organized into a closely knit clique. Members of the group cooperated in getting dates for one another. The clique went through "dating cycles" with several fraternities in the course of a year, starting when one of the girls got a date with one member of the fraternity and ending when all the girls had lost their desirability as far as that fraternity was concerned.

The example of the social system of the college just quoted shows clearly how a social system is plotted in terms of positions and the culturally patterned behavior expected of occupants of these positions; also how status, role, and prestige operate in such a system. The same situation may exist on other campuses similar to this one, where the sex ratio is unbalanced, six boys to every girl. On a campus where the ratio is more nearly equal, the culture may stimulate a different pattern, perhaps one in which "steady dating" would be more common.

OCCUPATIONAL CHOICE

The individual's position according to the occupation he has chosen is noticed on campuses, and cultural patterns arise in this connection. Certain attitudes and personality characteristics may be ascribed by students and faculty on the basis of the student's special occupation. At one college the art students occupied the favored position. They were not only ascribed prestige by the rest of the student body but they assumed prestige. They were the inventors of style on the campus. The art faculty developed within the students an individualism which they encouraged to be expressed on the campus. "They were art students and artists were different from other people"—such was the role ascribed to them by their faculty. Certain personality characteristics emerged; they were noted for originality and novelty, and were extreme "fad" adopters. One of the art students would create a new costume or a new habit and very shortly the entire campus would adopt it. From the whole artist group on this campus emerged specialists, a few students who had unusual art ability and originality. The behavior patterns and attitudes ascribed to these specialists played an important role in the selection by other art students of specialized art positions. On the other hand, the behavior and attitudes ascribed to members of the specialist group in which a student finds himself may be quite uncongenial and frequently a cause of maladjustment and psychological disturbance, leading eventually to inferiority complexes. After all, no matter how carefully the individual has been trained, nor how successful his conditioning has been, nor what prestige the groups wish to ascribe to him, he remains a distinct organism with his own needs and capacities for independent thought, feeling, and action.

In another college the engineering students hold the highest prestige. Certain standards of excellence are set up in the department, creating a prestige not only for the department but for the students as well. In still another college, the individual's position on the campus is decided by whether he is an agricultural student. The agricultural dances have the greatest prestige on the campus.

OPTIONAL RELATIONSHIPS AND RESIDENTIAL SOCIAL GROUPINGS

Lastly, students on the campus are classified according to optional relationships based on congeniality and common interests, and on common residence. But their position in the social system is also determined by the common culturally patterned behavior expected of these relationships and living units. The various kinds of social groupings will be treated in Chapter VI. Unfortunately, social stratification and social cleavages exist on college campuses and structure in an undesirable manner these optional relationships, living units, and social groupings. Similarly, racial and national discriminations and selective mechanisms operate in these social groupings and influence the structure of a student body.

Social Stratification. On one basis or another social stratification has existed on almost every American campus. A college student has specific characteristics associated with his "station on the campus"; he needs to go with the "right kind" of students to be certain of his ranking. If a student's past preparatory school is known, his father's occupation, his wealth, his race, his family, intimate friends, clubs, and fraternities, as well as his manners, speech, and general outward behavior, it is not difficult for his fellow students to give a fairly accurate estimate of his status. If only his special participation in cliques and his associations are known, he can be placed by the process of identifying his social place with that of others whom he resembles. The first generalization of this kind might be identified by such terms "the fellows in Phi Delts all have cars," "the Phi Sigs have grand cocktail parties," "the fur coats of the Chi O's." "The Phi Mu's are lowering their reputation by attending 'non-frat' dances"—such identifications as these can show the top of the hierarchy on a campus. Membership in Phi Beta Kappa shows a stratification of the intellectual elite. Then, too, there are the "off-campus and dorm students," the "commuters," the "town lodgers."

With regard to socialization on a campus, members of a group who occupy a high-prestige rating may mingle socially only with other groups of like status. Members of a girls' group, for example, may be required to date only with men belonging to a fraternity, or it may even be that the fraternity is ascribed among whose men they may date. Similarly, the same compulsions may be exerted by a social unit of men with regard to dating with girls. A student in an Eastern college for men relates that students during the week go with town girls and nurses from a near-by hospital with the idea of "let's go out and have a good time," but for the house parties the men bring the girls who are students at some girls' college of high rating or the girl back home who is socially accepted by their families. They have definitely a tendency to look down on "nurses and town girls," with the exception of the professors' daughters who happen to live in the town. Thus, there may be shown on the part of college men a discrimination against town girls in comparison with college girls. Personnel workers may rather easily learn something of stratification and class and caste structure on a campus by close observation or by actually finding out the proportion of girls attending fraternity dances who are college girls, non-college girls, sorority, or non-sorority, or who are local town community girls. They can also ascertain from what college they are invited, if they are not local college girls, or from what sororities on the campus they are chosen. The same information may be gathered through student leaders of groups on the campus: what girls the college men most often date, whether college girls, local town girls, out-of-town college girls, or out-of-town non-college girls. Social stratification may be evident in the ways the various types of girls are entertained: whether the evening is spent at movies or at other places requiring money or whether it is spent at the girls' homes; whether different amounts of money are spent for corsages and entertainment for different types of girls. The same information can be gathered about the college women in relation to dating. The criteria of popularity of men and women can also be estimated. Through casual interviews with student leaders, through analysis of social registers of clubs, perusal of permission records of rooming residences, check on college social calendars, much information concerning social stratification on a college campus can be gleaned. Interviewing students as to the satisfaction they have in the social life of the campus—what clubs they wanted to join that they had not been given a chance to join and why they wanted to join these particular clubs—can yield valuable information for understanding class and caste on the campus. Information can likewise be gathered as to what experiences unite or separate students and are pleasant or unpleasant to them.

It is to be remembered also that the student brings his outside life into the campus. He may be from the aristocracy of the social hierarchy in his own community or he may be seeking a higher social station in life. All these factors enter into the pushing and shoving that results in social stratification on a campus.

Social Cleavages. In a large state university a serious social cleavage exists between dormitory girls and town girls. A head resident of one of the dormitories on this campus remarked that the woman's student government decides the women's regulations and yet many of their officers have never been inside a dormitory and are for the most part town students who are under no written rules or regulations. The town girls hold most of the positions in the various campus organizations and that situation exists year after year. In a junior college in the Midwest, there are cleavages according to residential sections lived in—the southwestern part, residence section of professional people, and the southeastern and northeastern, where the "working people" live. There is a feeling that students from residential sections "get all the breaks" in campus politics and organizations. In a small liberal arts college for girls in a Middle-Atlantic state there is a cleavage between sorority and sorority instead of sorority versus non-sorority. A great deal of political jockeying goes on between the sororities for positions on the campus.

Social cleavage and religious discrimination on many campuses, particularly where there are sororities and fraternities, exist between Protestant and Jewish, and likewise between Protestant and Catholic students. Jewish students are excluded from Protestant clubs, and Protestants are excluded from Jewish clubs. There is no written stipulation in most sorority and fraternity charters against Jewish students. The real reason, as one personnel worker was told by the Protestant sororities in her college, was "the strong family bond" which the Jewish girls have. Because a Jewish girl of one family was in the sorority, it would necessarily follow that any relative would have to be invited in later years which to the sororities might mean undesirable members, perhaps, gaining entry. Apart from this discrimination Jewish girls gain prestige on this campus. In fact, there is a veritable social hierarchy among the Jews themselves. An outside Jewish Sister organization in the city obtains a list of Jewish girls from the college, selects a city college mother for them, who has them invited to her home and introduced into the city's Jewish society; she also gives them invitations to private Jewish dances in the city, where they can meet eligible Jewish men. It was thought by the personnel worker on this campus that many of the Jewish girls come to this college at the express desire of the parents merely to meet the famed eligible and rich Jewish men of the city through this social organization.

In some colleges social cleavages exist between football players and non-players and between students of rival colleges. In a New England college, according to a former student, social cleavages exist among the fraternities between those with "money and class" who come from the best homes in Boston and those whose family heritage is less distinguished.

During World War II, and since the war has ended, there has been in a strong church college in the East a definite cleavage between the conscientious objectors (CO's) and the armed services men. Quite a few ministerial students entered the campus as CO's. The CO's were a minority group on the campus and sensitive because of their role; consequently, they wore a mask of superiority which considerably irritated the girls on the campus. How the girls stood in regard to this cleavage depended on their backgrounds; the girls with most conservative church background sided with the CO's. In other colleges there are cleavages between certain prestige club groups on the campus and also between townspeople and faculty. In a Midwestern town where two girls' colleges are located, side by side, there has developed a cleavage mainly because one of them has much better publicity and financial and cultural status than the other. In a Negro college in the South, there are cleavages among the students according to their geographical origins—between those native to the region, those from other parts of the country, and those from New York whose parents and grandparents have been college students. There also are cleavages in this college, mainly in the sororities, between those of upper socio-economic class and those who live "on the wrong side of the tracks."

Racial, Religious, and National Discriminations. In the months since V-J Day evidences of race prejudice have increased and the alarming situation is that many of the discriminations have centered in educational institutions. The facts concerning race and color quotas in our colleges and universities are startling; likewise, the evidences of the anti-Semitic attitude among college and university students themselves. A student in a famous and traditional liberal arts college for women reports that it is virtually impossible for a Jewish girl to achieve social success or win a campus office. A chaperone at a man's university house tells of the heartbreak of a girl appearing as a "blind date," attractive and personable but of Jewish ancestry, abandoned by her escort and his friends to the permanent exile of the powder room. Gentile girls have been equally unfeeling toward Jewish boys. The blame rests with early home and community attitudes, or with the mores of the school social groups. Social distinctions, racial discriminations, class prejudices, misunderstandings, rivalries—all the material for creating unrest are alarmingly present in our college communities.

In conferences with over thirty personnel workers located in various colleges over the United States—in the North, South, East, and West—it was learned that racial cleavages and social stratification of one kind or another existed on every campus they represented. In a college in the West, Orientals do not win many posts of leadership. An Oriental within one personnel worker's experience, whom she had noted as having fine qualities of leadership, was asked by the worker why she did not express her ideas more often in a certain group. The Oriental student replied, "Oh, I could only use that influence among Chinese students." From a Western university also come reports of the cleavage between native Westerners and Orientals of Japanese origin. From a personnel worker in a teachers college in a Southwestern state comes a report of cleavage between the Western students and the Mexican students, arising mainly out of socio-economic differences and the expectancies of parents that their sons and daughters room with students of their same class or better.

According to an interview with a personnel worker in a college with a population of approximately 10,000 students located in a large cosmopolitan city, many cleavages and discriminating practices exist. There are five national sororities in this college plus ten others which are not under National Pan-Hellenic; there also are nineteen fraternities. The national Protestant sororities will not take Jewish girls, the Jewish sororities will take only Jewish girls, and the Italian fraternity will take only Italian men. The story of a returned veteran was told. He was bid to an Italian fraternity on the campus on the assumption that he was an Italian. He resembled the Italians in appearance but in reality was Spanish by birth. When the Italian fraternity learned that he was Spanish the bid was withdrawn. The Spanish boy was hurt and disappointed; he said to the members of the Italian fraternity: "What does it matter if I am Spanish? We have like interests and I like you fellows." The Italian spokesman for the fraternity said: "Some years ago we were discriminated against; we were treated as the scum of the earth. Our major interest became to organize ourselves into a strong association. We have done that and have become recognized on the campus. If you Spanish students feel the same way, start an organization of your own and develop as we have." Here we have an example of "discrimination because one has been discriminated against," of doing as one has been done unto. Another example was quoted of an Italian boy on the campus who had developed a hatred of Jews. Through mediation of college training and the work of a counselor, he decided to overcome his prejudices and invited two Jewish girl students to go to the drugstore meeting place with him; through conversation on a social basis he wanted to understand better their way of thinking. In reply to the invitation the Jewish girls said, "We don't go with Gentiles."

Students in minority groups often express the struggle they experience in achieving success. This struggle seems due to various social discriminations, difference in socio-economic status, and lack of positive attitudes on the campus toward minority race or religion. Many of these minority groups are sensitive to their religion and to the accent peculiar to their nationality. These strong cultural predispositions are playing havoc with personalities.

Selective Mechanism Structuring. The kind of selection that goes on in the college has considerable effect upon the tone of social groupings and the way in which they perform their various functions. The overemphasis on intelligence is offset in American colleges by the importance attached to activities. The able student very often does not attain the recognition that is accorded a football captain or the editor of a student paper. Family tradition and background counted for much in our older colleges; the influence of the family has by no means been destroyed. Again, according to Morison's history of the early days at Harvard it is clear that by the middle of the eighteenth century "the entire class was placed in the order of the presumed official or social rank of their parents."[14] As classes grew larger this process became more and more complicated and finally after a proud father complained that his son was placed in a class below a boy whose father had not been a justice of the peace as long as he, the overseers voted that the arrangement in the future should be alphabetical. There is no evidence that democratic feeling had anything to do with the change; social pretensions simply became progressively difficult to rate as classes increased, and the existing system caused too much vexation and jealousy. Facilities today by which parents can slip mediocre sons into the most desirable occupational niches have not decreased; it is still, unfortunately, a recognized function of some private schools to put into college boys whose ability does not actually warrant admission.

A Negro personnel worker in the South related how selective and political mechanisms operate sometimes to keep the cultural level low. If two Negro teachers apply for a position, in many cases the one less qualified may be chosen. Accreditation is given to students to enter college, but the accreditation does not mean a great deal. Poorly prepared students are accredited with the result that the cultural level, even in college, does not reach too great a height. This practice in the college means undesirable mores. The teachers must work harder for positive techniques in the development of higher cultural habits and customs. Teachers sometimes are poorly trained in understanding why these particular customs prevail, nor do they understand the means of changing them. They fail to encourage participation in activities, to discuss why these customs prevail, and to work with persistent effort toward changing them. Although the above selective mechanism may be true

[14] Samuel E. Morison, op. cit., p. 104. Reprinted by permission of the publishers from Samuel Eliot Morison, Three Centuries of Harvard, 1636–1936. Cambridge, Mass.: Harvard University Press, 1936. p. 104.

in only one particular college, the illustration may serve to show how a selective factor can present difficulty to personnel workers who desire to raise the level of student mores on any campus.

In a college in the East, according to an ex-graduate, selective mechanisms operate rather extensively in the fraternity world. The most reliable criterion for a good fraternity is that it is the one which has the largest number of players on the various sports teams. The second criterion is money and class—members from the best homes in the near-by city, those with "big" names. The third criterion is freshman congeniality with upperclassmen in dormitories.

The fraternity in this college is considered a luxury—a convenient place to take a date. There are seventeen Gentile fraternities and one Jewish fraternity. The Jewish students get along very well and are very often pledged into fraternities other than the Jewish one. However, some Jewish boys join only the Jewish fraternity even though they have been given a chance to join another. Here is another selective feature on this campus. According to the ex-graduate interviewed, "The Jews like to join their own fraternity because they feel more secure"; "are not always on the spot"; "won't have to be careful of what they say"; also, "the family will always feel at home." However, some Jewish parents do not want their sons to join a Jewish fraternity as it segregates them from the rest of the students and they will not have the benefit of meeting different kinds of people. It would appear that selective mechanisms here operate as basic defense mechanisms against insecurity. This insecurity may exist because the students consider it necessary to have wealth in order to achieve social status or it may be that a minority group wishes to foster "exclusiveness" for strength. Selective mechanisms also operate extensively in the admissions program of this college. The boy whose father is an alumnus will always be given preference, for it is the alumni who donate money and contribute to the college spirit.

According to the resident director of a girls' dormitory on a large North Central state campus, the selective mechanism set up by the administration for student admission in the spring of 1946 considerably limited the enrollment of girls. Preferences for admission were given, first of all, to the state veterans; second, to the students already in college; third, to new students of the state; fourth, to out-of-state veterans; fifth, to out-of-state students. Only the first three classes were admitted in the fall of 1946.

Selective mechanisms among various student groups on the campus create mores which are not always constructive. Selection of students for fraternities and sororities will be mentioned later in this chapter. A personnel worker from a Southern college has related how selective mechanisms even enter honorary societies of the campus. There exists a national honorary society for seniors, and three local honor societies for the other three classes. Members are taken in on the basis of scholastic rating, number of activities engaged in, and personality. The number is limited so that only fifty freshmen can be taken into membership of the freshman society, and only thirty-five sophomores can be taken into the junior society. Each year many more who are qualified wish to belong than are taken in. If there are, for example, more than fifty girls qualified for membership, then the process becomes one of selection mainly by personality. In this way the honor groups do not differ too much from the social sororities on many campuses except that they have greater prestige among the scholastically minded students.

The selectivity of a college is considerably affected by fellowships, scholarships, and other student aids. Nearly every scholarship is governed by a strict set of rules, and is restricted to only a certain type of student. Such terms in scholarship contracts as "boy of German origin," "girl of Irish descent," "Methodist boy south," "descendants of certain family," "reside in certain state," "must be Dissenter," "for one named Murphy," "eastern half of Pennsylvania" show some of the selective mechanisms of these student aids. There is no evidence in such partisan terminology of the important factors to be considered about students before granting them financial aid, such as academic record, health, general intelligence, evidences of character and integrity, evidences of future performance, or even the question of need. These conditions governing scholarships are important from the point of view of vertical mobility. Vertical mobility should be high in a college; a college must provide fair conditions of competition and not competition biased by hereditary rank, economic resources, or place of residence of a student's family. Any institution with such selective mores operative in the choice of students to be given financial aid is not bringing to its campus a number of those desirable students who perhaps in the long run would promote or create a more constructive type of student mores on the campus.

Cowley and Waller[15] cite the selective practices of student social groups, such as fraternities and sororities, who do not mold personality but obtain their unanimity largely by selection. They give the example of the boy "who had curly hair, and shook hands with the right elbow too far in the air." One group turned him down; the other brought him into line. One fraternity had exerted its control by not electing him; the other had expressed its control by molding him to its model.

The social hierarchy of the campus parallels that of the world outside. The athlete may have priority in campus elections; frequently elections to senior societies and other honors are largely determined not by ability but by the position the student holds, which in turn has been determined by previously applied selective norms.

To no small degree the control culture of the campus reflects the control culture of the larger society. Adult society variously affects campus patterns. Also the methods of big business are sometimes employed in fraternities where large public relations organizations undertake to help fraternities choose their new members. These organizations have devised an elaborate system of follow-up letters to the alumni asking for their recommendations of recent high school graduates who might be rushed. Other examples on the campus of methods of big business carried on by public organizations are found in intercollegiate athletics. That these influences work both ways is, of course, obvious, but as yet no comprehensive attempt has been made to canvass and plot them. An understanding of these selective mechanisms, however, should become an important objective of personnel workers.

In a study made of a Midwestern university from 1885 to 1937, it was shown that membership in three groups, alumni, friendship, and family, influenced the selection of new staff members during

15 W. H. Cowley and Willard Waller, "A Study of Student Life," *Journal of Higher Education,* 6 : 137, March 1935.

these years.[16] This internal selection, sometimes referred to as inbreeding, is natural, according to the author, for three reasons. First, the administrators are usually egocentric, prizing their own viewpoints above all others; second, they are personally familiar with the men and know whether they are sympathetic and reasonable; third, it is easier to engage a person who is on the ground than to spend time, money, and energy looking for outside personnel. Here we have administrators who may be egocentric and an institution which might become ethnocentric. Here there seems to be no desire to bring in new ideas, values, programs, or techniques. A person conditioned in the cultural values of an institution and not counter-conditioned by other values starts the vicious circle of an inbreeding static program that can only lead to further inbreeding, and more static mores. By this selective mechanism students are likely to encounter static institutional mores: if selective mechanisms operate also in the selection of students of a certain social class and status, student mores peculiar to this class and their value-systems also become inbred and static. Today, with the diversified student body and faculty, value-systems and needs different from those of a certain social class are likely to emerge. This, hopefully, may bring about a more dynamic quality in institutional and student mores.

Social Structuring Due to Material Equipment

As has been pointed out, the material equipment of a college campus plays an important role in structuring its social life. The setting of the buildings, their grouping, their compactness, or their spatiality affect student social life. An excellent example of this structuring of social life due to material equipment is furnished by Harvard during the early twentieth century, when the administrative attitude toward the social problems of housing was one of willful neglect. Residential facilities should have been established coordinate with Harvard College but this was not done. Consequently, private capital assumed the housing for the new increment of students and private luxurious dormitories were

16 A. B. Hollingshead, "Ingroup Membership and Academic Selection," *American Sociological Review*, 3 : 826–833, December 1938.

built as commercial ventures. The college retained its old buildings without modern conveniences and did nothing to meet the new competition. A sharp cleavage grew up between the "Yard" and "Gold Coast"—the more unfortunate because it was financial as well as social. Through this housing situation the students of Harvard became separated on a class and caste structure and Boston had better opportunity to become a "social leech" of Harvard College. Also, buildings were placed just outside the quarter-mile "prayer limit" so that its denizens need not attend chapel. The mores of college students thus were decidedly changed because of these material conditions.

To return to material equipment in terms of building structure, a majority of personnel workers interviewed in this study related how dormitory structure also leads to a social structuring of students. At one girls' college a pattern of exclusiveness arose from a housing arrangement of suites for six, with no central corridor. At another college, a fine dormitory spirit of friendliness existed in the residences where there were definite corridor groups and no suites. In another college a clique structure had grown up in sorority houses because of the separation of some of the girls by residence in annexes. A personnel worker in a junior college deplored its location on the third floor of a high school building. This situation made the students feel they were still part of the high school. They continued to attend the high school dances and their social mores remained the same as those of high school students.

There is no doubt that a dormitory with large rooms housing many students will tend to foster a different style of living and social-cultural pattern than one with private rooms and private suites with many different entries. At one college, the dormitory had one common entry to the building, three floors with L wings, each with from twenty to twenty-five double rooms, a common lavatory with three showers and tub, and one private telephone booth on the first floor beside the public one at an open desk in the front office. Girls were reached for the telephone by a bell system which rang in the hall instead of the room. At another college, the dormitory had ten or fifteen separate entries, each with eight or ten separate suites, each suite having its own private bathroom and telephone. These two types of buildings naturally will foster a different type of social life; in the latter the girls will be much more independent and in the former they will be more interdependent. In the former, if a girl has a date, the whole floor knows it; they also know who does not date. Under these conditions some girls might feel obliged to accept any kind of date rather than to appear unpopular before her more popular floor-mates.

Different types of building structure often are the means of forming cliques. A three-floor dormitory had well-developed culture cliques in the L wings where architectural segregation promoted common interests. In dormitories where architectural designs develop social-cultural exclusiveness, incoming freshmen who choose a room according to the ordinary stipulations of size, location, and price soon find there are other considerations. Very often they will ask to change rooms and, although complaints may not be verbalized, one can find upon investigation that the cause is uncongeniality in local clique structure.

The architectural designs of the men's fraternities on a large state university campus are the source of "exclusive" brands of social-cultural patterns. Fraternities on this campus are rated by men and women according to what novel things architectural design can create for each house. When one visits this campus, this factor is very obvious.

The existence of a common path from the dormitory to the classrooms and the location of a student union in the concourse of student traffic tend also to affect social patterns.

The technological factors of communication and transportation may likewise affect social life on the campus. Convenient transportation and communication facilities for out-of-town boy friends and parents can do much for the social morale of certain groups.

Status, Role, and Prestige
on a College Campus

In the social classification of student positions[17] in the college community lie status, prestige, and role conceptions. According to Linton,

[17] See page 115 of this study.

The place in a particular system which a certain individual occupies at a particular time will be referred to as his *status* with respect
to that system. . . . Role will be used to designate the sum total of
the culture patterns associated with a particular status. It thus includes the attitudes, values, and behavior ascribed by the society to any
and all persons occupying this status. . . . Every status is linked with
a particular role, but the two things are by no means the same from
the point of view of the individual.[18]

His statuses are ascribed to him on the basis of the classifications
previously mentioned, that is, age and sex, and the groups to which
he belongs. His role is the dynamic aspect of a status in which he
gets some consistent conception of himself in relation to other
people.

As a witness of how important status is to a student body, one
should glance through yearbooks of the past twenty years and note
the list of activities after each student's name. This gives some in-
dication of the number of students who achieved status by their
own efforts or to whom various groups and individuals ascribed
status. When a student carries out the duties of the status which
the group assigned to him, he is performing a role. Through these
roles the students organize behavior and attitudes congruous with
those of other students participating in the expression of the role.
Football might offer an example of such an organization; the position of quarterback is meaningless except in relation to other
positions. The members of a sorority all have status on the campus
by virtue of their membership in that sorority. The girls assume
certain functions which will justify their status as members of the
sorority. The members of a sorority, before arranging a special
social occasion, will make an assessment of the role each will play:
one especially gifted socially will be assigned a position as hostess;
another with talent in entertaining will be assigned that role.

A student operates sometimes in terms of one status and its role,
sometimes in terms of another. The status in terms of which an
individual is operating is his active status at that particular point
of time. His other statuses are latent during that time. The roles
associated with such latent statuses are temporarily held in abeyance, but they are integral parts of the individual's cultural equipment. A star on an athletic team is operating in that status during

[18] Ralph Linton, *The Cultural Background of Personality*, p. 76–77.

a football game; he may also be head chef in a dining-room; he may also be a comedian on the college campus. All these roles are necessary to an understanding of this individual.

In college social structures, the students' mores due to prestige seeking are an important factor. The first step taken by a student seeking acceptance into a group of high prestige is to assume the overt culture patterns of that group and to abandon those of his own. Also, membership in a particular age-sex group immediately provides the individual with a long series of patterns for the behavior which would be proper in his relations with members of the other age-sex groups. It is only necessary for him to recognize the category to which another student belongs for him to know how to behave toward the other and the sort of behavior he is entitled to expect in return. There is also a tendency to ascribe different roles in the culture of the campus to students of different age-sex categories. They are expected not only to possess different sorts of knowledge but also to have different value-attitude systems.

In the early pioneer academic community each member from the president to the lowliest freshman had his distinct place and precedence—seniority, it was called. According to Morison's history of early Harvard, "In order of seniority, written in Gothic letters, the names were kept constantly posted on the 'buttery tables'—tablets or bulletin boards which hung in a conspicuous place against the buttery wall. To have your name on the tables meant that you were a member of Harvard College; and to have your name 'cut out of the tables' or 'put out of the buttery' was the symbol of expulsion. The Harvard Order of Seniority was thus arranged:

The President of Harvard College
    The Senior Fellow of the House
Resident Master of Arts, if former Fellow-Commoners
        or Knights' Sons
    Junior Fellows, Masters of Arts
        Other Resident Masters of Arts
    Junior Fellows, Bachelors of Arts
        Fellow-Commoners
            Senior Bachelors
            Middle Bachelors
            Junior Bachelors

Senior Sophisters
Junior Sophisters
Sophomores
Freshmen[19]

"Seniority was not only fixed between one class and another, but within each class. Thus, a senior bachelor outranked a middle bachelor; and a middle bachelor who graduated first in his class outranked one who had graduated second."[20]

"Harvard never had more than two or three orders or vertical classes, we might call them, of undergraduates: fellow-commoners, ordinary students, and, possibly, sizars. Fellow-commoners are mentioned in the College Laws of 1642–46. . . . Alone of undergraduates, they were addressed and recorded as 'Mr.' They paid extra tuition, presented the college with a piece of plate valued at £3 or more, dined at the fellows' table, outranked all other undergraduates (even resident bachelors), and stood at the head of their respective classes in the catalogue of graduates."[21] "The important lines of division at Harvard, as ever since in American colleges, were those of years: the classes. But, within each class . . . there was an order of seniority which to the colonial undergraduate was a matter of great pith and moment. In this order the students were seated in the hall, served at table, and given choice of studies: in the same order their names were posted at the buttery hatch, entered in the Steward's book and on monitor bills, printed on the commencement theses, and in each successive catalogue of graduates, even to the last Quinquennial published in 1930."[22]

According to Morison, we have no certain knowledge of the principles of this ranking by which the seniority of undergraduates was determined. The English system of placement by date of entrance was not followed. Nor was age the criterion. Statements to the effect that the ranking was on a social basis can be found in almost every history of Harvard or Yale or of the Colonies. Morison has stated that intellectual merit was the determining factor in seniority at Harvard in the seventeenth century and well

[19] Reprinted by permission of the publishers from Samuel Eliot Morison, *Harvard College in the Seventeenth Century.* Cambridge, Mass.: Harvard University Press, 1936. Part I, p. 58–59.
[20] *Ibid.,* p. 59. [21] *Ibid.,* p. 59.
[22] *Ibid.,* p. 61–62.

into the eighteenth. "In the eighteenth century ranking by intellectual merit gave way to ranking freshmen by the Degrees of their ancestors; but whether this was a gradual evolution from the merit system, as influenced by provincial precedence, or whether it was an importation from Yale is still obscure."[23] From this early system of "prestige by seniority" has come today the seniority by class. Senior and upperclass privileges and underclass submissions still exist. Such occasions as "Moving-up Day" and "Promotion Day" are celebrated each year in some colleges with great pomp.

Besides the mores on a campus which arise from prestige expectancies in positions according to seniority and age, there are also prestige recognitions and expectancies in qualifications for specialized activities and association in groups. In the voluntary, spontaneous groups on a college campus the membership is usually confined to individuals of the same sex and age, such as the social fraternities and sororities, and some care will also be taken to include only individuals who are sufficiently congenial to be able to cooperate with a minimum of friction.

Certain groups bring unusual prestige. A student from a large city college mentioned in a conference a theater group, called "The Varsity," as having unusual prestige. In addition to this group there were other groups, called the "Little Theater," the "Masques," and "The Radio Guild," all open to speech majors. Asked why the "Varsity" group had unusual prestige she replied, "They are well organized socially, they have an air of social isolation, they are socially hard to penetrate, they dominate other theater groups, they think and know they are good, they carry over dramatics by being melodramatic off-stage, they want to be professional, there is a social elite about them. One often can hear students say, 'There's a girl from Varsity.' "

A personnel worker from this campus further ascribed the prestige of this group to "extreme confidence in themselves," and she added, "They have good programs," "they function well," "they think they are good," "they are grotesque, dramatic, and individualistic."

This illustration reveals the dynamics often underlying group prestige on a campus. The snobbish element is undoubtedly de-

[23] *Ibid.*, p. 64.

structive but the "confidence in themselves," "the functioning well," and the certain amount of individualism are well worth study, by both personnel workers and student leaders.

The personnel worker interviewed also mentioned other prestige groups on the campus. In fact, she said, "Prestige exists in each area of interests in student life on this campus." There is a special prestige group in drama, as mentioned, in politics, and in departmental organizations. The Bio-Medical Club has special prestige also, and for about the same reasons as The Varsity.

As regards membership in the system based on association, a student can hardly fail to be included in friendship units and workgroups. He may be debarred from belonging to clubs or other of the more formal groupings, but even so he occupies a very definite place in the system of which such groups are a part. He is one of the "outsiders," and it is the presence of this group which provides the "members" with prestige and most of their emotional satisfaction. It is inconceivable that a secret society could exist without a large audience of non-members to envy the members and speculate about the secrets.

The desire for prestige is universal, but the ways of obtaining it are determined by local culture and are infinitely varied. On one campus the way to prestige may lie in work and self-help; on another, in wealth and ostentatious waste. One group may accord it to the man who avoids competition; another to the one who is constantly trying to beat his neighbors. As soon as groups become strong, rivalry arises and a certain amount of prestige follows.

If the groups on a college campus were to rate each other in a prestige series, the ranking of individuals and groups in this series would be linked with the ascription of different forms of behavior to persons or groups occupying different positions in such a rating. There is usually a feeling that individuals of high prestige should behave in certain ways. They usually are expected to be cautious in the exercise of their real power and considerate of those below them, and failure in the exercise results in loss of esteem. Today on every campus there is a distinction between activities for underclassmen and upperclassmen. The freshman is expected to adhere to patterns of obedience; there are prescribed patterns of costume and behavior which they are expected to follow. The freshman eventually "emerges" as a sophomore, indicating that he now must adopt a new and more "grown-up" value-system. The sophomore "passes into" the body of upperclassmen, recognizing the assumption of more knowledge and prestige. The junior comes into the "grand old" senior class with an awareness not only of more dignity but of deeper responsibility.

The role of the individual with respect to his college is a dual one. Under ordinary circumstances, the more perfect his conditioning and consequent integration into the social structure of the campus, the more effective his contribution to the smooth functioning of the whole and stability of the mores. However, campuses have to exist and function in an ever-changing world. The unparalleled ability of students to adjust to changing conditions and to develop ever more effective responses to familiar conditions rests upon the residue of individuality which survives in every one of them after society and culture have done their utmost.

As a simple member of the social life of the campus, the student thus perpetuates the campus *status quo*. As an individual he helps to change the *status quo* when the need arises. Since no environment is ever completely static, no society can survive without the occasional inventor and his ability to find solutions to new problems. In order to function successfully on the college campus, the student usually must assume stereotyped forms of behavior, must abide by some established mores. However, a great many of these mores are oriented toward the maintenance of the college rather than toward the satisfaction of individual needs. A college cannot function successfully at any point in time unless its culture includes techniques for indoctrinating new students in the college's system of values and for training them to occupy particular places in its structure. It must also include techniques for rewarding socially desirable behavior and discouraging that which is socially undesirable. The behavior patterns which compose the culture must be adjusted to one another in such a way as to avoid conflict and prevent the results of one pattern of behavior from negating those of another.

The culture patterns upon which any college depends for its survival must, as in other types of community, be established as patterns of habitual response on the part of its members. The student's incentive for assuming these patterns and mores of the college lies in the satisfaction which they give him personally, especially with regard to his needs for favorable acceptance by others, for recognition and for stability. The ability to integrate into a single configuration elements of behavior, some of which serve to meet a student's individual needs, others to satisfy social necessities and group pressures, and to transmit such a configura-tion as a whole makes campus life harmonious.

The development of new social patterns on the campus calls for individual qualities of thought and initiative, but to achieve the integration mentioned above and to ensure the survival and suc-cessful functioning of a college society's mores, more and more statuses may have to be transferred from the achieved, in which the individual initiative is important, to the ascribed, in which the group or campus assigns certain positions to its members. Membership in such an organized college community may de-prive the individual of opportunities to exercise his particular gifts, but it gives him a strong emotional security by satisfying his so-cial-status needs, his needs for security and stability—needs which he must satisfy through the medium of his total group. Which of these needs is best or which makes for the greatest happiness to the greatest number, is a matter of constant observation and study on the part of the personnel worker.

Implications for Personnel Workers and Educators

The college community is a complex social environment. Its organization is a social system in which every part exists interde-pendently with every other part. It is impossible to detect the nuances of a college social system without knowing its operation from the inside. The composition of the groups in a college com-munity, the methods by which they are recruited, their organiza-tion, the status they occupy, the rewards and prestige each receives, their participation in the life of the campus constitute crucial data for understanding the operation of the social system. Special folk-ways and mores are the very base of a social system; they regulate status, prestige, and the functional aspects of college organization. Whether a college has a vertical or a horizontal administrative hierarchy depends on the mores of the institution and its clientele.

The college social system within which the teacher and the student function not only defines their goals, purposes, and interests, but also sets up a regulative structure. There is much competition and individual striving for ends that cannot be equally shared.

The prestige mores of the academic structure sometimes are damaging. Colleges by their narrow loyalties, by their insistence that students and teachers alike play the game according to the rules laid down in a jealous and self-contained community, dampen many progressive spirits and waste many creative and inventive personalities. The specific activities in which faculty members and students engage depend upon the positions which they occupy in the social system, the rights and duties expected of those positions, and the components of their wishes and needs for security and recognition. For those who are attempting to understand human relations in action, it should be clear that a large number of the relationships of a student in college, his activities, and his attitudes can be better understood by knowing the place he occupies or is striving for within the social context.

Personnel workers should know the norms of behavior which are imposed by a particular college in its social system. Only by discounting them as indicators of personality will they be able to penetrate social conformity and cultural uniformity in reaching the real individual. The personality often will be revealed, not by culturally patterned responses but by deviations from the culture pattern. Also, the way a college community feels about a particular episode is more important to a personnel worker than any overt behavior that may take place. By understanding feeling it may be possible to determine in part how far the behavior differs from the accepted mores. It may show wherein a personnel point of view may be needed to structure desirable mores of students, faculty, alumni, or townspeople.

As for status and role in the college community, the campus must be seen from the point of view of the persons involved in and going through the process of character formation and personality development. It is necessary not only to know the status and role ascribed to a student in the culture of the campus but also to know his own conception of his status and role, that is, to know his social personality. His behavior takes place in terms of his conceptions; in terms of his beliefs regarding the attitudes of others toward him. It is necessary therefore to know not only the cultural imperatives and group definitions but the student's conception of them, of himself, and of his place in the system. As to selective mechanisms, personnel workers and educators must do something about administrative policies that promote family inbreeding, a grandfather-father-son pattern, and favors for money and class. If the democratic pattern is to survive, must not more democratic mores be developed on the part of students? Must the college be peripheral to parent expectancies?

The fact that all personnel workers interviewed spoke of racial discrimination, stratification, and social cleavages of various kinds indicates the urgent need for intergroup education. With regard to racial discrimination, the problem is one not of race but of culture. Ideas, sentiments, beliefs are all acquired. Race prejudice is one of our widespread folkways. The question of difference between the American professed belief in equality, justice, and liberty and attitudes that are actually learned must be carefully worked on. The bases of discrimination, the prejudices of propaganda and of public opinion, the attitudes of majority and minority races, should all be studied.

The family mores of the students, and the mores of teachers and sometimes personnel workers themselves may include prejudices and group stereotypes concerning people of various races. Democracy is the major commitment of the American college campus. Intergroup education must be so developed on the campus that students will see the need for a sense of values that recognizes the rights and strivings of all individuals, races, and groups. This education must evolve from actual experiences in living together and the fostering of desirable human relationships in such living. The campus must be used as a laboratory for human relationships; its social system must be built by all working together. The social system must have a position and role for each person, and the contribution of each person must be recognized. Every student belonging to a group that is considered a minority group has thoughts, feelings, attitudes, and ways of behaving conditioned by that particular status in the college community. Above all other students he needs status and role. There must be successful integration of all groups. A personnel worker in a Western university related how a successful integration of Oriental women took place on that campus by working with the college women to have them accepted in their groups, by not segregating their living arrangements, and by having them appointed to leadership posts. This successful integration was accomplished through the mediating influence of a dominant personality, a former dean of women who had developed well-organized programs of orientation and group relations among the women students. The Oriental men were housed together in separate houses and were not accepted as were the women, mainly because the men had no strong mediating influence, no great personality from a personnel point of view, to modify their attitudes. Therefore, influenced by the culture which the students brought with them, viz., a parent culture reflecting a strong rejection of Orientals, the men continued in that culture.

In the new international world, wherein the college campus will have many foreign students, educators should recognize this new cultural heritage along with the language peculiar to the culture, accept the differences, and attempt to integrate them into a great unifying endeavor for a complete establishment of a cultural democracy.

A college social system includes structure and function. With the new groups of students and faculty who are appearing on the campuses the college community cannot help having a broader type of structure, and functioning must be carefully thought through to meet the needs of this new structure.

There are configurations in every college social system. Such configurations always include three elements, which this chapter has emphasized. First, it includes the human personalities who compose the college community; second, the culture of the college community, which comprises the whole set of techniques, types of structure, ascribed statuses, prestige series, and arrangements for living which are usually transmitted from one generation to another in order to ensure the existence of the college community; third, the natural environment to which the college members must adapt their lives. Social structuring is also affected by the physical aspects of this natural environment. Hence each personnel worker and educator must understand and study these configurations in order to work with the particular social system of his college.

Bibliography

Cattell, R. B. and Malteno, V. "The Concept of Social Status." *Journal of Social Psychology,* 15 : 293–308, May 1942.

Cooley, Charles Horton. *Social Organization.* New York: Charles Scribner's Sons, 1909. 436 p.

Counts, George S. *School and Society in Chicago.* New York: Harcourt, Brace, and Company, 1928. 367 p.

Dollard, J. *Caste and Class in a Southern Town.* New Haven: Yale University Press, 1937. 502 p.

Faris, Ellsworth. "Attitudes and Behavior." *American Journal of Sociology,* 34 : 271–281, September 1928.

Hollingshead, A. B. "Ingroup Membership and Academic Selection." *American Sociological Review,* 3 : 826–833, December 1938.

Johnson, Burges. *Campus Versus Classroom.* New York: I. Washburn, Inc., 1946. 305 p.

Katz, Daniel. "Attitude Measurement as a Method in Social Psychology." *Social Forces,* 15 : 479–482, May 1937.

Katz, D. and Braly, K. "Racial Stereotypes of 100 College Students." *Journal of Abnormal and Social Psychology,* 28 : 280–290, October–December 1933.

Katz, D., Allport, F. H., and Jenness, M. B. *Students' Attitudes.* Syracuse, N. Y.: The Craftsman Press, Inc., 1931. 408 p.

Lewin, Kurt and Lippitt, Ronald. "An Experimental Approach to the Study of Autocracy and Democracy; A Preliminary Note." *Sociometry,* 1 : 292–300, January–April 1938.

Linton, Ralph. *The Cultural Background of Personality.* New York: D. Appleton-Century Company, Inc., 1945. 157 p.

Linton, Ralph. *The Study of Man.* New York: D. Appleton-Century Company, Inc., 1936. 503 p.

Lundberg, George A. *Foundations of Sociology.* New York: The Macmillan Company, 1939. 556 p.

Lynd, Robert S. and Lynd, Helen Merrell. *Middletown. A Study in Contemporary American Culture.* New York: Harcourt, Brace and Company, 1937. 604 p.

Marks, Percy. *Which Way Parnassus?* New York: Harcourt, Brace and Company, 1926. 246 p.

Mead, Margaret. *And Keep Your Powder Dry.* New York: W. Morrow and Company, 1942. 274 p.

Moffett, M. L. *Social Background and Activities of Teachers College Students.* New York: Bureau of Publications, Teachers College, Columbia University, 1929. 133 p.

Morison, Samuel Eliot. *Three Centuries of Harvard, 1636–1936.* Cambridge: Harvard University Press, 1936. 512 p.

Morison, Samuel Eliot. *Harvard College in the Seventeenth Century.* Part I. Cambridge: Harvard University Press, 1936.

Myrdal, Gunnar. *An American Dilemma.* New York: Harper and Brothers, 1944. 2 vols. 1144 p.

"Results of the Survey of Social Life at Dartmouth College." *School and Society,* 43 : 664–665, May 16, 1936.

Sutherland, R. L. *Color, Class, and Personality.* Washington, D. C.: American Council on Education, 1942. 135 p.

Waller, Willard. "Rating and Dating Complex." *American Sociological Review,* 2 : 727–734, October 1937.

Waller, Willard. *The Sociology of Teaching.* New York: J. Wiley and Sons, Inc., 1932. 467 p.

Warner, W. Lloyd and Lunt, Paul. *The Social Life of a Modern Community.* Yankee City Series, Vol. 1. New Haven: Yale University Press, 1941. 460 p.

Williamson, E. G. and Darley, J. G. "The Measurement of Social Attitudes of College Students; I. Standardization of Tests and Results of a Survey." *Journal of Social Psychology,* 8 : 219–229, May 1937.

Williamson, E. G. and Darley, J. G. "The Measurement of Social Attitudes of College Students; II. Validation of Two Attitude Tests." *Journal of Social Psychology,* 8 : 231–242, May 1937.

Wilson, Logan. *The Academic Man. A Study in the Sociology of a Profession.* New York: Oxford University Press, 1942. 248 p.

Znaniecki, Florian. *The Social Role of the Man of Knowledge.* New York: Columbia University Press, 1940. 212 p.

V

THE COMPLEX OF INTERRELATIONS ON
THE CAMPUS

T HE purpose of this chapter is to describe how the interrelations of individuals and groups on a college campus affect the structuring of students' "ways of doing things." It will attempt to show how students' personality needs, adjustments and attitudes are strongly conditioned by interpersonal relationships. The chapter first treats the general over-all interrelations on a college campus, such as student-student, faculty-faculty, student-faculty, student-parent, and student-alumni relationships, and points to the necessity for successful total interaction. The chapter emphasizes how a social event of disturbing nature occurring in campus life affects all these relationships and must be analyzed in its entire relational context. Campus situations, as described by personnel workers, are presented to illustrate constructive mores in interrelations.

Second, the chapter deals with interpersonal relationships within groups and smaller units of campus life. It shows how leadership enters into interpersonal relationships and contributes to the effectiveness of a group as an agent of social action and as a bearer of the mores. Techniques of leadership which are valuable to a personnel worker in discovering the existing interpersonal relationships are also discussed. Suggestions are offered for developing good interrelationships among the heterogeneous student groups of today. Criteria for the evaluation of leadership and categories of dominance are discussed. Examples of various types of leaders are presented and the place of attitudes in interpersonal relationships is emphasized. Implications are drawn for campus workers to study more carefully their social environment.

Campus Interrelations and
the Total Social Configuration

As Warner and Lunt point out:

Society is a group of mutually interacting individuals. Hence, if any relationship of a given social configuration is stimulated, it will influence all other parts and in turn will be influenced by them. It is impossible, once the structure is in action, to determine which is cause and which is effect, since the several relations mutually determine the activities which take place at any given time in one or all of the relations.[1]

Social relations are so mutually dependent and interactive with the total social bonds within a college community that they can be best studied in this connection. The direct relationship between faculty and student is, for example, influenced by the relationship between president and faculty, as are also the direct student-student and faculty-faculty relationships. The faculty-faculty relationship influences student-faculty and student-student relationships. In interviews with personnel staffs two differing sets of mores were found evident in faculty thinking—the old-line conventional mores and a more modern, progressive, and liberal type. Quite often these two sets of faculty mores are in conflict in discussions of student social problems and in the development of the student program. This conflict causes divisions not only among the faculty but also among the students, and between students and faculty. Integration fails to take place in either student or faculty programs and this situation often leads to lack of integration in the whole college culture matrix.

GENERAL INTERRELATIONS—STUDENT,
   FACULTY, ADMINISTRATION, PARENT, COMMUNITY

A résumé of written discussions by approximately twenty students on the campus of a large city college emphasizes that most interrelationships on their campus are based on cliques. There is very little social mobility. Some students become close friends at

[1] W. Lloyd Warner and Paul S. Lunt, *The Social Life of a Modern Community,* Vol. 1, p. 13. Copyright, 1941, by Yale University Press.

college because they were graduated from the same high school. Each nationality group tends to stay within its own organization. The uniting factors are to be found in common interests, common ideas, and common attitudes developed through classwork. None of the students, however, know the faculty outside the classroom. The social research laboratory and the field trips of the geology department are mentioned favorably by students as means of getting better acquainted with the faculty. A difficult cog in the wheel of good student interrelations is that the students show a general disinterest in clubs. Each club tries to promote its own interests with advertising and posters and yet the response in attendance is generally unsatisfactory. Students even have to be recruited to hear a world-famous speaker. Although the students commute to this college and no doubt have outside interests, there must be some means to bring greater unity among them. It is a situation which requires study and above all the effective cooperation of the whole college community.

At another college a personnel worker said that the morale of the campus is colored by seething unrest on the part of students. There is an undercurrent of dissatisfaction over the lack of material things which the students feel they should have in return for the tuition paid. Any outburst of feeling is handled by administrative fiat on the part of the president. No effort is made to explain the issue to the students who are, on the whole, a capable, cooperative group. The parents and the local community are now urging investigations into the financial affairs of the college, and this in turn has its reverberations among the students. A town citizens' committee, interested in the athletics of the college but without confidence in the college's management of financial affairs, has established athletic scholarships that are to be handled by a town committee. This action has brought about an infiltration of a non-college type of student who enters the institution at the whim of a town politician. Because of the dissatisfaction resulting from this interference and the lack of administrative vision in handling it, the college is gradually becoming a prey to outside influences, with a resulting weakening of morale on the part of the students.

This situation illustrates how a poor president-student interrelationship can lead to destructive mores of students. It also shows how lack of successful interaction in a president-student relationship can bring about destructive mores on the part of other persons within and even outside the college community. This situation has been brought about through a rather common phenomenon in campus life relations, namely, "misunderstanding"; in this case it has been misunderstanding as to the financial management of the college. In this college, as in others over the country, failure of the administrative officer to explain adequately a disturbing situation has brought about poor president-student relations, president-parent relations, and town-college relations.

A persistent problem in the area of student-parent-college interrelationship has come from a personnel worker in a denominational college where the emotional effect of "liberalizing" the students whose beliefs are rooted in the faith of their church is very upsetting. Many of the students who are from rural sections want to make a change to a more liberal attitude, but their parents often are inflexible. This situation presents a difficult experience for the student, and often ends in his separation from the church and family. It is a much less difficult emotional experience for the young people, if the parents are striving also for more liberal ideas.

Parental Letter. With regard to the influence of parent-student interrelationships which are sometimes overlooked on a college campus, Hartshorne[2] mentions a largely unexplored documentary source, viz., the student letter, and takes in conjunction with it the parental letter.

The writing of letters to parents and the reading of the replies constitute activities of prime importance in the adjustment of the student. Hartshorne mentions that in the courtship letter there is a symmetrical relationship; that is, the functions for the writer are roughly equivalent to the functions for the reader, although there may be a certain amount of boy-girl differentiation. By way of contrast, the child-parent relationship is clearly asymmetrical; the functions of the letters exchanged will vary for the parent and for the child, for the writer and for the receiver. Moreover, some of the aims which the mother, say, intends to accomplish by writing

    [2] Edward Y. Hartshorne, "Undergraduate Society and the College Culture," *American Sociological Review,* 8 : 327–330, June 1943.

letters to her daughter at college may not be accomplished; while certain other effects upon the daughter, of which the mother may not be aware, may result from the reading. The effect on the daughter-reader may thus vary to some extent independently of the intentions of the mother-writer, and vice versa. There may be a reciprocal function, but it is useful to differentiate certain functions of the mother-daughter letter for the mother, since the mother's attitudes inevitably impinge upon the daughter in college. According to Hartshorne, among these functions for the parent are: (1) opportunity to feel useful and of service to the daughter by transmitting maternal values thought to be requisite for successful adjustment with respect to college work, health, psychic security, making friends, cooking, clothing, engagements, marriage; (2) opportunity to ask for and to receive response from daughter; (3) opportunity to express gratitude and appreciation for daughter's response; (4) self-praise, and especially pride in family and children; (5) sharing confidential information; (6) general projection of ego by recounting daily doings, attitudes, achievements, etc.; (7) opportunity for catharsis in a crisis, e.g., after death of husband or birth of first grandchild.[3]

The functions for the daughter who receives the letters depend upon the attitude of the daughter toward the mother. If the daughter's attitude is a hostile one, whatever the qualities of her mother's letters, they will have little or no effect. If the daughter's attitude is favorable, the effect will be to enhance the daughter's general orientation and socialization in the college community, that is, the daughter will acquire the values of her parent in all the phases of her life covered by the letters, and if such be the case, then college may be regarded as a relatively minor factor in the modification of attitudes which derive from the child-parent relationship. College educators sometimes tend to take a wholly one-sided view of the situation, assuming that parental attitudes are of importance only as a minor influence in the adjustment of the child to college. In many cases the influence of the college is peripheral to that of the family as an educative influence, rather than the reverse.

The parental letter thus sheds considerable light on the perpetu-

[3] *Ibid.*, p. 329–330.

ation of pre-college influences in the college culture as experienced by the undergraduate. Students' letters to their parents give evidence of the same pre-college influence. The decreasing frequency of child-parent letters in the course of the four college years neatly documents the role of the college in the weaning process.

TOTALITY OF INTERRELATIONS

The example of the failure of a group to function in a certain college comes to mind as an illustration of how important are all interrelations in a college community—student-student, student-faculty, student-administrator, and student-department. It was the dwindling in membership which brought to the attention of the dean this group consisting of non-sorority, off-campus girls who were majoring in something other than art—art being the chief field of this particular college. The purpose of the group was "personal and social development." There were in this instance of failure in group functioning several contributing factors. In the first place, the group worked under a feeling of inferiority due to clannishness on the part of the art students. Second, the program which had consisted of formal etiquette demonstrations was not meeting the needs of the members. Third, the faculty adviser did not visualize the role of the group in bringing about good student-student and other interrelations on the campus. The reasons for joining the club were reviewed for the dean by the few remaining members. Formal remarks were made until finally one of them broke down with "We wanted to be like the art students" and "to be in some social affairs." As to the question concerning who should be their adviser, one of them said, "If we could only have Miss——— [a popular art instructor] but she would never consider us." Encouragement was given to approach this person with whom the dean had quite often discussed the unfortunate cleavage on the campus. It was quite a different group who later announced their success when they obtained this adviser.

The first meeting, which had for its program "Interior Decoration," was held in the dormitory parlors. The meeting included a criticism of the parlor decorations. Immediately ideas came from the girls and the parlors were decoratively rearranged. This brought a glowing report in the campus newspaper. "Arrange their own rooms," the girls suggested as the project for the next meeting. Soon the whole dormitory was agog over attractive rooms. The group was then asked if they would like to visit and participate in a small art class specializing in coiffures. The instructor had prepared her class for this project. Criteria were set up for a successful coiffeuse; "she would create the most appropriate style, show courtesy, teach the customer how to do the coiffure herself." The experiment was extremely successful; not only did the club have a real experience but a friendly spirit was established with what in their estimation was an elite group, which raised social satisfaction and security. The art group also had the satisfaction and security of helping a non-art group whom they learned to know better. The next meeting was of the same type, the subject being the use of cosmetics. From insights gained from this experience, the art building was opened one evening each week to all who wished to delve into art as a hobby. Also, the annual art exhibit was held in the dormitory parlors instead of the classrooms.

The second semester brought increased enrollment in the club—art students as well as non-art. Art students and non-art students became personal friends. Reorganization of the club with capable leaders resulted, members gained seats in the Student Council, and a role for the group in the campus life was established.

The dynamics of the final success of this group seemed to be as follows: the breaking down of a social cleavage between two student groups through the media of socialized classroom work; the intervention of a strong faculty personality interested in cementing interrelationships between two groups of students; a faculty and administration willing to provide physical facilities for the social development of all students. Through such dynamics constructive student life in the area of social interrelationships can be built.

To show more clearly the totality of interrelations on a campus, at a large cosmopolitan college communistic thinking within the student ranks brought schisms in student-student relationships. Because there were some faculty sympathizers with the student movement toward communism, a schism occurred not only in the faculty-faculty relationships but also in student-faculty relationships. It later led to a break in president-faculty relationships, and eventually spread to president-faculty-alumni-community and societal involvements.

In this example, interrelations between persons in a college community are particularly tested in the occurrence of a disturbing event. Personnel people might therefore attack the problem of understanding interrelationships by studying a disturbing event, or a number of events which lead to destructive mores. They might do this by following the plan of the authors of the *Yankee City Series*,[4] who attempt (1) to place the events or activities under observation in an immediate social relational context, (2) to articulate the immediate relational situation with a larger one, and (3) to place the larger configuration in the total situation on interrelations which compose the whole community.

In the case of a disturbing event on a college campus which is likely to bring about destructive mores among the student body, a personnel worker or educator, in considering the Yankee City plan and the incident stated, might attempt to discover:

1. How does this event affect the social relations of the student body?

2. How did this event come about on this campus? Has it come from a certain stratum of the student body? What factors in the background of particular students have brought this problem to the foreground? Is it a problem peculiar to this particular geographical region of the country or is it a genuine social problem on all college campuses? Is it a problem with which youth are struggling alone or is it a problem of adult society as well?

3. How is the event related to outside influences? Is it due to alumni influence, to a local community, or to wider community influence? Or is it due to inside influence, as that of the faculty, or to a special student group? What pressures, outside and inside, are being brought to bear upon the issue?

4. How is this event going to affect the entire campus system of interrelations among students, faculty, president, and the whole college community?

In developing an analysis of a disturbing event by seeing it in

---

4 Warner and Lunt, *op. cit.*, p. 13.

these interrelations, much insight can be gained before making a plan of attack. The problems of the college community and of the students in college should be viewed as a complex of intricate interrelationships in a total conditioning situation. Schisms may develop in the process of working through an event but usually these are ironed out when the problem in its whole social relational context is brought to the surface. Interrelationships—student-student, student-faculty, faculty-faculty, faculty-student-president, student-alumni—should be studied as to their influence in the lives of all people in a college, and as to the means by which they can be developed or changed successfully.

CAMPUS SITUATIONS FOR CONSTRUCTIVE MORES IN INTERRELATIONS

The following résumé of conferences with deans, personnel workers, and counselors from different types of colleges presents the situations and means through which constructive interrelationships are developed on the campuses they represent.

General campus interrelationships—student-student, student-faculty, student-faculty-administration—are less tense and more wholesome where a spirit of friendliness, of loyalty, and of tolerance prevails. Cooperative interrelationships develop where a democratic approach to government and to campus living is in effect. Social interrelations are best developed where there are many *all-college* events, faculty-student banquets, faculty-student trips, student entertainment in faculty homes, faculty counseling of students, and discussion groups of both faculty and students. Relations are more friendly where faculty live in dormitories with students, where students and faculty are engaged in social service, community participation, and where there is student-faculty concern for the dignity and worth of each individual. Successful interrelationships are fostered where plans for social action are thought through by both students and faculty, and where students assume responsibility for their own behavior on the campus rather than follow traditional roles of authority.

Interrelationships are most satisfactory also where the administration has vision and understanding concerning student problems, and can handle dissatisfactions on the campus by explaining thoroughly to students the reasons for administrative actions. Effective student personnel and guidance programs, flexibility and adaptability in administrative procedures, and the willingness of an administration to accept change on the campus likewise promote good relationships.

Salutary relationships exist between students where there is a minimum of discrimination, social cleavage, and stratification, and where racial and national groups are not segregated in dormitories. It was especially observed that interrelations are better in situations where the students maintain a spirit of cooperation in spite of difficult housing conditions, where they have unification programs, such as interfaith movements, and where there is compatibility between college groups and community activities.

Good interrelations in a college community are most effective where there is not a divided campus in the location of physical facilities and college buildings; where there is not too strong a tradition, with its accompanying emotional effects. They also exist where there are well-trained house-mothers in dormitory residences, where psychiatrists are available to deal with severe emotional problems, and where mental hygiene services are administered. Classroom material that is suitable to student interests and well-developed orientation programs for new students also promote good interrelationships on a campus.

Interpersonal Relationships

Thus far, interrelationships have been discussed from a general point of view, such as a faculty role toward students as a whole, or an administrative role toward students as a whole. These interrelations depend on the culture patterns that each college community associates with the formal interaction of its members in different statuses. It has been shown how these interrelations have to be understood and sometimes changed for more constructive mores. There are also interpersonal relationships—the relationships that each person fosters toward another regardless of differences in status. It is a matter of individuals modifying the formal roles to make them more congenial to themselves. They may comprise an interpersonal relationship between two students or two faculty members, or one faculty member or student and president, which sometimes influences large segments of campus relationships or the campus relationships as a whole. Interpersonal relationships, that is, constructive individual development of personalities, are often effected through a cooperative enterprise —through students and faculty, through student leaders and followers, through group relationships, through the particular individual concerned and a counselor. It must also be remembered that individual-to-individual relationships form group reactions, so that it is impossible to discuss relationships between individuals without consideration of intergroup relations.

IMPORTANCE OF INTERPERSONAL EFFECTIVENESS

It must always be remembered that social interpersonal effectiveness on the part of college students can affect their academic work, and ultimately their success in life. The social qualities which students acquire through good interpersonal relationships are essentials observed, not only by their associates but by their employers, in any future positions in which the students may work. A successful interpersonal functioning is one of the most important factors in meeting the need for personal security.

Personality growth in interpersonal relations must be given consideration. Individual students must be introduced to small, congenial groups. There must be opportunities for each student to use his special ability for the good of the group and so achieve recognition and a sense of worth. There must be opportunities for leadership. Attitudes of acceptance of the individual and of genuine affection for the individual must be developed on the part of teachers and personnel workers. The teacher should be sensitive to the interaction of his personality with that of the individual student; he should know the student's developmental history, relationships with parents, and home patterns of adjustment.

LEADERSHIP

Perhaps the most important factor in interpersonal relationships and effective group work is leadership. Present in the activity of any social group are the phenomena of both leadership and apathy. It is, of course, a characteristic of group activity that within a certain group situation spheres of leadership and influence will inevitably be formed around certain individuals whose personal characteristics, in the minds of the other members of the group, fit them for leadership in the work at hand.

In an interview with a group of urban college students concerning student leadership on their campus, they characterized types of leaders who led particular activities and developed certain interpersonal relations in their college life. The leaders of the political groups, they say, are the ones who are best informed in their ideology and most vociferous in its expression. They are capable of managing their groups as well as of being active in most other activities of the campus. The leaders of athletic and dramatic groups are usually the heroes of the moment, bolstered by the admiration of the "hangers-on" of such groups. The leaders in House Plan are those with the most ingenuity in planning and organizing activities. The leaders of the professional organizations are leaders because they are good students and are interested in their field of specialization. They command respect as well as admiration, and they feel "that leadership in such an organization will lend prestige in their later careers."

The function of the leader is to guide the group process of interaction so that it contributes to the growth of the members as individuals and to the effectiveness of the group as an agent of social action, and as a bearer of constructive mores. In interviews with personnel workers, incidents were related of how a special group can bring about destructive mores which may exist over a number of years and disrupt good relations on a college campus. Then the dynamic and constructive influence of an effective student leader comes into play. The handling of a disturbing event through a dynamic leader can draw a whole college community into closer relationship. It has often been remarked by residence directors of large university campuses that it is impossible to effect good relations between various dormitories or between various colleges on the university campus. If the problems in these situations could be fully explained to student leaders, they might bring about the cementing influence. A deteriorated college community exists where spirit and morale are at a minimum and leadership is lacking. A constructive college community exists where public spirit and morale are highly developed and leadership forms a rich pattern of varied personalities excelling in ability and responsibility, and interacting cooperatively with one another. Indeed, the history of a college community may be written largely in terms of personalities—its leaders.

Today on our college campuses when we have students still retaining, through no fault of their own, "war mores" and other students knowing only "civilian mores," the process of assimilation of these two types of mores may be difficult. Effective group functioning and interpersonal relationships can help considerably in bringing about a successful integration of the two. Leadership can and will be a most important factor in this process. Criteria for evaluating more carefully the phenomenon of leadership will be offered in the following paragraphs.

CRITERIA FOR EVALUATION OF LEADERSHIP

Some criteria for the evaluation of effective leadership and group work have been suggested by Coyle from her study of groups of young people.[5] First in importance is the relation of the leader to the group. Is the leader accepted by the group? What positive contributions does he make to its activities? What is his function in relation to the mores of the group, and can he maintain his own integrity in the relationship? Second, the relation of the leader to individuals is important. How does he handle different individuals? How does he encourage initiative from the group? Does he distribute responsibility? Does he coordinate efforts? Is the leader sensitive to the personal needs of members of the group? Does he know how and where to refer the situations which he cannot handle? Third, the ability of the leader to handle social interactions is another criterion of good leadership and group work. Can the leader handle quarreling and factionalism? Can he manage conflicts between subgroups? Does he recognize that individuals are in search of different satisfactions from the group? The fourth criterion is the handling of the problem of group control. Is the group as self-directing as its stage of development makes possible? Is the group showing itself capable of selecting leaders? Does the

[5] Grace Coyle, *Studies in Group Behavior*, p. 4–16. Copyright, 1937, by Association Press.

power to carry through an enterprise arise out of the common concern for its accomplishment? The fifth criterion is the making of a program. What are the group's vital interests? What creativity is encouraged? Sixth, the handling of group feeling is important. Can esprit de corps be maintained? What cohesion takes place? Seventh, a final criterion for evaluating leadership is the relation of the group to the community. Has the group had contacts with other campus groups? How is this group affecting college community relations? Is this group taking an active part in outside community affairs?

On the campuses today, patterns of leadership may have to be studied rather carefully. A student who has had military leadership may also be an effective leader in peacetime. If the pattern, as expressed on one university campus in Pennsylvania,[6] is repeated on others, then the above seven criteria for leadership and good interpersonal relations in a group should be thoroughly understood by a student body. On this campus one civilian student remarked: "The only way you can get a veteran to do anything is to find a guy of higher rank in the war and appoint him head of a detail with authority to order the other veteran to do whatever's got to be done." Here we have an example, not only of a military role continuing on a peacetime campus, but also of a civilian role which is not democratic. The article further states, "Veterans refuse to share the dirty work around a fraternity house, the civilians complain, and where once a paddle was sufficient to bring a recalcitrant around, new diplomacy is needed."[7] Although the civilian does not exactly typify a follower of military mores, he does typify a follower of old-time authoritarian, autocratic mores. It is to be expected that both these types of roles and interpersonal relationships will continue on the college campus. After a student has spent from one to five years executing such a role, he cannot drop it quickly. The most hopeful part of the above statement is, "New diplomacy is needed." Certainly new diplomacy is needed on present-day campuses. But perhaps a constructive re-education program must be developed before any roles as typified in group

[6] Edith Efron, "The Two Joes Meet—Joe College, Joe Veteran," *New York Times Magazine*, June 16, 1946, p. 55.
[7] *Ibid.*, p. 55.

officers on a college campus can be established. A committee representative of the various elements of a student body today should work on qualities essential to effective leadership, and then discuss with the groups concerned these qualities of leadership, effective student interrelationships, and the hope for democracy on the campus.

The personnel worker will need to be sensitive to the process of assimilation of these two types of mores. He will need to study the process thoroughly and attempt to guide only after an evaluation of the situations at hand and of group reactions and interactions.

The aim of true democracy has been to secure active participation of every individual up to the limit of his capacity. More attention thus far has been paid to defending democracy than to developing the methodology by which it could be made to function in life. If the mores of democracy which students on college campuses should be more eager than ever to defend and strengthen are to be developed, it is not merely enough to have students "belonging" to college extracurricular activities. They must learn more definitely how to participate in them, why they should participate, and what they stand to gain through participation.

Are sound provocative group thinking procedures being developed? Given a situation and a problem, are the factors involved being explored? Have all possibilities for meeting the situation and problem been examined? What bonds seem to unite the group? What are the agreements and differences of opinion? Are the differences sufficiently well analyzed? What decisions can be reached which will meet the situation? Finally, what are the ways and means for putting the decision into effect? The conclusion should always include two parts: a decision as to a specific course of action which forms an answer to the problem and the reasons why this decision has been chosen. At the close of a discussion of a problem on which the group has been thinking, the leader should summarize whatever may be the status of the discussion. It may have reached an integrated solution or the question may still be unsettled, but it is important to recognize whatever stage the group thinking has reached.

Student bodies today have gone through a larger range of experiences than has ever been known in student life before, and it is to be expected that their whole outlook on life and interpersonal relations will be tinged emotionally by these experiences. The personnel worker more than ever must strive to develop by reasoning, difficult as it is, the implications of the problems of today. He must be able tactfully to guide, especially at the points where there is strong feeling. He must carefully analyze why the problem is of concern to the group, under what circumstances it arose, what interests important to the group are involved, where and how the group is facing the problem, and what difficulties are likely to arise in meeting it.

Now when an integration of the old and the new is being worked out on campuses and a superstructure of new mores is being erected, the personnel worker must be well qualified to guide interpersonal relations, to develop leadership and to recognize that it has qualities of permanence, to study the emotional components of students' experiences, in order to start desirable trends.

LEADERSHIP TECHNIQUES

It is important that personnel workers become familiar with the studies of Jennings, Moreno, and others, and use their techniques for studying interpersonal relationships on a college campus. Analyses of findings could be made and the results used in effective individual and group guidance. As Jennings notes:

. . . by means of a prolonged and systematic study of the reputation which the individual has built up in the eyes of peers and superiors, supplemented by specific records of what the individual has done to earn this position in the group, it is possible to define situationally the qualities that appear wherever leadership is present. The result is to document fully a functional conception of leadership in which, instead of defining a leader in terms of the possession of certain static traits, one defines leadership as a function of inter-personal relations, dependent upon the complex give-and-take between members of groups; it is relative to the group processes concerned.[8]

Each student on a campus lives his life interacting with other persons. His happiness and effectiveness are to a degree a product of his interpersonal relationships. Personnel workers must give at-

[8] Helen Jennings, *Leadership and Isolation,* Foreword, p. xiii. Copyright, 1943, by Longmans, Green & Co., Inc.

tention therefore to the growth process and attempt to broaden and deepen the student's participation in the social milieu of which he is a part.

The Sociometric Test. The sociometric test, as outlined in Moreno's studies,[9] allows the student to express his personal feeling for others in the form of choices for functioning with them within the group of which he and they are members. It can be used as a technique for a process of grouping; through it individuals who are capable of harmonious interpersonal relationships can be brought together and a social group can be created which will function efficiently. It is a means of studying the emotional relations between individuals functioning as a social group. This test may show what factors are the bases of friendship and leadership structures on a college campus. Common interests, family relationships, and geographic factors may appear and these can be correlated with socio-economic status. A mapping of the psychological geography of a college community can be made that will enable one to survey its psychological currents, that is, the feelings of one group toward another or feelings within a group. One or two individuals may contribute more than the rest toward determining what feeling is directing the current. Psychological currents may further be studied with respect to their sex, racial, social, vocational, and cultural bases.

Group formation, according to Moreno, can be studied in three ways: first, through observation and interpretation, where spontaneous groupings are watched for isolates, pairs, and the "bunch" that cling to the leader; second, through entrance into the group, becoming a part of it, and registering its intimate developments; third, through member experimentation, that is, making the members of the prospective groups themselves the originators of the groups to which they belong. The sociometric technique would show the "position of each individual in the group in which he has a function, for instance, in which he lives or works."[10] Differences in structure of groups based upon different functions and different age levels could be noted.

The questions used in a sociometric technique that might be

[9] J. L. Moreno, *Who Shall Survive.* Copyright, 1934, by Nervous and Mental Disease Monographs. With permission of the author.
[10] Moreno, *op. cit.*, p. 11.

administered to the members of a group to discover their choices for social or work functioning are illustrated by the following:

1. With whom in this group would you like to attend a movie?
2. With whom would you like to sit at your table in the dining room?
3. With whom would you like to share a room?
4. With whom would you most like to associate?
5. With whom in this group would you like to work on a committee?
6. Whom would you like to help you represent this group at a faculty committee meeting?

A confidential popularity index might be worked out as to number of "isolates" and "stars of attraction." This technique would furnish information which later might be the basis for interviews with isolates in a discussion of their special problems.

Through the sociometric technique, administered at intervals during the year to a student population, one could show what process is at work in interpersonal relations—whether it be assimilation, clique structure, or integration. One could determine also at intervals what influence is controlling choices, the military role, for example, or influences of social class distinction, or more democratic influences. Sociometrically, leadership might be mapped as to place of residence, overlapping of leadership, mobility of leaders, and interaction among leaders of various groups. Still further, the social backgrounds of leaders might be compared with the social backgrounds of the groups led.

Choice Analysis. Jennings also notes that even more closely related to the problem of intensity of choice than preference levels is the contact range of the individual.[11] A first choice drawn from a contact range of 300 people, for example, is likely to be more valid than one drawn from a contact range of ten or fifteen. The choice analysis must then be accompanied with behavior data related to specific individuals, if elements underlying the expression of choice and rejection are to be understood. The process should determine in what directions choice differs among individuals, whether there are similarities between different individuals at the same times or at different times, and whether there are similarities between the same individuals at different times.

Also, to understand the struggle for security, role, and status on

11 Jennings, *op. cit.,* p. 21.

the campus, a study of students' choices and rejections over a period of time, and over a number of years, would be worth while. These choices would show the group's stability, or lack of it, and their ambitions concerning the types of individuals whom they want for natural leaders. For example, college student A is a typical leader. Of the twenty other students in his social group, he shows mutual attraction for six; they choose him for an intimate friend and he chooses them. He is indifferent toward ten others who are definitely attracted to him. He feels repulsion for three members of his group but they are indifferent to him. Between him and one other student there is mutual antagonism. In an emergency or critical situation within the group he could command the loyalty of more than two thirds of the group and could hope to win support with some effort from all but one. From such an analysis of "followers" and "leaders" in their relationship to one another, one could predict how a group would act in a crisis by understanding the thoughts and attitudes of the accepted leader. This demonstrates, too, the need to give expert education and guidance to those accepted leaders who command the loyalty of a group.

Other Aids. Price,[12] in a study of the genetic process of group life among students, based on a recording of the social life and its development of interrelations, considers many group techniques for adapting situations on the college campus so as to foster interpersonal relations. Roethlisberger and Dickson,[13] by their experiments in the industrial field, have shown the interpersonal setting of the worker in the factory and home situations. These studies may be significant for a college campus.

LEADERSHIP AND DOMINANCE

A leader's behavior usually takes some form of dominance which has a counterpart in the submission of others. Young states that "Dominance is a particular interactional pattern which implies submission or acceptance on the part of another, and that such an interactional form is given meaning only by cultural definitions."[14]

[12] Louise Price, *Creative Group Work on the Campus.*
[13] F. J. Roethlisberger and W. J. Dickson, *Management and the Worker.*
[14] Kimball Young, *Social Psychology* (second edition), p. 226. Copyright, 1946, by Appleton-Century-Crofts, Inc.

There are three categories, according to Young, that distinguish the forms of human dominance: (1) dominance more or less voluntarily accepted by those controlled, which is called "leadership" and which may take both democratic and autocratic forms; (2) dominance resulting from institutional arrangement, which may be termed "leadership"; (3) dominance resulting from the class system, which is called class dominance or status dominance. All three types of dominance may exist on a college campus; there is a form of dominance among students in which the followers more or less willingly accept direction and control by the leader. It may be autocratic, however, as well as democratic. Headship, or institutional dominance, is the kind that comes from culturally transmitted power, such as that of the appointed head of a college. Status dominance is an expression of power on the part of the upper strata, the elite of a campus—perhaps the fraternity groups which have acquired a special social status. These socially elite groups induce in their members an expectation of ascendancy and stimulate the feeling of dominance. According to a large number of students in the college world today, it is the veterans who have status dominance. The majority of the leaders are veterans and many of the organizations on the campus revolve around their welfare.

Individual Status Dominance. Besides this usual conception of status dominance, there is also a dynamic status dominance on the part of certain unique individuals on a campus. It is often difficult to understand and to explain why groups rally to these individuals. They are the natural, spontaneous leaders who attain positions of influence, voluntarily accorded them by their fellows. These leaders are a product not only of their particular personality characteristics but also of the situation which calls for some sort of leadership. Brief descriptions of a few such leaders, culled from conferences with college students and personnel workers, follow.

On a certain campus, Sally was the leader because she always had an original idea. When college life became monotonous and uninteresting, she had suggestions for doing something different from the usual humdrum of the campus. She had plans for the dull week-ends when most of the students left the campus for a week-end at home. She might suggest some new place for dancing, organize stunts in the "Rec" room, or present a clever dialogue in assembly.

Jack was a leader because of his entertainment value. He was the person whom the students would urge to the piano to sing witty songs and popular chants. He was the comedian of the campus, and would be called upon at any time to enliven a party.

Anne was the executive type—she could map any program and carry it to completion. She was bossy, but the students would take it, believing in her efficiency and utter dependability. One could count on Anne.

Jane was the radical; she talked well and fast. She was always "sold on an idea" and could rally followers to its support. Sometimes her ideas led to disruptive influences, such as strikes.

Dolly was the social leader who was a master at whipping up enthusiasm. "Everyone out!" was her slogan. She backed the pep meetings and in fact all meetings in which good attendance was a goal. "Come on, everybody! Get behind this!" was her favorite appeal.

Bill was also a social leader. He had a genius for building good relationships on the campus. With his friendly attitude toward all he was able to cement differences. He had a fine physical appearance, was intelligent, and possessed a good sense of humor. Invariably one could hear his classmates say, "Maybe Bill can get us out of this!"

Eleanor was the meditative, subtle type of leader. She would think through a situation very thoroughly and then start action slowly but surely to change it. She would work her way quietly through small groups and change opinion in an unostentatious but nevertheless dynamic manner.

Dick was the athletic leader. He was eager to unify the student body in support of the team; he would make dramatic speeches at "pep" meetings. He was the hero of the underclassmen and moved the student body by vigorous appeals for the pride and love of "good old ———."

On every campus there are many such leaders who emerge in many different situations and have the characteristics and enthusiasm necessary to gather followers for their cause.

The Followers. Followers or "the masses" are important to leadership. This is true on the college campus as elsewhere. One is reciprocal to the other. The masses carry the culture patterns, the mores, upon which the special functions of leadership rest. In any field which touches the mores or folkways, leadership must fall in line with what the masses hold to be true. Change and resistance to change lie in the folkways. In the mores relating to culture the conservatism of the masses often restrains the inventiveness of men eager to be leaders. There is an interactional pattern between follower and leader and also between follower and follower. Dominance in any form likewise implies some kind of corresponding submission. There can be no leaders without followers, no upper class without a lower, no headship without individuals under authority.

In attempting to understand a leader, personnel workers are confronted with the question of whether a leader can be understood best by analyzing his particular personality features or traits, by studying him as a total personality, or by the social-psychological and cultural approach. The latter varies somewhat from the other two methods, for it deals with the leader chiefly as a personality who has a certain role and status, whose conduct is an integrated combination of biopsychological features, interaction, and culture. Young believes that each method may make its contribution, but it would be more profitable to coordinate some features of one with those of another.

Implications for Personnel Workers and Educators

Personnel workers and educators must understand the system of interrelations in their college and guide the social structure that their campus is likely to assume. They must create a fuller group life and attitudes of relationships which, both in their constancy and their changefulness, sustain and modify the college's social system. To create a better functioning of student groups, each member of the personnel staff must constantly relive his personal experiences and relationships as a member of groups. Beyond that he must turn personal experience so as to enter imaginatively into the lives of students, seeking to interpret the experiences which have left their effects in their relations with other people. But, first of all, he must be keenly aware of the limitations within himself and within the college in which he is located. As has been said repeatedly, it is only through a study of a local situation that interrelationships acquire meaning and realism. Each local college community has a system of interrelations on its campus perhaps peculiar to that situation only.

Student life is not made up just of social life, religious life, aesthetic life, economic life, and group life. The greater coherence of the campus consists in the ever-changing pattern of the totality of the social, religious, aesthetic, and moral relationships of diversified groups. Lack of successful interaction in interrelationships in one segment of personnel can bring about destructive mores in the whole system of interrelationships. Disturbing events must be studied in the totality of interrelationships. It is as one sees the total situation of interrelations and the social relational context in which a disturbing event arises that one can work adequately for its solution. How does a proper social structure become rooted and grow within the environment of a particular college? What is the moving equilibrium on the campus of changing structure and of changing environment due to interpersonal functioning? What are the main trends of these interpersonal relationships and the forces which determine their direction at any time, the harmonies and the conflicts, the adjustments and the maladjustments within the structure as they are revealed in the light of students' desires and needs?

The content of interpersonal relations is the result of a very complicated interplay of mutual understanding, non-understanding, and misunderstandings. Attitudes toward one another and images of one another are basic elements in interpersonal relations. Researches in this area mention four types of interpersonal relationships: acceptance, rejection, leadership, and isolation. These afford affective valences among persons working together in situations and functioning in groups. These valences of personalities are influenced by their common needs. Moreno has brought out in his studies that the social structure of functional groups is a composite of the affective valences between individuals. One group can accept a project without appearance of tension; another group will have "bickering" or open quarrels. Mutual rejections exist between teachers of the same faculty, between students in the same classes, and between students and teachers thrown together in functional relationships. These mutual attractions and rejections between teachers and students and between students should be recognized and used to improve the effectiveness of classroom and extracurricular activities. Isolates should be brought into effective group participation; those rejected must be helped to acquire greater understanding of conditions of belonging. Opportunities for socially useful behavior must be multiplied. Perhaps the best way to bring about sympathetic and objective relationships among students is to develop with their cooperation dynamic purposes which all want to strive to achieve.

Interpersonal relationships are crucial in determining the influence which institutions have upon developing personalities. Affective relationships between persons in a college community are powerful factors in the satisfaction or frustration of personality needs. In this connection Prescott states, "Many times, the intellectual aspects of school are secondary in importance to the personal relationships established or lost."[15] He also states that "Not only do personal relationships directly satisfy or frustrate basic needs; they also teach good or poor techniques for dealing with other people and are instruments by which a child measures his own personal success or failure."[16] A college campus is the place where students must make satisfactory interpersonal relationships that will carry over in successful dealing with people in future vocations and daily living. Educators must also realize that the test of all theory ultimately comes in the personal relationships established within an institution.

The need for a study of interpersonal relationships must then be realized, and all techniques possible for understanding and measuring them should be utilized. By these means personnel workers can see how an individual or a group grows and changes. The cross-currents of emotions as they play back and forth between individuals can be studied. The position of each student in the group in which he has a function and is emotionally related can be noted.

[15] Daniel Alfred Prescott, *Emotion and the Educative Process*, p. 281. Copyright, 1938, by The American Council on Education.   [16] *Ibid.*, p. 290.

Since the mores concern "the ways of doing things to satisfy human needs, together with the faiths, codes, beliefs, and standards of well-living which inhere in these ways of doing," attention should be directed to the role and social control that interrelationships have among persons and groups in a college community, in the organization of patterns of behavior, development of attitudes, beliefs, and faiths, and the realization of value-concepts.

In fact, interpersonal relationships are based for the most part on attitudes. Young states that "social changes begin with changes in the conditioned attitude in individuals."[17] If one is interested in a change of relationships, attitudes change first; the changing attitude of the individuals in a college community toward interpersonal relationships will be a barometer indicative of changes in the mores of relationships peculiar to that particular community. Today, with vast heterogeneous student bodies on the college campuses—students whose needs cannot be met in like functions—and with relations of all kinds in a state of flux, there is offered an opportunity to evaluate, study, and change undesirable attitudes in interpersonal relationships. Personnel workers, teachers, and students will be called upon to study their usual affective valences, understand the conditions from which they have arisen, and broaden them to meet the different personality needs of individuals conditioned by many diverse experiences of a war period.

All interrelations, whether general and traditional in character or interpersonal, should be regarded consciously by a personnel staff as a part of the whole plan for a student personnel program and should be carefully and constantly evaluated. Leadership should be considered a most important factor in all effective interrelations. One must realize that from wholesome, constructive mores of interrelations desirable and emotionally satisfying behavior, attitudes, and values result in a college community.

Bibliography

Bogardus, Emory S. *Leaders and Leadership*. New York: D. Appleton-Century Company, Inc., 1934. 325 p.

17 Kimball Young, *Social Attitudes*, p. 43.

Busch, Henry M. *Leadership in Group Work.* New York: Association Press, 1934. 305 p.

Chapple, E. D., "Measuring Human Relations: An Introduction to the Study of the Interaction of Individuals." *Genetic Psychology Monographs,* 22 : 3–147, February 1940.

Coyle, Grace. *Studies in Group Behavior.* New York: Association Press, 1937. 258 p.

Efron, Edith. "Old Jobs, or New Ones, for the Veterans." *New York Times Magazine,* 94 : 11, March 18, 1945.

Faris, Ellsworth. "Attitudes and Behavior." *American Journal of Sociology,* 34 : 271–281, September 1928.

Hartshorne, Edward Y. "Undergraduate Society and the College Culture." *American Sociological Review,* 8 : 321–332, June 1943.

Jennings, Helen Hall. *Leadership and Isolation.* New York: Longmans, Green and Company, 1943. 240 p.

Johnson, Alvin D. "An Attempt at Change in Interpersonal Relationships." *Sociometry,* 2 : 43–48, July 1939.

Landecker, W. S. "The Functional Analysis of Intergroup Relations." *Sociology and Social Research,* 25 : 431–440, May–June 1941.

Lewin K., Lippitt, R., and White, R. K. "Pattern of Aggressive Behavior in Experimentally Created Social Climates." *Journal of Social Psychology,* 10 : 271–299, May 1939.

Moreno, J. L. *Who Shall Survive?* Washington, D. C.: Nervous and Mental Disease Publishing Company, 1934. 440 p.

Pigors, Paul. *Leadership or Domination.* New York: Houghton Mifflin Company, 1935. 354 p.

Prescott, Daniel A. *Emotion and the Educative Process.* Washington, D. C.: American Council on Education, 1938. 323 p.

Price, Louise. *Creative Group Work on the Campus.* New York: Bureau of Publications, Teachers College, Columbia University, 1941. 437 p.

Roethlisberger, F. J. and Dickson, W. J. *Management and the Worker.* Cambridge: Harvard University Press, 1939. 615 p.

Strang, Ruth. *Group Activities in College and Secondary School.* New York: Harper and Brothers, 1941. 361 p.

Sumner, William G. *Folkways.* Boston: Ginn and Company, 1906. 692 p.

Tead, Ordway. *The Art of Leadership.* New York: Whittlesey House, 1935. 308 p.

Warner, W. Lloyd and Lunt, Paul. *The Social Life of a Modern Community.* Yankee City Series, Vol. 1. New Haven: Yale University Press, 1941. 460 p.

Wickman, E. K. *Children's Behavior and Teachers' Attitudes.* New York: The Commonwealth Fund, 1928. 247 p.

Young, Kimball. *Social Attitudes.* New York: Henry Holt and Company, 1931. 382 p.

Young, Kimball. *Social Psychology.* New York: F. S. Crofts and Company, Inc., 1946. 558 p.

Zeleny, Leslie Day. "Sociometry in the College Classroom." *Sociometry,* 3 : 102–104, January 1940.

Zeleny, Leslie Day. "Leadership." *Encyclopaedia of Educational Research,* edited by Walter S. Monroe. New York: The Macmillan Company, 1941. Pp. 662–666.

Znaniecki, Florian. "Social Groups as Products of Participating Individuals." *American Journal of Sociology,* 44 : 799–811, May 1939.

VI

THE ROLE OF GROUPS IN THE
CAMPUS MORES

THE PURPOSE of this chapter is to show the various social units through which college students participate in the culture of the campus, are assigned roles in the corporate living of the campus, and abide by the mores sustained by the group. It aims to describe the groups of formal and informal organization and to suggest ways in which each group regulates and structures campus life. The problems of informal clique behavior, on the part of both students and the faculty, are particularly treated because out of these problems very often arise the real pervasive student mores. A plan is given for the study of such informal groups with respect to their internal and external functions.

The chapter aims to discuss the factors which underlie the organization, structuring, and functioning of groups. It postulates that evidences of organized behavior embodied in a charter, personnel, rules or norms, activities, material apparatus, and function should be carefully studied to find how mores operate in the organizational life of students, what group mores are strong, and how the origin of groups has influenced the contemporary individual and group mores. Specific techniques for studying group structure are reviewed—techniques which can be used in the discovery and understanding of student mores in a campus group structure. The chapter also describes intergroup relations and the way in which they are exclusive, overlapping, and inclusive; also the place of role and status in group relations. It aims finally to treat and describe the social processes at work in the evolution of a group structure.

The underlying thesis of this chapter is that mores imply an element of force, and the essence of social control on a campus is to be found in the organization of students. It is in understanding and studying the organization, structure, and function of student groups that personnel workers can discover how to build satisfactory group mores on the part of a student body.

"The mores are the ways of doing things which are current in a society to satisfy human needs and desires, together with the faiths, notions, codes, and standards of well-living which inhere in those ways, having a genetic connection with them."[1] Groups on a campus have long satisfied basic personality needs of students and for that reason are important to consider in a study of the mores. The developmental, therapeutic, and diagnostic values of group activities for the individual have been rightfully recognized by personnel workers but the faiths, beliefs, codes, and standards of well-being which have inhered in groups have not been studied to any great extent.

Group activities and social situations constitute the phenomena of social behavior on a campus. According to MacIver,

In all conscious behavior there is a twofold process of selective organization. On the one hand the value system of the individual, his active cultural complex, his personality, is focused in a particular direction, towards a particular objective. . . . On the other hand, certain aspects of external reality are selectively related to the controlling valuation, . . . become themselves value factors, the means, obstacles, or conditions relevant to the value quest. The inner, or subjective, system is focused by a dynamic valuation, and the outer, or external system is spotlighted in that focus.[2]

But there is a style of the group as well as of the individual which the group

. . . is always seeking to perpetuate, by establishing conventions and standards, by institutionalizing in an at least semi-compulsive form the main lines of its system of assessment, though individual variations and deviations forever play upon them. The thought-forms, the valu-

---

[1] William Graham Sumner, *Folkways*, p. 59. Copyright, 1906, by Ginn and Company.

[2] R. M. MacIver, *Social Causation*, p. 292. Copyright, 1942, by Ginn and Company.

ational constructs, thus perpetuated among the members of a group, serve as the group focus of dynamic assessment.[3] . . . Individual assessments are not independent, self-contained operations, especially where issues of moment to the whole group are involved. They are responsive, alike in stability and change, to the group sustained mores.[4]

MacIver further illustrates how the culture complex of the group lies back of the dynamic assessment of the individual. Both types of dynamic assessments are operative in student life. With the many customs, traditions, folkways, ritual, and group activities which dominate the college campus, it is not difficult to see that the *group focus* of dynamic assessments in these situations is of vast importance. The degree of consistency as well as integration on a campus is due to these dynamic assessments of individuals and groups. In each college there will be a particular patterning of culture and particular styles of groups, institutional complexes of various sorts, and schemes of social relationships. Also within each campus there will be a particular patterning of its own groups. It is through the organization, the structure, and the functioning of groups that their particular style, manner of living, patterns of behavior, and group-sustained mores become known. The structure, function, and organization of groups, therefore, must be analyzed in order to perceive the role of group-sustained mores on the campus.

Social Grouping

One must know how the students on a particular campus are grouped, classified, and organized, since it is through these mechanisms that all members of the college are assigned their roles in the corporate living of the campus, and through their roles build group-sustained mores. The first step in understanding the social structure of the campus is therefore to determine what sort of social units are primarily responsible for establishing the individual's participation in the college culture. When one looks through a college handbook one readily sees that the college campus is an aggregate of small organized groups.

---

3 *Ibid.,* p. 301.
4 *Ibid.,* p. 309.

Roucek writes that "There are many different ways of classifying social groups: by the functions which they perform, by the type of organization, by the degree of permanence, by the type of structure and many other ways."[5] Sumner's in-group and out-group divisions may make a classification of at least subgroups. Slavson classifies according to means of motivation: "the threefold division of 'compulsory group,' 'externally motivated group,' and 'voluntary group.' "[6] Compulsory groups on the campus would be the class, in many colleges the chapel or assembly, and, generally, the departmental organizations. Externally motivated groups would be those in which the individual participates for the rewards and prestige involved rather than for the sake of the activity or friendship—athletics, dramatics, student government, honorary fraternities would fall in this classification for many members. Voluntary groups in which young men and young women participate purely for the enjoyment of the activities or the friendship of other members would be such groups as hobby clubs, musical organizations, fraternities, sororities, and the many informal unorganized groups that permeate every college campus and dormitory.

Hartshorne has mentioned "the official college culture and the unofficial college culture"[7] as areas of study. The official college culture consists of the formal organization, such as the club organized by charter, rules, etc.; while the unofficial consists of the informal organization, such as the spontaneous clique, developed by students in their process of adjusting to the official culture.

Gavit divided students into four groups:

Group I. The socially prominent and personally popular. Active in all the more conspicuous athletic and undergraduate enterprises. . . . Few in this group are of notably high standing in scholarship. . . .

Group II. Men of lesser prominence. Engaged in minor sports and activities. . . . Members of the less prominent clubs and fraternities. . . . Here again are few if any Phi Beta Kappas. . . .

[5] J. S. Roucek, *Sociological Foundations of Education*, p. 511. Copyright, 1942, by Thomas Y. Crowell Company.
[6] S. R. Slavson, *Creative Group Education*, p. 170.
[7] Edward Y. Hartshorne, "Undergraduate Society and the College Culture," *American Sociological Review*, 8 : 321, June 1943.

Group III. The students personally inconspicuous socially, but monopolizing the Phi Beta Kappa material and the high scholarship grades generally. Perhaps twenty per cent are working their way and have hard sledding financially. These men take college very seriously as regards both scholarship and college regulations. . . .

Group IV. The recluses; totally obscure. Half or more of them are in serious financial straits, earning their way, often by menial drudgery; pinched in food and clothing, and with difficulty of hanging on. . . . This group is small or perhaps even totally absent in colleges in small towns but it is characteristic of those in or near large colleges where they can live at home or in nooks, corners, and attics within reach of the college. . . .[8]

Cole makes somewhat different classifications: She lists formal activities of college students under five main headings: cultural, ethical, athletic, political, or purely social.[9]

Combining the different classifications of these authorities one finds that on most campuses social units comprise units of some form of formal organization: residence groupings, such as dormitory women, off-campus men, non-sorority women, non-fraternity men, men commuters, women commuters; campus governmental groups, such as student government organizations, men's union, women's league, house councils; departmental groups, such as engineering, foreign language, and science clubs; religious groups, such as the Y.M.C.A. and Y.W.C.A., Catholic and Jewish organizations; honor groups, including various Greek letter honor societies; athletic groups for men and for women; special interests groups, such as etiquette club, crafts club, hiking club; the four-class groupings—freshman, sophomore, junior, senior; occupation groupings, according to specialization field, courses pursued, etc.; in-groups and out-groups, such as fraternity and sorority versus non-fraternity and non-sorority, the clubs versus "independents"; optional relations as racial or national groups, such as Jewish clubs, Orientals, and Puerto Ricans, and along with the racial groups, international clubs; work groups, such as N.Y.A. and student self-help; especially today there will be political groups, well set up in formal organization, such as AYD, Marxist Group, League for Industrial Democracy, and the like.

[8] John P. Gavit, *College*, p. 117–118.
[9] Luella Cole, *The Background for College Teaching*, p. 142.

Besides these well-known groupings there are others with which a personnel worker is not always familiar; for example, groups which come from certain geographical areas and which have a mutual relation with their environment—"The Texans," "The Farmers," "The New Yorkers"; family or genetic groups, and the sons' and daughters' cliques of families which have proud lineal connections with Alma Mater.

On most campuses, also, social units comprise informal organization. The informal, spontaneous groups or cliques—the "bull session," the "poker-party," the "after-the-game" gang, the Saturday Evening Cocktail Session, or the "strollers"—express most often the freedom of college life. In spontaneous groups, such as these, often one finds the pervasive mores of the campus.

FORMAL ORGANIZATION

Formal groups are well organized, tend to perpetuate themselves, and usually have definite purposes and activities. They also regulate and structure the behavior patterns or mores of students under their influence. The residence groups or the groups which experience a living situation together are the most influential of all in personality development. Hand says, "A student's adjustment to society, his scholarship, his attitudes, and his mental and physical health are as a whole largely determined by where and how he lives."[10]

The athletic activities have been utilized as a means of control on a college campus. Waller would account for "the favorable influence of athletics upon school life in terms of changes effected in group alignments and the individual attitudes that go with them."[11] Athletics are the means of unifying an entire college group. There has been a tendency for the college population to split up into its hostile segments of teachers and students and to be fragmented by cliques among both groups. According to Waller, by furnishing all the members of the college population with an "enemy" outside the group, and by giving them an opportunity to observe and participate in the struggle against that

[10] By permission from *Campus Activities*, by Harold C. Hand, Copyrighted, 1938, by McGraw-Hill Book Co., Inc. p. 147.

[11] Willard Waller, *The Sociology of Teaching*, p. 115. Copyright, 1932, by John Wiley & Sons, Inc.

enemy, athletics may prevent a group tension from arising between students and teachers. Also, athletic groupings may motivate students in prestige behavior patterns. The prestige of the college letter, the place of the hero in the eyes of the girls on the coeducational campus, the newspaper publicity—these rather than the enjoyment of the game may be the principal incentives to many.

The groupings by departmental clubs, according to Warren,[12] have special sociological significance because of the many types of students which they draw. First, they number those students who are particularly interested in the college subject around which the club is built; second, they draw students who are only marginally interested in the subject but who are of the "club type"; third, and particularly significant, they offer an avenue of activity for those students whose social techniques would condemn them as sub-marginal to fraternity membership or leadership in key school positions.

The social campus groupings, such as student union, men's and women's organizations, and fraternity and sorority groups, regulate and structure to a large degree on many campuses the politics of student life. The non-fraternal and non-governmental groupings are generally much weaker in structure and influence. Much of the zest of the activities of these social groups is derived from a spirit of competition. Each gathers the most influential students it can get, knowing that power is cumulative; these in turn have their own spheres of influence and positions on the campus.

The classroom group, although not a social group, meets two, three, or five times a week for a semester or more and forms the occasion for students to "get to know" one another as interests are manifested in academic work. Casual meetings before and after class are often the basis of lasting friendships. Many campus cliques have their origin in some class. The class provides constant contacts with those members of the school group still considered by many students to be "on the other side of the fence"—the faculty.

As to the assembly or chapel group, it can be, according to Hosman,

12 Roland L. Warren, "A Sociological Analysis of Student Activities." *Educational Forum*, 5 : 446, May 1941.

. . . an important center of college life, unifying and tying together the many diverse and heterogeneous groupings of the campus. As such it has a definite control value. As the one group where *all* students and *all* faculty members are supposed to participate, the assembly theoretically cuts across the barriers of class, sex, social position, and academic achievement.[13]

INFORMAL ORGANIZATION

Such unorganized, spontaneous groups or cliques as "our crowd," "our bunch," and X's gang very often regulate and structure most definitely the college culture. They usually are small congenial groups easily formed and as easily dissolved, and are fitted to every possible taste and whim of youth. They most often represent the real college life, where originality and individualism flourish, where there is no pressure to conform, and much opportunity for development of talents. These are the least tangible social units because of their informal, transitory, and often secret character.

These groupings are not structured as units of formal organization, with objective forms expressed in written constitutions, buildings, and other material equipment, and are not charged with functions by the college community. Yet they have an influence in determining the functioning of the more formal groupings. Clever leaders will realize that the success of a student program must take into consideration cultural, psychological, emotional, or other types of clique alignments. The existence of these cliques is highly dependent on the continuation of the common interests of their members.

Perhaps the most common spontaneous unorganized form of group on the campus is the "gang." One hears a great deal of gangs in the early adolescent period; however, in late adolescence, these informal groups also form and function in much the same way as in early adolescence. It is difficult to study the dynamics of their behavior, and personnel workers are prone to let them go unrecognized and unaided. Thrasher[14] has contributed greatly to our

[13] E. M. Hosman, "Convocations in Urban Universities," *School and Society*, 47 : 316–318, March 5, 1938.

[14] Frederic M. Thrasher, *The Gang*. Copyright, 1936, by The University of Chicago Press.

understanding of gang behavior in community life on the part of boys in the early adolescent period—the nature of the gang, its structure, its characteristics, personality patterns, and control. Much of this information can be used to study gang behavior on a college campus.

As to the nature of the gang, it constitutes the spontaneous effort on the part of some segments of college youth to create a society for themselves because none exists on the campus adequate to meet their needs. Its members usually have a common interest. There is an individuality about this kind of a group. Thrasher states, "Wide divergency in the character of its personnel, combined with differences of physical and social environment, of experience and tradition, give to every gang its own peculiar character."[15] It may vary as to membership, type of leaders, mode of organization, interests and activities, and finally, status on the campus. It usually has an unplanned and unreflective beginning. It may assume the character of a "bull session," a rehearsal of an adventure, or a common social get-together, such as that of gambling, drinking, smoking, or loafing at a corner drugstore or "campus hang-out." It is in this type of behavior that it usually develops its spirit, loyalty, and esprit de corps. When the informal group begins to have a degree of continuity of experience, the common interests lead to the development of a common tradition, a heritage of memories which distinguishes the gang from other groups. The roles and status of the members individually are determined not by formal choices but by interaction in social situations.

As to characteristics of a gang, according to Thrasher, an outstanding one, first of all, is its attachment to a local "hang-out," which the members are always ready to defend against criticism. Second, the gang may develop features of a secret society—ritual, passwords, codes. It may imitate a secret society which it observes on the campus. The desire for new experience may prompt the formation of a gang which gives its members the desired escape from, or compensation for, monotony. Third, there is a great fund of energy among gang members which they can express in the freest and the most spontaneous manner possible. Thrasher states that "Behavior in the gang often takes the form of movement and

15 *Ibid.*, p. 45.

change without much purpose or direction."[16] The gang is a type of disorganization within the social structure of the college community and is thus a product of interaction between the nature of the members of the group on the one hand and the environment on the other.

As to organization in the gang, Thrasher states,

> The gang develops as a response to society. The social group of which the gang boy is a member has failed to provide organized and supervised activities adequate to absorb his interests and exhaust his energies. The gang solves his problems, offering him what society has failed to provide. . . . The demands of common activities and the opposition of its natural enemies—other groups and superiors with authority—necessitates an effort to act as a unit, out of which it develops a code, methods of control, and a structure.[17]

Without a wholesome direction from the larger community, the gang adopts the social patterns which have prestige in its own social environment. Their codes and activities must be studied with reference to the moral codes and activities they meet in the community in which they live. The gang in its organization very often has a language of its own whose meanings are based on past experiences peculiar to the group, such as catchwords, jokes, and songs linked to memories of the group. "Although the gang is not always unified and harmonious within, discord is usually eliminated by the conditions which collective action imposes."[18] Unity is further aided by the songs and traditions of the group. Thrasher states that "every gang tends to develop its own code of conduct, of which its members are more or less aware and which may be more or less rigidly enforced upon them. The code of the gang is in part reflected from the patterns of behavior in its own social world, in part the result of the development of primary group sentiments, and in part the product of the individual group in its own special environment."[19]

As to mechanisms of control in the gang, the individual member of a gang is almost wholly controlled by the force of group opinion. The way everybody in the gang does or thinks is usually sufficient

[16] Thrasher, *op. cit.*, p. 85.
[17] *Ibid.*, p. 251.
[18] Charles H. Cooley, *Social Organization*, p. 24–25.
[19] Thrasher, *op. cit.*, p. 284.

to persuade or dissuade the gang member. He feels the pressure of public opinion in that part of his own social world which is most vital to him and in which he wishes to maintain status. Another important form of control is ridicule, commonly known as "razzing," making fun, teasing, or sarcasm. The gangs, as represented in college fraternities, use this pressure above all in enforcing conformity. There is, however, a positive mechanism of control which contributes to the desire for recognition; this is applause and hero worshiping. The gang member is much concerned with the interpretation that his group will put on his behavior. Thrasher mentions as a basis for control the rapport engendered in the gang as an intimate primary group with a common social heritage shared by every member. Collective representations embodied in signs, symbols, such as the badge in a fraternity, secret grips and words, and the argot of the group, all promote mutual responsiveness in this communication. This rapport is sometimes so complete in a gang, such as a college fraternity, which is akin to a gang, that there seems to be a type of personality common to all. Common habits, sentiments, and attitudes become so strongly unified that individual differences appear to be submerged.

As to the structure of a gang, it is the two-and-three-student relationship which must not be overlooked in discussing its composition. It is a relation of this sort, existing before the gang develops, that serves as a primary structure when the group is first formed and that shapes the growth of its future organization. The security of the two-and-three relationship is often much more important to the individual member than his relationship to the gang. The two-and-three combinations very often form into teams, each member having a special function to perform for his team, and each team a special function to perform for the entire group. When gangs thus acquire special functions, they develop special relations and structure to correspond. Very often it is these relations that eventually bring about dissensions and finally dissolution of the gang.

As to personality and action patterns, every member of a gang tends to have a definite status within the group. As the gang develops activities, the positions of individuals within the group are defined and social roles become more sharply differentiated. Each person in the gang acquires personality and a name—he is a person; that is, he plays a part and gets a place with reference to the other members of the group. He cannot be studied intelligently or understood apart from this social role. There is usually a struggle in the gang which takes the form of both conflict and competition; the gang becomes a constellation of personal interrelationships with the leader playing the central and guiding role. Sometimes the leader grows out of the gang; the gang does not always form about a leader. A gang will often become whatever the leader makes it and this will be determined by the forces that already have played upon him and molded his character.

According to Thrasher, the chief trait of the natural leader is "gameness." He goes where others fear to go. A quality that seems requisite is quickness and firmness of decision. "Lacking the traits of a natural leader, a boy often manages to exert control in the gang through the possession of some special qualification."[20] He may be the oldest resident and "know the ropes"; he may possess the knowledge of some special technique useful to the gang, or he may control some material advantages.

These traits characterize leaders of gangs in a college community. Fraternity gangs are quite common on a campus; a group within a fraternity, for example, will rally around a leader who has a dilapidated automobile in which they can make themselves conspicuous. Other gangs will rally around students who have homes in town, to which all can go for "grub and gab" fests. Some gangs will form around a leader who always has an idea for something new. The leader of a gang often possesses some rare piece of equipment, interest in which may have caused a gang to form. The equipment may pertain to athletics, particularly equipment for athletic games not played on the campus. The possession of horseback riding equipment by a student on a campus where this sport is not engaged in may cause that person to have a following. Or, the leader of a college gang may be one who is seeking adventure or who is fighting for an idea.

Informal Clique Structure. Many formal functional organizations on a college campus are influenced by cliques such as these or other informal groupings with common backgrounds. The cliques

[20] Thrasher, *op. cit.*, p. 351.

select new members in the formal organization, not according to the organization's functional requirement, but according to their acceptability in terms of the clique's standards. Eventually, if the process continues, the informal or latent function of the group may become as important as the formal functions. Analyses of membership patterns may throw light on these latent functions. An excellent example is the situation in a college located in a large Eastern city where communist students formed secret cliques in the important formal organizations of the college and exerted a dominant influence in the recruitment of new members, in voting on important issues, and in electing officers.

Informal cliques are likely to exert their influence in every large social unit, such as a dormitory, a fraternity, a large club in undergraduate society, and should be recognized as both a positive and a negative force. In a positive way, a clique satisfies the wishes for response, recognition, security, and new experience. It protects its members in the meetings of the larger college community. No one who is in such a group need ever fear social rejection; there is no sense of inferiority within the group. There each individual's talents are recognized and genuine friendship is the basis for solidarity.

On the negative side, the formation of close cliques within the larger groups on the college campus inevitably leaves a large number "outside." One may check this finding by analyzing the dormitory dance programs, the table reservations for special dinners, the room parties, and compare the choices of students with the clique structure. The larger parties are usually monopolized by cliques.

Morison relates[21] that it was almost a necessity after 1890 for a Harvard student with social ambition to enter from the "right" sort of school and have been popular there, to room on the "Gold Coast," and to be accepted by Boston society in his freshman year, in order to be on the right side of the social chasm. Family and race did not matter: an Irish-American, Jew, Italian, or Cuban was not regarded as such if he went to the right school and adopted

---

[21] Reprinted by permission of the publishers from Samuel Eliot Morison, *Three Centuries of Harvard, 1636–1936.* Cambridge, Mass.: Harvard University Press, 1936. p. 422.

the mores of his fellows; conversely, a lad of Mayflower and Porcellian ancestry who entered from a high school was as much "out of it" as the most undesirable foreigner. The factors of school, site, and the Boston hallmark determined the socially eligible class; consequently, an ambitious freshman had to watch his step very carefully. No Harvard Individualism for him! You must say, do, wear the "right thing," avoid the company of all ineligible, and eschew originality. Athletic success was not much help at this college.

Similarly, pressures of the informal group train its individual members in adjusting to social situations, in "getting along" in college. It was related by a personnel worker that in her own undergraduate sorority the group gathered together before some special social occasion and made an assessment of themselves as to what role each could play best. The girls would agree on the one who could best meet people, or who could best serve the tea. It was a democratic assessment of each one's potentialities.

As to faculty cliques and college organization, Cole[22] relates that the emotional atmosphere within a department may vary from open hostility to brotherly love, and cites instances of departments in which there were two or three cliques so antagonistic to each other that an outsider had to be brought in as head; and others in which all members of the group were completely congenial. The problems of adjustment within any given department vary with its size, the personalities involved, the extent of domination by a single person, and the position of the group in the minds of similar groups. The typical organization of a college may easily lead to jealousy and rivalry between departments, because in the ultimate analysis, teachers are sometimes dependent upon enrollments for keeping their positions.

As stated in a previous chapter, these problems of maladjustment and clique structures among faculty have a counter-effect upon the mores of students. The students take sides with certain faculty cliques and this situation in turn creates cliques among students. They feel a certain psychological security in creating a clique structure. Very often in such a structure the students are influenced in the way of thinking that is peculiar to a particular fac-

[22] Luella Cole, *Background for College Teaching*, p. 487–488.

ulty clique; this tends to create a college provincialism. Instead of a well integrated campus structure there are a series of disintegrations. The duty of a personnel administrator here would seem to be to devise intradepartmental and interdepartmental committees to try to effect a harmonious integration among faculty and to show as clearly as possible the constructive results that such an integration would have upon a student body.

Plan for Study of Informal Groups. It is the informal group which is most likely to enforce the dominant culture-patterns but it may also restrain members to mediocrity. To direct or guide into constructive channels the student life on a campus, one must understand and study these informal groups which very often exert a tremendous influence in structuring the larger groups on the campus. Hartshorne and others have suggested some of the following areas of approach.[23] First, one might begin with the relatively simple process of studying the personnel data as usually listed on office personnel forms or in the registrar's office or admission officer's office, observing such objective characteristics as ethnic background, religious affiliation, occupation of parents, residence, school background, field of concentration, age, and sex. A study of these characteristics often gives clues to factors which may be at the base of schisms. Certain students might feel a cultural inferiority, might be representing the influence of a certain regional problem, or might feel socially or economically inferior because of the occupation of parents.

Second, the personnel worker who wishes to get at the roots of informal, spontaneous clique behavior could make a thorough study of the social personality of each individual member, the past roles he has performed, and the present role he is trying to express. Through interview, one may be able to discern the role of the student in the family group, other pre-college roles he has had in school, in church, or in community organizations, and his role at present in the informal group. Is he the leader or a follower? Lastly his future expectancies and levels of aspiration might be ascertained with respect to socio-economic status, occupation, and marriage.

[23] Edward Y. Hartshorne, "Undergraduate Society and the College Culture." *American Sociological Review,* 8 : 327–328, June 1943.

Third, another field of study would be to determine the origin of this clique, to discover the crises which served to crystallize it and to outline its general lines of growth. What evolutionary and revolutionary concepts do the group have? What were the motives for associating with this clique and remaining a member? What symbols are evident of the group's purposes or solidarity?

Fourth, a personnel worker might study how the group is functioning. What are its common activities? What are its common characteristics? Against what customs and what part of college life are the members rebellious? Where are they seeking influence? When do they band together most closely? What rejections of students who are not in their cliques do they show? What seem to be the internal functions? How is self-protection shown? Does the informal group assist and protect its members in competing for grades, in competing for dates, and in other competitive situations? Also, what is the amount of mutual molding of social roles within the group? Even within a small informal clique there may be intragroup stratification. Perhaps each could rank the other on certain criteria which they themselves might choose. Does membership in the clique work to the disadvantage of the individual in his relation to the larger college society?

Next, one might discover the group's *external* functions. One should notice the place of this clique in the next largest social unit, for example, the dormitory floor, the dormitory as a whole, the class, the college, the home, or the community at large. One should observe the specific behavior patterns which the group adopts toward specific out-groups, and groups of other ages—such as the older members of the family, parents, teachers, or leaders of one type or another. Also the patterns they adopt toward other informal groups or formal groups—whether the clique is functional or disfunctional in its effect on student adjustment in the various areas.

Again, the personnel worker could work on a definition of the particular culture this spontaneous group shows: common interests, common tastes in dress, books, and movies; common style of humor, stereotypes, private group vocabulary, the group's own definitions of appropriate behavior in various types of activities, and the behavior patterns toward the other sex, if the group is composed of one sex only.

Organization, Functioning, and Structure of Groups

As to a concept of group organization, Malinowski states that,

The essential fact of culture as we live it and experience it, as we can observe it scientifically, is the organization of human beings into permanent groups. Such groups are related by some agreement, some traditional law or custom, something which corresponds to Rousseau's Contrat Social. We always see them cooperating within a determined material setting: a piece of environment reserved for their use, an equipment of tools and artifacts, a portion of wealth which is theirs by right. In their cooperation they follow the technical rules of their status or trade, the social rules of etiquette, customary deference, as well as religious, legal, and moral customs forming their behavior. It is always possible also to define and determine sociologically what effect the activities of such an organized human group produce, what need they satisfy, what services they render to themselves and the community as a whole.[24]

He also states that each group

satisfies a set of needs of the inmates and of society at large, and thus fulfills a function. . . . Home and business, residence and hospital, club and school, political headquarters and church, everywhere we find a place, a group, a set of by-laws, and rules of technique, and also a charter and a function.[25]

This organizational framework and concept of group functioning pertains also to student groups organized on a college campus. The history of each group on a college campus would show that it was organized originally to satisfy some need on the part of students.

The Porcellian Club in early Harvard, for example, was organized to gather a group of select aristocrats together to dine on roast pig. Their need was social rather than academic; no pretense was ever to be made of cultivating literature or public speaking. The first Harvard clubs, however, were founded by the pious students in self-defense against the student "rakes and blades" who

[24] Reprinted from *A Scientific Theory of Culture*, by Bronislaw Malinowski by permission of The University of North Carolina Press. Copyright, 1944, by The University of North Carolina Press. p. 43.
[25] *Ibid.*, p. 47.

brought in profane swearing and riotous actions. The Philomu-
sarian Club, according to Morison, was founded "in order therefore to stem that monstrous tide of impiety and ignorance."[26] The
Hasty Pudding Club, on the other hand, for a long time the largest
of all campus societies, started as a folly amalgam of literary, con-
vivial, and patriotic elements.

On "Pudding nights," when the bell tolled for the scanty evening
commons, two members might be seen bearing on a pole an iron pot of
steaming hasty-pudding from some near-by good wife's kitchen to a
member's room, where the brethren supped on that simple but filling
fare, concluding their repast with "sacred music" which became less
and less sacred as the years rolled by.[27]

If one were to look more closely into the functioning of these
groups down through the years, there would be concrete evidences
of organized behavior embodied, according to Malinowski, in such
forms as charter, personnel, norms, material apparatus, activities,
and function.[28]

Charter, referred to here, means a system of values in the pursuit
of which students organize new groups or enter organizations already existing. Personnel refers to the definite principles of authority, division of functions, and distribution of privileges and
duties on which the group is organized. Norms or rules refer to
technical skills, habits, legal norms, and ethical commands which
are accepted by members or imposed upon them. Material apparatus refers to the place of meeting and profits accruing from
concerted activities. By activities is meant actual behavior depending on ability, power, honesty, and good will of members.
Function is the integral result of organized activity; it is the satisfaction of a need.

In studying these evidences of organized behavior, one might see
more clearly how mores operate in the organizational life of the students, what group mores are strong, and how the genetic origin

[26] Reprinted by permission of the publishers from Samuel Eliot Morison, *Three Centuries of Harvard, 1636–1936.* Cambridge, Mass.: Harvard University Press, 1936. p. 62.

[27] *Ibid.*, p. 82.

[28] Reprinted from *A Scientific Theory of Culture*, by Bronislaw Malinowski by permission of The University of North Carolina Press. Copyright, 1944, by The University of North Carolina Press. p. 53.

of the group has influenced the contemporary individual and group mores. In analyzing the charter, personnel, and activities, a personnel worker would find the following questions helpful:

1. How was this group formed? What are its admissions criteria?
2. How did it grow? What are the transitions through which it has gone?
3. What are the structural and functional differentiations in transitions?
4. How have its objectives and interests changed?
5. What bases of authority have shifted? In regard to initiation practices? Domination by other groups? Pressures to conform? Means of maintaining morale? Means of eliciting or suppressing behavior?
6. Has the group had increasing or decreasing cohesion? What bases of stratification—in-group, class, and caste?
7. What activities or service projects does it perform?
8. Where is its meeting-place? Is it permanent or temporary?
9. What cultural norms does it carry out especially in regard to (a) ritual, (b) ceremonies, (c) insignia—pins, (d) group folkways and traditions, and (e) material culture symbols.

For an analysis of this kind, the personnel worker will make use of the club's charter, minutes, newspaper write-ups, yearbook, together with interviews with students within and outside the group and faculty opinion, with this underlying thesis in mind: that the essence of social control of a student body is to be found in the organization of students.

In conjunction with the functional analysis of student organizations on a college campus, a structural analysis would also be necessary. For this sort of analysis, Chapin's "Sociological Graphs"[29] would be valuable to show the structure of each group. These graphs would show size, sex, homogeneity; number of other clubs in which one club's members are participating also as members; socio-economic status of its members; residence groupings; work-status; religious and political affiliations. In this way the interrelation of structure and function in each group can be seen—how

---

[29] F. Stuart Chapin, *Contemporary American Institutions*, p. 17. Copyright, 1935, by Harper & Brothers.

the composition of groups affects their norms, structure, and control, what differences are due to a composition or structure of students of a certain age, of varying socio-economic status, difference in home residence, work status, extracurricular affiliations, and type of curricula pursued.

Often a study of the structure of a group will show why the group is or is not functioning well, or at least indicate areas for research into the causes of the non-functioning of a group. Homogeneity as to age, sex, participation in other clubs, and interests of the members of a certain group may tell the story of its success. One must be careful, however, not to state that the structural or functional configuration of one group on a campus is typical of that group on campuses in general. Groups of the same name may have a totally different configuration from campus to campus. The Sigma Betas may have a high rating on one campus but the lowest on another. There are distinguishable patterns in groups from campus to campus. Just as the patterns of various types of colleges, such as liberal arts, teachers colleges, state schools, private schools, are different, so the structure and function of groups on these particular campuses will be different. The Y.M.C.A. and Y.W.C.A. may be flourishing, successfully functioning groups in the liberal arts denominational colleges, while in state universities they may merely survive. Membership in sororities and fraternities may be the highest symbol of social prestige in the colleges of the East; in the West it may be a last resort for a girl who cannot achieve prestige in any other way. The AYD may be a flourishing group in a large cosmopolitan college and may not be known at all, or may be forbidden, in a small rural college. Political affiliations usually do not have as definite a configuration in small colleges as they do in large cosmopolitan centers.

Social Status and Role within Each Group

As we have just seen, campus life is divided into a series of groups and to each group are ascribed degrees of social importance. A group may originate through the conscious formation of some social unit, such as the first college fraternity, which is usually followed by the formation of a series of similar units organized along nearly the same lines. A varying number of statuses can be achieved by individual effort.

Speaking for the informal social life of the campus, clothing and personal style often indicate social status. The girl who is always well dressed commands a certain respect from her peers; on the contrary, the girl who is customarily dressed in blue jeans and lumberjacket creates a certain camaraderie about her on the part of the rest of the students. Different types of food and what use is made of it in one's own group also is indicative of social status. In a particular crowd there are always a few who receive from home the largest cake, the most fried chicken, and the best cookies. The gab-fests and get-togethers in their rooms and around the food are always gala events. Sometimes there is rivalry in these groups as to who can get together the best food. The girls living off campus likewise have food from their homes but it is not so often an occasion for a gala celebration. These girls cannot afford to live in the dormitories; they live in homes in the community where facilities for preparing their own meals are provided. Since these girls must prepare three meals a day, food has a more serious and practical significance to them. If they have some special food, they are likely to gain social status by inviting friends for dinner to share it with them rather than by having an "extra party" in their rooms.

Closely related are the off-campus afternoon and evening snacks. Local and regional habits modify student customs in this respect. One cannot imagine a Midwestern campus without a corner drugstore; other campuses may have the "co-op" corner in the student union. Social status differentiation comes also into play with recreational equipment that students display in their rooms—equipment for horseback riding, lacrosse, hockey, skiing, with all the accompanying paraphernalia.

There are in each group two different types of membership, the active and the latent. An active member has status and a role and acts through his duties and obligations. Latent members have status but do not assume a role. The hope of gaining prestige or the fear of losing it does more than anything else to hold the average individual to the proper performance of his roles. The functioning college campus is that in which there is a high degree of interaction among all members and in which actual roles bring everyone into patterns of cooperative behavior.

In such an ideal situation, individuals not only may achieve status through one group but may also achieve status in another group or in many other groups. The status of student John Doe would be the sum total of all the statuses which he has from membership in various groups of the campus. Membership in the various smaller groups established by the total college community cuts across the lines of the primary groups and integration takes place with respect to the configuration of the whole. Thus the fact that one organization, such as a departmental club, includes individuals from several different primary groups, such as the fraternity and governing associations, serves to draw these groups together and aids them in functioning as integral parts of the larger whole. The various groups incorporated into the larger configuration of groups will normally be arranged in a system of prestige ranking and will exercise greater or less influence in the formulation of the groups' policies according to their positions in this system.

Intergroup Relations

Landecker shows that a systematic treatment of intergroup relations requires their analysis from three different points of view, which are mutually supplementary: qualitative, structural, and functional.[30] All studies in which a specific intergroup relationship is characterized as either friendly or antagonistic may be termed qualitative. Outstanding as qualitative analyses are the investigations of the social distance between groups by Bogardus,[31] who attempts to locate specific intergroup relations on a scale of attitudes ranging from nearness to farness.

An analysis of intergroup relations is structural if it examines social groups as circles which establish geometrical relationships with one another. Considered from this point of view, three fundamental forms of intergroup relations are conceivable: exclusive, overlapping, and inclusive. Two groups are mutually ex-

[30] W. S. Landecker, "The Functional Analysis of Intergroup Relations," *Sociology and Social Research*, 25 : 431–440, May–June, 1941.
[31] Ruth Strang, *Group Activities in College and Secondary School*, p. 239.

clusive if they have no members in common; they overlap if each is partly composed of members of the other; and they are inclusive if they form a whole-part relationship, i.e., if all members of one group are also members of a larger group comprising others, too.

To explain these intergroup relations more concretely, an exclusive relationship would be said to exist between two groups, such as science and dramatics, if no members of the science club belong to the dramatics club, or vice versa. An overlapping relationship would exist if some members of the science club were also members of the dramatics club, or vice versa. An inclusive relationship would be one in which all members of both clubs belong to a larger organization, such as the Y.M.C.A. or Y.W.C.A. Similarly, the relationship may be extended to outside groups, such as churches, lodges, or town organizations of Y.M.C.A. or Y.W.C.A. This overlapping of relationships extending to the outside community is especially important in that it may help orient the college to a place within the social order. So long as groups do not become exclusive, do not absorb all the devotion of their members, but leave each one free to join in the life of other and larger groups, their influence is good, and the group spirit of each minor group contributes to the strength of the larger group and the spiritual life of the whole is thereby enriched.

The qualitative as well as the structural approach takes the existence of intergroup relations for granted; but not so the functional approach. We can determine neither the quality nor the structure of intergroup relations until we know what these relations are. Are they relations between individuals or relations between groups? Landecker asserts that intergroup relations are relations between individuals, modified by the fact that they belong to different groups and that they are either transmitted or direct. Transmitted intergroup relations are relations not between an "I" and a "he," as in direct relations, but between a "we" and a "they." The subjects face each other not directly, but by using their groups as intervening media. For example, there is individual A, a member of group 1, and individual B, a member of group 2. If A enters a relationship with B, he undergoes two psychic processes: through the "we" attitude A identifies himself with his own group; i.e., he submits to the collective representations proper to his group; in particular, he accepts those attitudes and prejudices against group 2 which prevail in his group. In this sense, group 1, of which A is a member, functions as the first medium of the relationship. Second, by approaching B not as an individual, a "he," but as a representative of a "they," A identifies B with the "they" to which the latter belongs. By this process of identification he transfers his attitudes toward group 2 to subject B. In B he sees group 2 personified. Thus, group 2 is the second medium through which the relation between A and B is transmitted.

Direct intergroup relations take place only if both subjects belong not only to different groups but also to a group of which both are members. In other words, direct intergroup relations are always a mixture of out-group and in-group relations. The directness of the relationship is due to the fact that both subjects have something in common; they are able to communicate with each other as individuals, not simply as group symbols. In organized intergroup relations an imputation of *behavior* takes place, whereas simple transmitted intergroup relations are based on an imputation of *attitudes*. What happens in a simple transmitted intergroup relation is that those stereotyped actions of an individual which are called his attitudes are imputed to his group, i.e., they are considered "typical." Similarly, the attitudes which are considered typical for his whole group are imputed to the individual. Individuals are considered as acting *for* the group; consequently, their actions are imputed *to* the group, so that the individual's actions appear as actions *of* the group.

Specific Techniques in Studying Groups

Among the techniques which are particularly valuable for the discovery, functioning, and understanding of student mores in a campus group structure, as noted earlier, there are Moreno's sociometric technique for interpersonal relations, Jennings' choice analyses for leadership and isolation, Price's genetic study of student life,[32] Malinowski's organizational diagram, and Chapin's sociological graphs for group structure.[33] A plan for the study of

[32] See pages 160–164 of this study.
[33] See pages 189–192 of this study.

informal, spontaneous groups has also been mentioned.[34] Besides these, there are other informal methods which may prove valuable for studying certain other aspects of group life. Group description may be mentioned as one of these methods.

GROUP DESCRIPTION

Sanderson states that "Until we take the trouble to describe different kinds of groups with the same care that a biologist describes a species, genus, or family of plant or animal life, we shall fail to have any adequate understanding of the nature of the group." He feels that the description of the structure of a species which will establish its identity is only the beginning of the zoologist's task. The zoologist then proceeds to study the life history of the species, even going back into its embryology, and carefully observes its behavior and habits under different environmental conditions. What is now glibly called "a group" varies from an association of two persons to the whole college proper, from informal intimate associations with a high degree of behavior control, such as a gang, to a loose association of large numbers of students, such as the "Y" organizations. The college or university is itself a group. Further, the word college may be applied to groups with very different structure. A plan for describing groups should be worked out so that by comparison and analysis of exact descriptions the likenesses and differences and characteristic forms of behavior can be determined. Sanderson believes that an adequate description of a group seems to involve five major sets of characters.[36]

1. Identity—Whether its group limits are exclusive, restricted, or inclusive.
2. Composition—Size, homogeneity or diversity of membership, stratification or uniformation, permanent or shifting membership.
3. Intergroup Relations—Whether the group is independent or controlled from without.
4. Intragroup Relationships—Forms of interaction between members—quality or type of participation, group folkways and mores, place of role of certain individuals.

[34] See pages 186–188 of this study.
[35] Dwight Sanderson, "Group Description," *Social Forces*, 16 : 311, March 1938.
[36] *Ibid.*, p. 313.

5. Structure and Mechanism—The established procedures and division of labor for performing specific functions—aims and purposes, means of consensus, extent of institutionalization, mechanisms for group maintenance or preservation.[37]

According to Sanderson, group description will include the following practical objectives.[38] First, it will aid in understanding the relation of individuals to the group, and the influence of the group on the individuals composing it. This will answer, for example: What is the difference between the relationship of individuals to the religious groups as contrasted with their relationship to the fraternity? Second, it will be a means of interpreting the clinical use of the individual group: determining how the group may be improved, what factors within the group condition its success, and likewise, what sort of organization and type of relationships are essential for its success. Third, a group description can determine the adaptability of group structure to certain functions. Consequently, it will show which groups meet certain needs or functions, as, for example, whether there is a relationship between small size and intimacy and large membership and power to personal relations in a group. Is the "Y" organization, for example, adapted to the same functions as a religious council in a camp? Fourth, it can be used to understand the relation of a given group or group-class to other kinds of groups, as a basis for determining policies of group relations. What should be the relation, for example, of the "Y" organization to politics on a campus? Fifth, it will determine policies affecting the general group pattern. For example, should the "Y" stress its ritual or minimize it? Should it be interested in spiritual affairs or in clean politics? Should it stress charitable living or sponsor philanthropic projects?

One sees that the purpose of group description is not mere taxonomy, but the bringing out of differences in *structure* that are associated with differences in *behavior* in order to predict what one may expect under given conditions and to give direction to group functioning.

---

[37] For more detailed plan by Sanderson for the description of groups, the reader should see Appendix, pages 290–292 of this study.

[38] Sanderson, *op. cit.*, p. 319.

GROUP RECORD

Wilson has shown how the technique of the group record shows not only the interaction of members who make up the group but also the process which they create in so doing.[39] The criteria for the group record, as outlined by Wilson, are as follows:[40]

1. History, including how the groups were formed.
2. Roster sheet, including "raw statistics" from registration card: name, address, telephone, native tongue, age, sex, race, occupation of both parents, school or occupation of member, religion, marital status, date enrolled.
3. Attendance record: totals showing number present, number of visitors, new members added, old members dropped, and enrollment to date.
4. Group meetings. What significance did the meeting have for individuals? For the group as a whole.
   a. Group problems.
   b. Plans of procedure of leader and of group members.
5. Individual contacts—behavior characteristics which contributed to development or blocking of group activity; behavior characteristics indicative of individual blocking.

Wilson's outline makes it possible for the group worker to describe the process of the group meeting in such a way that the various kinds of adjustments to conflict or competition can be recognized. Records show the various processes at work in group activities. They reveal, first, *elimination,* through which members or groups of them have been dropped; second, *subjugation,* by which the recalcitrant is forced through threats, or even physical powers, into line; third, *compromise,* or log-rolling, which makes a bargain possible; fourth, *alliance,* by which different subgroups with different goals may agree on the same idea or project to attain a different end; fifth, *integration,* an ideal toward which most group work aims, a situation in which a problem, thoroughly discussed, is understood and eventuates in a unanimous decision for action; sixth, *dissociation,* through which the results of these adjustments may be seen in the individual or group which "went

[39] Gertrude Wilson, "Record Keeping in Group Work as a Contribution to Sociology," *American Sociological Review,* 2 : 237–246, April 1937.
[40] *Ibid.,* p. 238.

home mad"; seventh, *cooperation,* which results in a majority vote or in the achievement of corporate action.

Conflict of personalities, struggle for power, clash of interest, competition in achievement, desire for prestige, and other forms of ego expression are described by the person keeping the record under either the caption "participation of members" or "indications of conflict." In keeping such a record it would be possible to watch a new member come into the group, make many attempts to gain acceptance from first one person and then another, attach himself to a pair or to an individual only to repulse and be repulsed, and then make other attempts until he finally has found his place. During this process one could describe the relationships of every member of the group to each other. There is nothing static about the structure of groups. They are as dynamic as the personalities of which they are composed.

GROUP DIARIES

Hartshorne mentions group diaries as a means of showing how groups function and are structured.[41] A group diary is a kind of chronic complaint book in which any group member who chooses can air his view on the group's program, on the group's members, or on the group's purposes. Feuds which might otherwise disrupt group unity are fought out on the pages of this book. Looking through such a diary, one can find reflected part of the unrestrained fantasy life of a group with all its ideals, its hates, its witticisms, and its group culture values. One can see in its pages direct expressions of attitudes.

Through personal diaries of members of groups, through poems, autobiographies, and other personal documents, one can glean youth's philosophy of life, hopes for the future, and the role played because of their successes and failures. Diaries sometimes expose the techniques of control in the adolescent group, showing how the behavior of newcomers is brought into conformity with the standards of groups. They also show the relative importance of factors that fix the status of each individual in the group. They likewise furnish records of activities, reveal the interests with which they

[41] Edward Y. Hartshorne, "Undergraduate Society and the College Culture," *American Sociological Review,* 8 : 327–330, June 1943.

are preoccupied, and show the ways in which they occupy their time. The documents show for both sexes the activities controlled by various institutions, those less conditioned by the culture group and those not social at all in origin and character. They show the groups which the student joins and the status he achieves in them, the emotional satisfaction he derives from this membership and status, and the significance the contacts have in determining the conception he comes to have of himself. The run of attention is evident from the things students talk and write about. The diaries show the factors that determine particular interests as well as the shift, change, and progress of interests. They portray the mores of the group, the demands and compulsions of a young people's world, and the codes of behavior. They also show the variation in attitudes in various environments.

The last three techniques for the study of groups would, more than any other types of study, demonstrate in a practical way an understanding of the latter part of Sumner's definition of mores: ". . . the faiths, beliefs, codes, and standards of well-living which have inhered in these ways of doing, having a genetic connection with them."

Social Processes in Group Work

Many social processes may be seen operating in the social laboratory of the college campus. Wilson in her plan of record keeping of a group's activities has shown what evidences of social processes are at work in group functioning. There are also other places in college life where these processes operate. Roucek has mentioned some of the processes which take place on a college campus.[42] The material in this study offers from time to time examples of social processes at work on college campuses. First is *competition,* the basic process in our culture, which takes place from the time the student enters the doors of the college until he is handed his diploma or falls by the wayside. He competes as an individual with other students for scholastic honors, for a place on the team, for a student body office, for a part in a dramatic production, and for the attention of the prettiest coeds. He competes as a member

[42] J. S. Roucek, *Sociological Foundations of Education,* p. 509–511.

of a group in an athletic contest against another college or as a participant in a musical contest.

Second is *conflict,* which appears in many forms in college groups. Race conflict is constantly showing itself. If a high school graduate is a member of a racial minority group, he may find it impossible to gain admission to the college of his choice. Certain groups tend to discriminate against Jewish students, which situation results in a degree of voluntary or involuntary segregation for members of that race. Conflict between fraternities, between classes, between ideologies, between departments, between faculty and students is the rule rather than the exception on most campuses. One of the types of conflict most frequently found is the conflict between the college as a whole and the outside community —the traditional clash between "town and gown."

The third basic process, *cooperation,* is found to a lesser extent on the campus, just as it tends to be less prominent in our "greater society." Cooperation is demanded of all toward the success of the athletic teams, and probably it is in this realm that a greater degree of college unity is achieved than in any other activity.

Fourth is *assimilation,* which is constantly in operation in the college at large and in the classroom. The incoming freshman or transfer-student soon learns to accept the folkways and mores of the campus culture, and to become a living part of that pattern.

Fifth, *domination and exploitation* are evident—the domination and exploitation of the unorganized groups by the organized; the domination of students by faculty, and in some institutions even of faculty by students; of the lowerclassmen by the upperclassmen; of the newer departments of study by the traditional ones; of the non-athletes by the athletes; of the few by the many. Fraternities have particularly wielded an undue influence on many a campus because of their organization.

Sixth is *stratification,* as illustrated by a class and caste structure which exists on some campuses, the selective mechanisms, and various clique structures.

In addition to the above processes, the process of *construction* exists on campuses when the college group as a whole possesses good morale, that is, when all its members are actively engaged in furthering its common aims and ideals, each individual performing his particular function enthusiastically and with due regard for the interests of the whole.

MacIver describes a process in the following manner:

A process is continuous. Since, therefore, it cannot be explained by the conjuncture of forces at any one moment we must look for determinants that are themselves persistent, that work more deeply in the soil of society, that are congenial and understandably related to the direction of the process.[43]

If the process is that

in which domination and submission are reciprocally established within a group, we must view it as the shaping of a pattern of adjustment between the variant interests and attitudes of individuals or groups within a given situation.[44]

In every instance of a social process what we have before us is the continuous change of a dynamic system emerging from the interactivity of its components.[45]

Implications for Personnel Workers and Educators

To quote Lloyd-Jones concerning the lack of social understanding:

Every college campus constitutes a complicated network of social connections; those who direct group programs differ widely in their ability to sense and understand lines of social cohesion, the patterns of the natural groupings, and how the larger social organizations are constituted.[46]

This statement inspired the writing of these several chapters on the many and intricate social relationships and group formations which exist on a campus, with the hope that a description of them might arouse an interest not only in recognizing them but in studying them carefully. To aid in the understanding of the total group configuration on a campus, a part of this chapter has been devoted to a description of techniques that might be used in disentangling the groups on a campus, seeing their functioning, their structure, how function and structure are interrelated, the social

---

[43] R. M. MacIver, *Social Causation*, p. 133.   [44] *Ibid.*, p. 133.   [45] *Ibid.*, p. 134.
[46] Esther Lloyd-Jones, *Social Competence and College Students*, p. 28–29.

processes involved, and how the mores of the college are sustained through the group. The description shows the need for trained staffs in group work. Do the educational and personnel fields have enough information about college groups to outline adequately objectives, resources, and techniques for work with them? Do teachers, personnel workers and administrators understand thoroughly enough the role of group experience in the development of persons? Staffs in these areas must be greater students of human relations and dig deeper into the dynamics of behavior and into the role of group experience to determine attitudes and the satisfaction of basic personality needs on the part of students. Group life is the fundamental basis of personality and culture. It is in and through the processes of interaction that behavior patterns are transmitted, and personality developed as a product of such group life.

One can easily observe the interest of students in groups and activities. That seems to constitute the *raison d'être* for the group, but the genuine educative process is the range of interaction, relationships, responsibilities, and other experiences that emerge around these activities. What social action emerges? Have the leaders been well trained in guiding the group process of interaction and experience so that it contributes to the efficiency of the group? Are the functions of the various groups in a college community worked out in the light of the nature and needs of the college and of the stage of development and resources of each group? The interrelationship of structure and function must be seen; functions develop relations and structures to correspond. There must be the right students for the right jobs. There must be a reciprocity between the individual and the group whereby basic needs of both are satisfied. The group needs interaction among all members; it needs to make it possible for each member to carry specific responsibilities and to possess a definite status and role in the group. The leader must understand each member as an individual.

College campuses must become laboratories of experience in cooperative or democratic living. MacIver states that

Democracy was born of the struggle of groups—religious groups, economic groups, ethnic groups—against the intolerance and abuse of power. We need to explore the nature and functioning of social groups, the formation of their value-systems, the role of leadership in them, the conditions under which group images emerge, spread and change.[47]

With regard to group images, more direct functional instead of transmitted relationships are needed in which there is always a mixture of out-group and in-group relations. In these relationships groups are able to communicate with each other as individuals, not simply as group symbols. Every college clique, gang, fraternity, sect, tends to be an in-group that is suspicious of competing out-groups. The fear of out-groups will foster in-group solidarity; the spontaneous response to in-group security, however, may give rise to fixed prejudices. Witness from a previous chapter the social cleavages, racial and national discriminations, and social stratifications that have occurred on the campuses represented by the personnel workers interviewed. It can be observed that the term "group" extends from a single pair to the total college community. If the whole college community could have the experience of working as one group toward a common goal, viz., democratic living, one could spot the various smaller groups and find out in what way they do or do not contribute to the larger purpose.

As to the informal, spontaneous group, leaders must work *with* the natural forces in the gang or clique rather than against them. Their function is to lead and direct rather than to impose something foreign from without. They must take account of the students' own conceptions of their roles in the group. In attempting to understand the conduct of a student who comes into conflict with social patterns, one can gain much from a statement of his experiences and attitudes. From such a statement, one may become familiar with his social background and experience as *he* sees it, with his attitudes and wishes, and with his conception of the role he plays. One can see his problem behavior as he sees it, *his own reasons* for his behavior, and can become familiar with other experiences and attitudes which are likely to bring him often into conflict with socially defined standards.

The real problem in gang behavior, according to Thrasher, is

47 R. M. MacIver, "The Power of Group Images," *The American Scholar*, 14 : 222, Spring 1945.

not so much one of increasing the activities as one of having leaders who can organize the activities of the members, direct them into wholesome channels, and give them social significance. Every individual member of the gang feels that his gang gives him what he wants most and he is more interested in maintaining his status in the gang than in any other group. The alternative for a leader is to deal with the gang as a whole. This may be done by recognizing the gang and making a place for it in the program of the college community, gradually redirecting its activities into socially significant channels. It may be done by including the gang leader and each member of the gang in some larger activity, toward which loyalties can be developed. The gang might be made into a club; it might also be separated by redirecting some of the separate members into a larger group or enterprise. When once they see what their activities mean in relation to the larger program and their own future plans, there is seldom difficulty in controlling their behavior. The student in the gang must be led into seeing the meaning of what society wants him to do and its relation to some rational scheme of life. The energies in these haphazard activities need to be redirected and integrated with the student's own ultimate purposes. A leader must understand the experiences today of these young people, and what is going on not only in their own social world but in the larger community as well. Strikes today on the campus seem to grow out of the students' own experiences and the exploits of society in general.

The college student today, however, should possess something more than gang behavior. He is going to live in a society where tolerance of other groups, responsibility toward them, and cooperation with them are essential to social order and general prosperity. To this end there is need for an *intergroup* morality and behavior. One of the shortcomings on the campus is the failure on the part of each group to recognize obligations to other groups. The kinds of groups on a college campus parallel those of the outside culture—there are government groups, residence groups, athletic, political, social, religious, ethnic, common interests, occupational interests, and international. There are those of formal organization and those of informal. Values are inherent in all types of groups if they are constructively directed. Since the campus groups parallel those of the outside culture, the college community would seem to be an excellent place for students to acquire training in an intergroup morality leading to democracy which would remain functional when they enter the outside world. It is through an intergroup morality that a well-functioning social organization exists in society. If group-sustained mores are to include democratic action, intergroup morality must include a sense of group responsibility. A student is not only responsible for his individual actions; he is responsible for the level of action of the students he lives with. Loyalty to a group has long been understood; *responsibility* to a group is a more difficult and adult concept. The individual wants to feel that his own contribution is good and also that he is responsible for helping to keep group standards high. Group pressures should center around a core of college community standards which would be framed not by the administration alone but by representatives of the *whole* community. There should be a *planned* democracy involving the participation of all members of the college community on a basis of individual and group responsibility. Then and only then would group-sustained mores of the campus include some design for living, such as the one which has been so well worked out at Antioch.[48]

Thrasher has defined the code of the gang as, first, reflections of the patterns of behavior in its own social world, second, the result of the development of primary group sentiments, and, third, the product of the individual group in its own special environment. It would seem advisable for personnel workers and educators to study these three realms and know how constructive behavior patterns, codes, or mores can be built in them on the college campus. This is particularly true today with the broader socio-economic base of student composition, with the greater mixtures of races, and with the more varied student interests. Much must be done, therefore, in the way of establishing security by group status, in sustaining roles of good relationships, and in encouraging group patterns of cooperative behavior.

Again, it is emphasized that a total picture of cooperative intergroup relations working for a common purpose, such as campus

[48] Algo D. Henderson and Dorothy Hall, *Antioch College: Its Design for Liberal Education.*

democracy, must be visualized. Intergroup and intragroup relationships, composition, structure, function, and organization of campus groups must be understood by personnel workers for the realization of this democracy as a total campus group configuration. It is only by understanding the interactivity of all these group components that one can see how group mores arise and in what particular way on the campus they sustain social control of student life. Sociological graphs, organizational analyses, group diaries, studies of processes are aids in visualizing more objectively the factors that are causing the particular group mores to be operative on a campus. It is, however, in understanding the interactivity of *all* group components in a college community that policies of group relations can be formulated, functions of particular groups analyzed, techniques of control discovered and perhaps redirected, and social processes understood. It is only in this way that group-sustained mores can build a planned democracy on a campus.

Bibliography

Albrecht, Arthur E. "A Student Venture in Cooperative Living." *Journal of Educational Sociology*, 10 : 262–268, January 1937.

Blumer, H. "Social Disorganization and Individual Disorganization." *American Journal of Sociology*, 42 : 871–877, May 1937.

Bogardus, Emory S. "The Philosophy of Group Work." *Sociology and Social Research*, 23 : 562–567, July 1939.

Busch, Henry M. *Leadership in Group Work*. New York: Association Press, 1934. 305 p.

Chapin, Francis Stuart. *Contemporary American Institutions*. New York: Harper and Brothers, 1935. 423 p.

Cole, Luella. *The Background for College Teaching*. New York: Farrar and Rinehart, 1940. 616 p.

Cooley, Charles Horton. *Social Organization*. New York: Charles Scribner's Sons, 1909. 436 p.

Coyle, Grace. *Social Process in Organized Groups*. New York: Richard R. Smith, Inc., 1930. 245 p.

Coyle, Grace. *Studies in Group Behavior*. New York: Association Press, 1937. 258 p.

Elliott, H. S. *Process of Group Thinking*. New York: Association Press, 1928. 222 p.

Ellsworth, Allan S. and Bogardus, Emory S. "Measurement in Group Work." *Sociology and Social Research*, 23 : 62–70, September–October 1938.

Gavit, John Palmer. *College*. New York: Harcourt, Brace, and Company, 1925. 342 p.

Hand, Harold. *Campus Activities*. New York: McGraw-Hill Book Company, Inc., 1938. 357 p.

Hartshorne, Edward Y. "Undergraduate Society and the College Culture." *American Sociological Review*, 8 : 321–332, June 1943.

Henderson, Algo D. and Hall, Dorothy. *Antioch College: Its Design for Liberal Education*. New York: Harper and Brothers, 1946. 273 p.

Hosman, E. M. "Convocations in Urban Universities." *School and Society*, 47 : 316–318, March 5, 1938.

Landecker, W. S. "The Functional Analysis of Intergroup Relations." *Sociology and Social Research*, 25 : 431–440, May–June 1941.

Leigh, Robert D. *Group Leadership*. New York: W. W. Norton and Company, Inc., 1936. 259 p.

Lloyd-Jones, Esther. *Social Competence and College Students*. Washington, D. C.: American Council on Education, 1940. 89 p.

MacIver, R. M. *Civilization and Group Relationships*. New York: Harper and Brothers, 1946. 177 p.

MacIver, R. M. *Social Causation*. Boston: Ginn and Company, 1942. 414 p.

MacIver, R. M. "The Power of Group Images." *The American Scholar*, 14 : 220, Spring 1945.

Malinowski, Bronislaw. *A Scientific Theory of Culture and Other Essays*. Chapel Hill, N. C.: University of North Carolina Press, 1944. 228 p.

McDougall, William. *The Group Mind*. New York: G. P. Putnam's Sons, 1928. 418 p.

Morison, Samuel Eliot. *Three Centuries of Harvard, 1636–1936*. Cambridge, Mass.: Harvard University Press, 1936. 512 p.

Patrick, James G. *The Role of Intimate Groups in the Personality Development of Selected College Men*. Los Angeles: University of Southern California Press, 1935. 43 p.

Price, Louise. *Creative Group Work on the Campus*. New York: Bureau of Publications, Teachers College, Columbia University, 1941. 437 p.

Roucek, J. S. *Sociological Foundations of Education*. New York: Thomas Y. Crowell Company, 1942. 771 p.

Sanderson, Dwight. "Group Description." *Social Forces*, 16 : 309–320, March 1938.

Slavson, S. R. *Creative Group Education*. New York: Association Press, 1937. 247 p.

Strang, Ruth. *Group Activities in College and Secondary School*. New York: Harper and Brothers, 1941. 361 p.

Sumner, William G. *Folkways*. Boston: Ginn and Company, 1906. 692 p.

Thrasher, Frederic M. "A Study of the Total Situation." *Journal of Educational Sociology*, 1 : 599–613, April 1928.

Thrasher, Frederic M. "How to Study the Boys' Gang in the Open." *Journal of Educational Sociology*, 1 : 244–254, January 1928.

Thrasher, Frederic M. "The Boys' Club Study." *Journal of Educational Sociology,* 6 : 4–17, September 1932.

Thrasher, Frederic M. *The Gang.* Chicago: The University of Chicago Press, 1936. 605 p.

Thrasher, Frederic M. "The Gang as a Symptom of Community Disorganization." *Journal of Applied Sociology,* 11 : 3–21, September–October 1926.

Waller, Willard. *The Sociology of Teaching.* New York: J. Wiley and Sons, Inc., 1932. 467 p.

Warren, Roland L. "A Sociological Analysis of Student Activities." *Educational Forum,* 5 : 442–457, May 1941.

Whitley, R. L. "Interviewing the Problem Boy." *Journal of Educational Sociology,* 5 : 89–101, 140–152, October–November 1931.

Wilson, Gertrude. "Record Keeping in Group Work as a Contribution to Sociology." *American Sociological Review,* 2 : 237–246, April 1937.

Znaniecki, Florian. "Social Groups as Products of Participating Individuals." *American Journal of Sociology,* 44 : 799–811, May 1939.

VII

THE COLLEGE IN TRANSITION

T HE PURPOSE of this chapter is to show how a new structure of the campus today is bringing about new norms. The chapter aims to indicate how the culture which the student is bringing today, as symbolized in the various types of composition of student clientele, is to a large degree reshaping the campus. Second, it aims to show by examples taken from student periodicals and weeklies from colleges and universities throughout the country how the established and traditional culture of the campus is being reassessed, and re-evaluated. It attempts to show how the new impact of student government is changing the established mores of dominance to mores of a different pattern, centered around a larger concept or role of student action. The chapter also discusses the problem of present-day student housing in relation to the physical culture and social structure of a campus and the potentialities of the change in housing conditions for good group interrelationships. The discussion emphasizes how the culture of the campus is impinging on that of the wider culture and is bringing the campus into a realization of the realities of community life.

The chapter points out that the new organization and functioning of student groups should be built on a reassessment and re-evaluation of existing group charters, personnel, norms, functions, and activities, and the establishment of satisfactory direct group interrelations. It likewise suggests the importance of studying and trying all techniques possible for understanding a student body in order to build better social patterns, relationships, and mores on the campus.

Moreover, it shows by specific examples how present-day happenings on some campuses are indicating that processes of change are in operation and are bringing about a superstructure of new mores.

Impact of the Culture Which the Student Brings with Him

Sherif states that "Important changes in the structure of society usually determine the formation of new norms appropriate to the situation. These new norms may not eliminate the old ones right away; by inertia they may persist for a long time, and eventually disappear."[1]

The college world today is experiencing a veritable contortion of structure in the clientele of its student body. Because of the G.I. Bill of Rights, the diffusion of more wealth among all classes of people, and the agitation of broad-minded educators, a greater social mobility among students is coming about on the campus. Up to the present time, in spite of the spread of state universities, junior colleges, and other public institutions of higher learning, the mass of students have come from the higher socio-economic group. Studies of the occupational status of fathers of college students have shown "a much larger percentage of fathers in the proprietor, professional service, and agricultural service groups; a smaller percentage in the managerial, clerical, and commercial service class; and a negligible number in the skilled and unskilled labor groups."[2] Today are found among the students on college campuses more varied backgrounds, wider experiences, and more diversified patterns of behavior.

In 1939 there were 1,250,000 students in American colleges. In 1946 there were more than 2,000,000, of which number 880,000 were veterans. These statistics alone would indicate a broader socio-economic base among the college students. For the first time in American college history, economic and social position is playing a smaller part in the determination of who shall go to college.

This broadening of the base so far as socio-economic status is

[1] Muzafer Sherif, *Psychology of Social Norms*, p. 44. Copyright, 1936, by Harper and Brothers.

[2] Ruth Strang, *Behavior and Background of Students in College and Secondary School*, p. 279.

concerned will have various effects on the established mores of a college culture made up of a student body of the higher socio-economic status. It may bring a more purposeful, serious, democratic, and hard-working group than has ever before been on the campus. The culture which this new student body is bringing will be of a different sort. There are going to be more students who do not know anything about tradition; who will not be at all acquainted with social etiquette and formality. There will be students seeking to climb the social ladder. If a student is successful in passing from one class to another, his behavior will, however, show the contrast between the mores in which he was bred and those in which he finds himself. His mistakes and misfortunes will reveal the nature of the old mores, their power over him, their pertinacity against later influences, and the general confusion in character produced by trying to change them. One will readily observe the grip of habit which appears both in the persistence of old mores and in the weakness of new ones. Personnel workers, teachers, and educators will need much more patience in trying to reach social goals on the campus and much more persistency in bringing students to see these goals.

THE HETEROGENEITY IN COMPOSITION
OF THE STUDENT BODY

Besides the socio-economic factors there are other differences in the structure of a college student body which have not heretofore existed. The different types of students on the campuses today are presenting a heterogeneity of student composition such as the college world has not seen before. The veterans alone make up a large part of a heterogeneous student body. Besides the dissimilarities in their home backgrounds, there are wide differences in experiences. Some have never left the United States; others have been in many parts of the world. Some have been in battle areas; others have seen foreign service without battle. Some have spent most of their time on college campuses; others are entering college for the first time. Some are re-entering the college they left; others are entering a different one. There are the wounded and non-wounded; the commissioned and non-commissioned. There are differences in the kind of experience they had in the Armed

Services, depending upon whether they served in the Army, the Navy, or the Air Corps.

On the campus there is the married veteran without his family, the married veteran with his wife, the married veteran with wife and children. The veteran's wife may also be a student. There are the veterans who are physically handicapped. There are the 4F's and CO's; Wacs, Waves, and Spars, who have also had varied experiences; the married women students whose husbands have been killed, who have children, or who are divorcées. The college clientele consists also of some girls who stayed in college during the war, and others who left college to work, but are now returning to the campus. Also included are youth who went to work after leaving high school and are only now entering college, many of whom had many kinds of work experience. Furthermore, young high school graduates are also in the student body, boys and girls who have had no work experience of any kind. There are also the older men and women who are returning to the campus for enough study to qualify them to retain their positions.

In addition to the differences arising out of family background, socio-economic status, age, kinds of experience, there are also differences in the value-systems of members of this diversified student body, in the ways in which they have reconstructed their experiences and formulated them into attitudes and a philosophy of life. In other words, we now have in the college world the mores of those who live in the suburbs, and of those who live "on the wrong side of the tracks"; the mores of the "upper-uppers," the lower-uppers," the "upper-lowers," and even some "lower-lowers"—to make use of Yankee City terminology. Students reflect the mores of the farm and the factory, the mores of the young and the old, the mature and the immature, the rich and the poor.

What is the significance of this diversity? It will mean that today with this diverse student body, college life must be built upon differences as well as likenesses. The likenesses are what students have collectively, what they share, the experiences in which they participate together. It is because they have like wants that they associate in the performance of unlike functions. All this must be fitted into a philosophy and a program of action in dealing with and developing new mores among a postwar student body.

NEEDS OF A HETEROGENEOUS STUDENT BODY

Students on our campuses today, no matter how great their differences, will have the same needs students have always had, that is, the need for security, for response, and for recognition. All are alike in this respect and will share and participate together in meeting these needs. The functions they assume, however, or the particular overt behavior they assume will be very different in meeting these needs. All students are seeking security today. Perhaps the college campus will present a picture similar to the following.

The veteran will express his need for security by wanting to crowd just as many studies as possible into his schedule so that he can finish quickly and catch up economically on the years he has lost out of his youth. He will have a social maturity in many respects and will want it recognized. Veterans perhaps will not readily accept supervision of their hours, amusements, and morals. They may resent the deans and their occasional use of housemothers as regulators of behavior. They have managed to take care of themselves in various corners of the world and will not permit having their lives regulated in a college world. They will not easily see the point of view of the younger undergraduate to whom football, fraternity, big campus jobs, and social affairs mean everything. A dean in a Southern college tells how the veterans say "that they feel they can fit in everywhere on a college campus except on the social dance floor where they can't see the 'jitterbug' and such social immaturity of the younger undergraduates."

The college girl who has remained on the campus during the war and who has not had a "regular boy friend" may in her search for security react as one girl expressed it in an interview with the same dean, "I've got to get myself a man before leaving college." The Wacs and Waves on the campuses today may in their need for security react in the same manner as this girl, except that they have had wider experiences and are more likely to possess and to demand in men greater social maturity.

The younger high school graduates entering the colleges are also seeking social maturity for themselves in this older student body of today. But social maturity to them may mean taking part in all the social affairs, knowing the last dance "hit," and being recognized socially in as many ways as possible.

In these large heterogeneous student bodies, whose needs are fundamentally the same but whose attempts to realize them will be vastly different, members of a personnel staff may constantly ask, "How can good interrelationships be brought about in this student body?" There will be opportunities for group relationships in which all can be an integral unit, but many kinds of activities and group relations will have to be worked out to meet the particular ways in which these students of today can satisfy their needs.

STATUS AND ROLE
ON THE PRESENT-DAY CAMPUS

Under the present necessity of reorganizing the social structure on college campuses because of this heterogeneity of the student body, the system of statuses and roles will be breaking down. Since a new system, compatible with the actual conditions of modern life, has not yet emerged, the student will thus frequently find himself confronted with situations in which he will be uncertain both of his own statuses and roles and of those of others. He will not only be compelled to make choices but will also feel no certainty that he has chosen correctly. He will fear that the reciprocal behavior of others will not be what he expects on the basis of the statuses which he has assumed that they occupy.

For examples of the uncertainty of statuses and roles today on our college campus, we turn again to the veteran. The veteran may have had the rank of lieutenant-colonel in the Army but he returns to the campus and finds his most esteemed professor was only a lieutenant. As he sits in his class and must return what the professor "hands out," he may confuse his Army status with that of a junior in an undergraduate college. Or again, the veteran might return to the college with a wife and child but be asked to attend the meeting in which the dean of women outlines the social regulations. Are these expectancies for him? Also, coming to the college as a freshman is the recent high school graduate, one who, because of the war, may not have had either in his family or in his school the balancing dominance of a father, older brother, or older boy classmates. He also resents, but perhaps in a different emotional way, the rules and regulations of the campus.

To return to the married veteran, his status, while he is a member of the college community, is that of a student; his status in his home is that of husband and father; his status in his country is that of a soldier, made evident by the Distinguished Service Medal and other badges of merit he may have won, plus his rank in the Armed Forces. In his home community, his status is that of civilian. The roles involved in these statuses may be in the stage of being assumed. One must realize that the veteran is playing several roles; when he fails to comply with certain requirements of the college, perhaps his role of father has taken his attention to his home and away from the college. The dependency on the "father role of Uncle Sam" may still operate in civilian life.

The status of the Wacs and Waves on the campus, like that of the male veteran, will be conditioned by their experiences in the Armed Forces. These young women have been required to function as efficiently as possible. They have been accustomed to orders and may find their role difficult on a campus where they must rely on their initiative and popularity without the enhancement of a uniform.

There is also the girl who has stayed in college and has become a leader on the campus. She is intelligent and capable, but withdraws her talents for the benefit of the service man, a former college student.

There are the students who left college for work in industry and earned exceptionally good wages. They have not been associating with people of college interests; these students find annoying their own lack of culture in the social and intellectual aspects of the college community. They may feel much less secure in their student, parasitical role—as they see it—than they did in their money-earning role.

There is the 4F who probably more than ever before will feel a sense of inferiority among so many of his classmates who have been in the war zones in the far-flung corners of the world. The social popularity which he won during the war because of the dearth of men will now wane, or he will fear that it will.

There are also the married women students whose husbands,

former students, have been killed. Many of these women are returning to a campus. For some it is a place of sacred memories; for others a place of stern reality where they must obtain enough education to earn their own living; for others a place to meet an eligible man.

There are also the older people, men and women adults, who are returning to the campus for further study to qualify them to retain their positions.

There are those veterans who are physically handicapped, uncertain of the role they can play, or who may even feel inferior about the pre-war "girl friend."

Lastly, there are the veterans' wives, who are perhaps more dubious than any of the others concerning their role on the campus, and who are struggling to live on a G.I. income. Many of these wives have had a year or two of college work; others have had no college training. Many of them will feel "out of the picture." All these students are seeking a more secure status and wondering what their role will be on the campus in relation to other members of the college community.

The individual's social behavior consists of a continuing series of interactions with other individuals within a set of relations. The relations are part of a social system continuing in time, while the interacting individuals who make up the continuity of generations change by the entrance of new units and the departure of old ones.[3]

Today new units have entered the campuses. The relations, as "part of a social system continuing in time," may have to be changed. Major conflicts may develop between these groups; social change on the campus may be accelerated; the mores that controlled the behavior of the former college students will lose their efficacy. The resolution of these conflicts will produce a new equilibrium; new mores will develop and perhaps a changed social pattern. The task, therefore, of the personnel worker and educator today is to plan, work for, and achieve the reconciliation of conflicting social groups and tendencies—to integrate these groups into a life on the campus befitting the campus clientele, resources, and potentialities.

[3] Lloyd Warner and Paul Lunt, *The Social Life of a Modern Community*, Yankee City Series, Vol. 1, p. 22. Copyright, 1941, by Yale University Press.

In resolving these conflicts into a wholesome integration there is, first of all, the necessity for the personnel staff to have a social understanding of the heterogeneous student body—its background, needs, experiences—and especially an understanding of what experiences mean and do to people. These workers should be sensitive to the particular social problems of the different types of students. They should also have a clear idea of the function of the particular college culture in which they are working and formulate in conjunction with faculty, administration, and students what they feel can be standards of social behavior for this particular college and also society at large. The diversified student body should then be informed of the *social function* of their college and be encouraged to *work out their role within this function*. For this purpose they must realize how groups on the campus belong together in working out their goals.

The fact that a student is eager to have a higher position in the social scale and wants to get it as quickly as possible is all the more reason why he should take time to learn effective social education and group functioning. Social education will require, first of all, that a candidate can effectively live and work with others. The veteran's war experience has not given him altogether the kind of training he needs for effective peacetime relationships. The civilian group of students, just entering from high school, must know and understand the veterans, and interact with them. From this interaction and understanding of the veterans' experiences, the civilian group can perhaps attain greater social maturity. The dominance which the civilian students feel the veteran group exercises may be helpful to them and take the place of a lack of it in their families which has arisen from the dislocations of war. The veteran likewise must realize that because he may have had a sharp rise in social position as a result of his experience in the Armed Forces, he must win a certain esteem, prestige, and role to retain such a position in society. The college campus will probably offer him his first opportunity to prove to his college classmates his qualifications for that role.

Thus, all types of students have had experiences which must be blended for the mutual working out of compatible relationships and roles, and for developing growth of the entire student body.

IMPACT OF THE VETERAN

The veteran is especially selected here because of the depth of his experiences and because his problem of adjustment is in some respects more difficult than that of other students. It is a sound conviction, however, that the veteran should not be segregated for special attention, except, perhaps, with regard to the administrative details of the Veteran's Administration. Veterans in college wish, first of all, to be students and should not be considered differently; they are members of campus groups and must function as such in relation to other student units on the campus. The heterogeneity of the veterans in composition and in experiences has already been discussed. It can be expected that these experiences will bring about different types of behavior on the part of various segments of the veteran student body.

The Conditioning from Military Mores. In conferences with veterans, both men and women, who had seen foreign service, it was often mentioned that experience in the military mores of the Armed Services was a conditioning factor in civilian life. They spoke of how uncertainty in the foreign field, of not knowing whether they were going to live or die, the crowding of ten years' experience into three, and experiences with Army hierarchy, were all strong conditioning factors for maladjustment on their return to civilian life. The constant move, pressure, impatience, and idea of "Where are we going next?" was carried over into the civilian atmosphere. Their first purpose upon return was "to get what they wanted and to get it quickly." Because of the experiences they had been through they felt resentment toward the complacency of civilian life, the pushing in subways, the nylon line—when half the world was starving. In the classroom, they said, there is lack of real appreciation among the faculty of the vast experiences they have had. Their war experiences are not drawn on in motivating them in college work. The presentation of classroom material offers no challenge to their experience. The feminine side of education is stressed too much; there is definitely a lack of virility and strength. Besides, they came from an experience of exactness to a situation which seems to them to lack direction. A personnel and statistical officer in the Air Force with rank of captain spoke of the veteran being in "open revolt against 'wishy-washy' types of teaching plans with no crystallization of thought or action." One hears veterans saying, "This bores me terrifically"; there is sheer disgust in the "up-in-the-air" presentation of material. Organization, method, and efficiency in presentation seem to them to be lacking.

A veteran of the Signal Corps branch remarked that "the men imbibed a devil-may-care" attitude from the environment of the Army. Their uniform carried certain power; they had freedom from the regimentation of their own social mores—that of their family, their church, and their community. But this veteran felt that whatever the social mores of the veteran during the war period, his main aim now is to seek a stabilizing influence.

That the military mores have exerted a conditioning on the veterans can be seen in their maladjustments to civilian life. The veteran's pressure and impatience to get something quickly, resentment against the complacency of civilian life, feeling that educators lack appreciation of their experiences, desire for organization, efficiency, and method, and longing for stability in social life are all impacts in one way or another of the military mores. A tinge of criticism has been noticed in the interviews with veterans; this would likewise appear to be in the "mores of the military." As one veteran remarked, "A study of our complaints would be worth while." It is true that many of these complaints do have significance for the educational field; organization, efficiency, methods, and action are much needed in the institutional and instructional mores of the college world. Several personnel workers have remarked that the veterans "want to know" what are the rules and regulations on the campus. They want it to be clear what can be done and cannot be done. This attitude seems without doubt a carry-over from the military mores in which duties and rules were clearly defined and outlined. This would seem to be an opportune time to take charters, norms, and rules, and go over, define, restate, and critically evaluate them in light of present-day situations. Perhaps it would take a year to discuss adequately in student organizations and forums the social problems of college youth and determine what ideals, standards, rules, and regulations can exist under present circumstances. Can these rules, made many years ago, abide in this age of easy communication and transportation? Youth will go many places, unattended by chaperones, in the years to come. What kind of faith can we build in these young people, and what kind of faith can we have in them? What responsibility should students assume for out-of-town behavior? These problems must be ironed out by students themselves under the guidance of strong leaders, both students and faculty. Some faculty are still saying, "Why doesn't the dean decide these matters?" It is time for faculty to awaken to the fact that a study of these problems is exactly what they should be preparing their students to make. It is largely because they have not integrated their class work with student problems and activities that these situations exist. Wanting to know "what the rules are" but not having rules handed to them ready-made may make students realize their responsibility for bringing about more desirable mores of social control.

Adjustment of the Veteran on the Campus. As has been stated earlier, the veteran because of his particular type and depth of experiences has an adjustment perhaps somewhat different from that of other students. There is an adjustment to his home and the particular social relationships involved, to his community, to college, and, above all, to a less active life. When the veteran arrives on the college campus he resents immaturity. His return to college brings him into contact with a younger age group. He does not share the normal interest of college boys in the undergraduate culture. He cannot become as excited as they do about such activities as football, fraternities, freshman rules, and hell week. He has few convictions concerning the best kind of fraternity rushing. An article by Efron,[4] with the setting on a university campus in Eastern Pennsylvania, describes what has been taking place on many college campuses. The article emphasizes that there is unrest among young civilian students; the Joe College lads are not content around their big wooden fraternity houses because the Joe Veterans, on the average twenty-three years old, are reforming the college in their own mature image, making it less boyish, less playful, more serious.

The civilians on this campus charge that "The veterans are kill-

[4] Edith Efron, "The Two Joes Meet—Joe College, Joe Veteran," *New York Times Magazine,* 95 : 21, June 16, 1946.

ing traditions; freshmen are required by time-honored law to wear brown ties, brown socks, and brown 'dinky' caps. They must also light the cigarettes of upper classmen." Because the 400-odd freshmen who had seen military service flatly refused to play this game, the school paper—a civilian organ—instantly printed a series of editorials, plumping for traditions, for school spirit, pointing out the advantages of hazing, paddling, and dinky caps and concluding with appeal, "Veterans, you mustn't let ———— College down."

The few veterans, according to Efron, who bothered to answer said, "Amusements for seventeen-year-olds could not be imposed on veterans." The civilians continued: "They go on drinking sprees, steal civilians' girls." "The Dean tightens up house party regulations by instituting a forty-eight-hour chaperone system." The veteran replied: "Basically, the kids are jealous of us—they have an inferiority complex because they weren't in the service, so nothing we do pleases them. We didn't come to school to play games. We've come to study."

The faculty is also split into pro- and anti-veteran camps. The official view is that the veterans are a success in college. "Veterans are more mature, more responsible, noticeably more polite, more respectful than non-veterans," say the professors. Most professors are secretly delighted to see the Joe College activities dying out, and are grateful to the veterans for their influence. The minority point of view as expressed by three instructors in this one institution was approximately as follows, "That the G.I. Bill of Rights was a political weapon and as such would eventually destroy the colleges; that the veterans, because of their intense interest in careers, were 'vocationalizing the school and intensifying an already dangerous trend'; that the G.I. Bill was being interpreted to mean that every veteran was entitled to go to college, bringing about a 'non-sensical' situation in which every empty grocery store would soon be converted into a 'college' to satisfy the demand."

In this example of effort on the part of the veteran for an adjustment suitable to his maturity, personnel staffs and others can see many of the characteristics of the mores fully operative. The same need for social recognition, for response, and for status is operative on the part of both civilians and veterans, but the same needs are sometimes satisfied in unlike functions. The use of the forty-eight-hour chaperone system illustrated the use of the element of force in the established institutional mores. This incident also bears out that an event occurs in a relational context, as mentioned previously in this study, and that a disturbance in one part influences all other parts and, in turn, will be influenced by them. The disturbance here in student social life disturbed also the faculty who wished to bring into play their own particular mores. This incident would appear to indicate that perhaps it is time for *all* people in a college community to define and re-evaluate such terms as social maturity and college spirit. The fact that the veterans have labeled the customs as "childish" might raise the question whether it may not be necessary to build a new maturity. This college community might also see that social maturity is more than just ability to study, that it also includes such elements as successful relationships and social responsibility. Waller says,

While the veteran resents the assumption of immaturity, it would be an error to suppose that he is actually mature. . . . The veteran is not immature in the same way in which the ordinary college boy is immature. He knows more about sex, perhaps less about love. He knows how to fight, but is less likely than the college boy to have had a satisfactory work experience. . . . The veteran who has become a commissioned officer or a noncom has some organizing ability; he knows how to run things. What is certainly indicated is that, if the veteran returns to school or college, *some way must be found to capitalize on his experience and to remedy its lacks.*[5]

The difficulty in academic adjustment has been a disturbing influence to veterans upon their return from the Armed Forces. Two chief nurses in the Army Nurse Corps, one of whom served three years and the other three and one-half years overseas (one in England, and the other in England and France) described the difficulty in their academic adjustment as graduate students on a university campus after they returned from a period of service in the Army. Adjustment to study was particularly difficult. Early in the semester both were ready to give up, feeling an inability to think and function effectively. They had not been exposed to professional literature in the Army and felt completely out of date. They had

[5] Willard Waller, *The Veteran Comes Back,* p. 152. Reprinted by permission of the publisher from *The Veteran Comes Back,* p. 152. New York: The Dryden Press, 1944.

been subject to a lack of freedom and need for initiative and now when they had freedom their inability to function effectively interfered with their use of it. Because of the pattern of conformity to which they had been subjected, both for some time felt incompetent to measure up to the originality and scholarship required in a college. It was a comforting experience to them to talk with other nurses and realize that they all were having the same difficulties. One of the nurses said that the most morale-building information she had had in her effort to get herself functioning effectively was that from a psychologist who told her it would take six months to make such an adjustment. Also, their vocational choice upon return from the service gave them serious thought. Professionally, they were eager to try something different, but their conscience and sense of responsibility to the nursing profession limited their choice to a line of work within the nursing field.

In another conference with two recreational directors of the Waves and one from the Marine Corps, all three stated that they felt that undue maladjustment would not exist on the campuses among returning girl veterans. They believed that maladjustment was overemphasized; the Navy residence unit was not very different from the college dormitory. They felt that the girls in the Waves would be adults in age; they had been treated by the Navy as adults and would assume that they should be treated in the same way in college. One of the outstanding gains from their own experience in the Armed Forces was that they had found "they could do something different and do it well." New vistas were opened to them; many of them in returning to civilian life would continue to do what they had done in the Navy. They would also be seeking to get into the kind of job they wanted or at least would be willing to experiment until they found the job that would be most satisfactory to them.

Many of the girls in the Armed Forces have no doubt had this same experience. This willingness to experiment vocationally, this experience in flexibility—"the doing of a job that they never thought they were capable of doing"—will perhaps condition many young women to higher aspirations and desire for more education and varied experiences. If the colleges can meet the social expectancies of these veterans, an adjustment will take place which will lead into more useful and socially desirable mores because of the satisfaction in developing one's greatest potentialities. If, on the contrary, the mores of the college are such that these expectancies cannot be met, then much dissatisfaction and emotional distress will result.

The differences in adjustment among these women veterans represent the fact, mentioned earlier in this chapter, that there are differences in the experiences of the Armed Forces, and also that there are differences in the *depth* of experiences which lead to various degrees of difficulty in adjustment. What the veterans have reconstructed from their experiences into value-systems of their own will undoubtedly affect the mores as factors of social control on the college campus.

Again, with regard to problems in the adjustment of the women veterans on the campus, an educational Service Officer in the Waves spoke of how much prestige and status meant to the girls in educational off-duty activities. The tendency for "upward-downward looking" from the point of view of prestige and status would exist on the college campus; "they will look up on the campus to those who had been officers, to people of good organizing ability and efficiency, and will look down on anything not well planned and executed. Unless some prestige and status could be acquired on the campus, many of the girls will have heartaches and dissatisfactions."

As to interrelationships in the Armed Forces, all the veterans interviewed spoke of the existence of social cleavages. Cleavages existed between officer and enlisted men, among officers according to rank; at first there was one officers' club; then there were officers' clubs and officers' clubs for field grade only. Other veterans spoke of dissension between commanding officers and executive officers in handling of battalion, discipline, and regimentation. Some of the cleavages which they definitely thought would exist on the campus are: service men versus civilian, wounded service men versus non-wounded service men, overseas service men versus non-overseas service men. The service men who had been closest to the battle line would have the greatest prestige.

Because of these cleavages, differing attitudes and values will exist on the campuses. Techniques for good group relationships will be essential to bringing about a reconciliation and adjustment to these differences. Mores of cooperative living must be sanctioned more than ever. These differences will not yield to lectures only but will demand time-consuming processes.

Together with the veteran's urge for haste, for organization, and for new, up-to-date methods of doing things, there is also his nostalgia for the old, including the old-time carefree and rather irresponsible college life. At one college, one reads of the veterans wanting college customs, such as hazing practices, thrown overboard; at another, they do not want any customs changed as they would have nothing in common to talk about in the future with their families. On other campuses, the nostalgia for the old includes the possession by the college of certain buildings, preservation of material objects, and retention of accustomed spots of beauty on the campus. The veteran's sense of security may be tied up with this nostalgia. This nostalgia for the old must be reckoned with in advancing to the new in campus life.

There is, too, a strong impact for the good coming from the veteran-student. All personnel workers have spoken of this "good" in various ways. A dean of men in a Negro Southern college sums up as follows the impact of the veterans on his campus: "They believe they have a place and role in community life and are anxious to fill it. They are creating an atmosphere of scholarship; they are coming back with strong religious convictions; they will exert pressure to get the things that are rightfully theirs; they will, however, not be unfair." All these things indicate the potential resource and strength out of which leadership should develop on a college campus.

Again, regarding the problems of the returning veteran, the veterans interviewed unanimously agreed that the two uppermost problems concerned, first, how long it would take them to get through college; second, when they would receive their subsistence checks. It must be remembered that many veterans are in college because they do not wish to return to the old job. Efron gives four reasons why the veteran refuses to go back to his old job.[6] First, the opportunity for careers offered by the G.I. Bill of Rights

---

[6] Edith Efron, "Old Jobs, or New Ones, for the Veteran," *New York Times Magazine*, 94 : 11, March 18, 1945.

opened up new vistas for the veteran. Second, he learned a new trade while he was in service; at separation centers there were many such men. Third, a veteran refuses to return to his old job because he has had a sharp leap in "social position" which often occurs in the Army. Fourth, there is a basic reason—perhaps it is more an attitude—which explains the veteran's rejection of his old job. According to experts it is an attitude composed of a tremendous desire for security, an awareness of the magnitude of their sacrifice of time and of economic progress, and a fierce resentment against civilian workers, who, they think, have been living off the best of the land. These four reasons for a veteran returning to a college campus instead of the job represent four of his important needs—the need for response, the need for new experiences, the need for social status, and the need for security.

Can the institutional mores of the colleges, particularly mores which refer to curricular practices, meet these new needs? As one looks at these four reasons why veterans are not returning to old jobs, one readily sees that they have significance in the college for instruction, guidance, and campus living, and through these three areas can likewise be visualized a longed-for change in the institutional culture. The faculty usually can be depended upon to make the transition if the whole institution is moving with them. Surveys from colleges show the "seriousness of purpose" of the veteran. It seems that now is the time to integrate instruction with the life purposes and professional ambitions of these students. If, as the professor in the Pennsylvania college believed, the veterans are vocationalizing the college, it would seem that this vocationalizing ought to be used for building desirable mores in the lives of students. In the realm of guidance the veteran should have a share in planning his own future and learn to see himself in relation to the veteran's problem in general. It would be the function of guidance to teach him to live as well as to make a living. Lastly his campus should offer opportunities to live and develop desirable ways of doing things in fitting him for the highest potentialities in his vocation, and attaining security in his social relationships. This calls for a re-establishment of a group relationship that will sustain him in returning to civilian life.

Veterans' Groups. Veterans' organizations have been discussed pro and con, many veterans feeling that they narrow their contacts with the other groups of the campus. However, participation in one group pulls members into relationships with other groups and eventually a group-wise participation is effected on the campus. The head of a junior college in the West spoke of being criticized by some of his faculty members for allowing so much freedom to the veterans in their organization, by not forbidding them to have "beer" parties. The only requirement was that they not be held under the sponsorship of the college. In other affairs and activities the veterans were given full support. Very soon on this campus the all-college activities and dances of the college's social program went into full swing and the veterans' "beer" parties vanished because the veterans became more interested in the college affairs, which were less expensive and through which could be made more contacts. The treatment of this group is an example of what Waller believes: "Tolerate, recognize, and guide such groups and they become socially useful. Oppose them, alienate them, antagonize them, force them underground, and they become dangerous."[7] The group is tolerated, is permitted to meet, is given status, is endowed with respectability; in return, the group often changes the nature of its leadership in the direction of social acceptability.

The veterans are making a period of readjustment between two worlds. In this period all the morale-building activities of the institution will have to be focused on aiding in the transition to the new lives the veterans are going to lead. Social activities, recreational pursuits, avocations, and hobbies all loom large as vehicles by which the transition can be made.

In interviews with veterans, the following suggestions for successful adjustment of the veteran to campus living came out. The common interests among all different types of students should be stressed. Differences should be forgotten and action as one unit promoted. "To belong" was particularly stressed; all must have group life. Many all-college events should be held in which faculty and students should socialize together; this would prove to be decidedly good morale-building.

Social affairs should be well organized and under good leader-

[7] Willard Waller, op. cit., p. 195.

ship. More intensive orientation should be devised; talks should be given on the cultural expectancies of the college. Personnel staffs and educators should realize in their social programs that the experiences which the veterans have had are not substitutes for normal experiences.

Impact of the Present-day Campus on the Traditional and Established Culture of the College

CURRICULAR INNOVATIONS

To consider another phase of the present-day campus, the writer systematically observed during 1945, 1946, and 1947 the changes in established mores and the rise of new mores in the academic realm of the college world which might have a marked effect in the social control of student life. In this area college campuses appear to be considering an evaluation of old practices and beliefs common to their culture and the formation of new norms. Cultural change is taking place on many campuses through the processes mentioned earlier in the study; inventions and innovations of all kinds, on the part of both students and faculty, seem to be the commonly accepted means of meeting the new situation. The following changes in curricula in colleges in Northern, Southern, Eastern, and Western regions of the United States were mentioned in the Magazine Sections of *The New York Times* during the year 1946–1947:

Marshall College, Huntingdon, West Virginia, is sponsoring a new program of forum discussions, speakers to include prominent persons in international politics, outstanding radio commentators, and editors of weekly and monthly magazines.

Russell Sage College is offering a series of lectures, entitled "Our Pacific Island Neighbors." The series is designed to acquaint families of returning service men and women with the physical and cultural background of places mentioned in letters to military dispatches.

Radcliffe is presenting a new program offering for the first time an opportunity to combine a complete liberal arts education leading to a bachelor's degree with professional education in nursing.

Marietta College is giving free instruction in regular college courses up to six credits a semester to wives enrolled in order to give them an opportunity to keep up with their student husbands in cultural interests and to provide a place for them in campus life.

The faculty of Southwestern at Memphis, in order to create an understanding of what has made the American way of life, is presenting a symposium on "Our American Heritage."

Indiana University offers a new program in music to those who do not wish to follow a professional career as soloists or music teachers in order to fit these students for music-related positions—music criticism, music publishing, radio announcing, music promotion and advertising, managing of opera, and other musical organizations.

Wilson College will offer an expanded course in public administration designed to familiarize students with the work of their state and federal governments.

Barnard College will have an enlarged program of international and area studies designed to make good citizens and to provide a foundation for advanced training for students who will later specialize in the field.

University of Michigan will have an Institute of Public Administration to conduct research on matters of public interest.

Wesleyan University will have a course in the mechanics of motion picture production, arrangements being made with one of the large motion picture companies for the showing of exceptional films.

The University of Notre Dame through its Industrial Relations Institute will conduct five labor sessions and five management sessions to promote industrial peace and understanding between labor and management.

Wellesley College, under supervision of its Department of Speech, is having a small group of specially qualified undergraduates help in treatment of veterans in the Neurological Section of the Cushing General Hospital, Framingham, Massachusetts.

Vassar College will conduct a regional study on Tennessee Valley Authority in order to have students investigate the scientific and social factors contributing to the development of the region.

City College, New York, is combining theory and practice by having its students supplement classwork in race problems by practical investigation of techniques used in New York City groups engaged in counteracting race tensions.

Lincoln University, Pennsylvania, oldest school for higher education of the Negro, shifted from pre-theological to the training of professional leaders on all levels.

Ohio University is offering a short course of six evening classes to teach the wives of their veterans the art of sewing, mending, knitting, darning, food planning, hospitality on a limited budget, etc.

University of Denver will have an Inter-American Education Workshop in which there will be conversational language groups in Spanish or Portuguese.

Sarah Lawrence College will have three labor forums, which have been arranged by the college and Labor Education Committee of Yonkers, to be held at the headquarters of the Textile Workers Union.

Mississippi Southern College in its English Department has introduced the tutorial system so that the instructor who may not have refreshed his lecture course with new material during the past ten years will find himself obliged to talk about books the student has read and wishes to discuss.

Florida Southern College, through the establishment of a part-time division in the Agricultural School, will have students retain jobs in packing plants, grove service organizations, nurseries, dairies, and farms while taking formal instruction.

New Rochelle College, to combat the breakdown of family security resulting from the war, has introduced a series of family-life conferences for seniors. In a comprehensive round-up, weekly lectures bring together the information of various departments which contribute toward making a better home life and toward fitting women for better home management.

Rollins College, Florida, unlike colleges that are now building their curriculum around a "core" of required subjects, is attempting to tailor the curriculum to the capacities and character qualities of the individual student, thus creating a core curriculum for each student.

In regard to an abrupt change in the mores on college campuses, the following instances may be cited:

The University of New Hampshire will hold classes at noon hours. Other colleges are holding evening sessions, carrying on extension work and full-time sessions at near-by high schools. This use of time and all facilities available have had to be considered for the first time in the history of many colleges.

Cedar Crest College in Pennsylvania has sponsored the revived school for girls at Laon Cité du Nord in France, a school with two hundred pupils now meeting in an abandoned Army barracks. International good-will will be furthered by correspondence between the girls of the French and American institutions.

Where once the strains of Wesleyan's "Alma Mater" rang through the paneled halls of Delta Upsilon, the prattle of babies now is heard. The fraternity house has been converted into a nursery school operated by wives of veterans studying at Middletown (Connecticut) University.

Although it is not a coeducational institution, Williams College will admit to its classes the wives of enrolled veterans. Faculty wives have "listened in" on courses from time to time at Williams but this is the first instance that any official recognition in the form of a certificate has been given.

Wilson and Vassar Colleges and other women's colleges, for the first time in their history, will admit off-campus men students.

Vassar breaks the strongest tradition that she perhaps has ever had, viz., that of a male president, electing for the first time in her history a woman president. Young Vassar women this fall will find the proof of the concept for which they all, theoretically, are fighting—woman's equality—will be staring them in the face.

What do these curricular expansions and changes mean in the study of the student mores of a college campus? They mean many breaks with former academic traditions and much effort to satisfy the needs of youth today, particularly the need for security as evidenced in provisions for the veterans' wives and in the greater number of offerings in fields in which students are especially interested. They mean that in some colleges more attention is being given to ego-integrative needs by "tailoring the curriculum" to fit the capacities and character qualities of the individual student.

These curricular innovations also mean closer integration of the colleges with the communities in which their students will work and better ways of doing things on the part of students because of this broader relationship with the outside. This community consciousness is not only local but national and international in scope. New group techniques are making possible social interaction and interrelationship between a larger representation of persons in and outside the college community.   What the various colleges are offering reflects, too, the influence of society and societal issues on a college campus. Through a combination of theory and practice in the area of instruction more constructive student mores may be built, meeting more adequately than in the past the student's need for recognition, response, security, and stability. The effect of these innovations in curricula on the student bodies of the future may mean less chance for social stratification and more chance for social development through knowledge of what constitutes good public relations and means of using "public relations" instruments of communication, through training for good citizenship and for more harmonious working relations, through practical investigations into the areas where democracy is not at work, through work experience, through study of family life, and through individualized experiences.

If one were to regard carefully the innovation made by each individual college or university, one might say that these innovations were made according to the institution's particular philosophy. This is aptly illustrated by the Community Participation Plan of Sarah Lawrence College, by the genetic connection with a college of certain interests, such as the "public" interests of the University of Michigan, and the race interests of City College in the City of New York. Innovations according to each institution's philosophy are evident also in the persistent efforts of some colleges to conform to the demands of the times, as is shown at the University of Denver and Ohio University. Innovations are also the product of a particular history and environment, such as the part-time work of Florida Southern College in its immediate geographic environment. They may also come about according to the desire to experiment with progressive ideas, as at Vassar. These innovations show that some colleges are willing to reconstruct institutional and academic mores to accord with needs of present-day youth, on the basis of what is indigenous and possible in their particular culture. These innovations may foretell the future mores of both faculty and students in the teaching and learning realms. There is evidence now that colleges are extending a greater influence into the province of community and societal problems, This influence is perhaps the most far-reaching.

In a student newspaper of an undergraduate student body within a large Northern university, dated May 7, 1946, one reads: "Emergency Council meets today with officials on dorm rent hike. Veteran leaders to attend as opposition to increase continues unanimous."

"Teachers leave! Why? Why does ———— College lose its faculty? A book could be written on the subject but briefly the situation can be summed up in one sentence: The administration has no faculty-personnel policy."

In a newspaper of the same student body, dated May 14, 1946, one reads the headlines: "College Budget Required; Progressive University President also Needed." "We have suggested the establishment of an 'all-college' promotion group for making personnel policy decisions. We would like to see established a completely independent and unhampered college budget."

In this same issue, one also reads that the "Undergraduate Committee is to study plans for Social Center, to pass on the type of facilities available, to approve the condition of these facilities, to formulate policies regarding the administration of all the social activities that will center in the building."

In a newspaper of the city in which this university is located one reads in the issue dated October 15, 1946, that a strike on the part of maintenance workers in the university is taking place. On the fifth day of the strike students of the university joined the pickets, "bearing signs urging their fellow students not to 'scab' and carrying handbills addressed to the university community." Student organizations that banded together in a Strike Aid Committee included the American Veterans Committee, the American Youth for Democracy, Young Citizens PAC, Law School Student Council, Graduate Science Society, Graduate Psychology Society, Sociology Club, Marxist Study Group, Liberal Club, University Christian Association, Permanent Peace Committee, and the Law School Moot Court Committee.

Similar incidents reverberate on campuses in other parts of the country. The list of student groups which banded together in the

Strike Aid Committee mentioned above reveals the mores of students which are operative on this campus; they are the mores which bespeak interest in the social problems of the society in which they live and interest in action on principles. In the forces of the university at work in the molding of these mores, there is evident the influence of teaching and the influence of the wider culture. This is also an illustration of the use of force and criticism on the part of students against an administration.

THE NEW IMPACT OF
STUDENT GOVERNMENT

In a student paper of a Southern university, dated July 10, 1946, one reads:

The hottest issue to come before student government in many years will be discussed by authorities tonight when the Dialective Senate convenes to consider the bill: "Resolved, that the student constitution should be accepted without amendment by the faculty, administration, and Board of Trustees. Special invitations to attend the meeting tonight have been issued to all members of the student legislature. Five articles are being held in abeyance while groups confer over questions of student authority. Parts of the new constitution considered in conflict at present are: (1) the fee structure; (2) the form and administration of coed self-government; (3) the right of the student council to hear appeals in disciplinary cases; (4) the fact that the new constitution does not provide for faculty members on the Dance Committee; and (5) whether dormitory counselors paid by the University should serve on the Interdormitory Council.

In the student weekly of the same university, dated July 17, 1946, this article appeared:

Student government officers yesterday reached a decision permitting the student council to operate under the provisions of the new constitution. Previously this point had been "held in abeyance" pending results of a series of discussions being held by a joint student-administration committee studying the student government document.

One also finds in the same paper the headline: "Meeting of All Students Called Today—Will discuss possibility of increases in dorm rent—rise is part of self-financing plan to pay for building new dormitories." The paper states further that unless the dorms are erected under the self-financing plan, the construction will have to be postponed until after the state legislature meets in January. Administration leaders and members of the Board of Trustees are interested in knowing what the students think of such a move.

In a student newspaper from an old college in the East, dated October 14, 1946, appears the headlines, "Student Government Recognized—Trustees Grant Specific Powers. Undergraduate Council Decides Constitution Tomorrow Night." The article continues:

Marking a new high in the placing of democracy and responsibility in the hands of the student which is unprecedented and unparalleled by any other college in ——— and possibly any other college in the nation, a new student body constitution, recognized provisionally by the Board of Trustees, has been drawn up by the Committee on Social Organization and will be presented for approval to the Undergraduate Council tomorrow night at 8:30. The most significant feature of this constitution is the recognition it will receive from the Board of Trustees of the College which is the first time in the history of ——— that a student government body has been granted this distinction.

The student editor of the newspaper writes:

This recognition by the trustees marks the disappearance of the old time ———, former student governing body, whose chief functions consisted of donning white sweaters several times a year to usher at convocation exercises, referee the freshman-sophomore football rush, and form a human barricade before the doors of the old nugget during the annual Nugget assault. Instead of relying upon the authority of proctors, the students of ——— will discipline their own schoolmates in student courts and recommend their own remedial methods for the improvement of educational methods and instruction.

However, in a student newspaper of the same college, dated October 31, 1946, one reads concerning the rules and regulations that had been drawn up for the students:

We suggest that every undergraduate acquaint himself with the rules printed on pages three and four and their reasons. They are the result of nine months' labor of seven men. The seven were not unanimous; two opposed the 7 P.M. curfew. But we suspect that the same rules would have been evolved by any group selected by the Administration, whether seven or seventy, whether deliberating nine months or nine years.

The seven-point achievement plan appearing in a February, 1945, issue of a college newspaper in a large cosmopolitan area is of interest here:

First, the need for a new constitution for student government designed to eliminate the evils of the old. Also revision of outmoded and antiquated documents of all other student activities.

Second, the arousal of a sluggish electorate to its political responsibilities.

Third, the support of an intelligent literary magazine.

Fourth, the maintenance and improvement of the high level of cordiality existing between the V-12 unit and the civilian college student.

Fifth, the publication of a series of articles dealing with the origin, history, and functions of the various extracurricular activities.

Sixth, the projection of plans for improvements in the educational and recreational facilities and in the landscaping of the university.

Seventh, the deliberation and decision on a stand in national issues.

As to what is happening to student government mores in different parts of the country, *The New York Times'* Magazine Section on Education for the current year again furnishes clues:

Students at Williams College voted to reinstate the Honor System which was dropped during the war; it will round out the first half century of its institution, the college having been persuaded by the Class of 1896 to accept its principles.

A special faculty-student committee has been designated to make a survey of Dartmouth College Regulations.

At Cornell University, the leading student organizations are developing a model organization of the United Nations for the purpose of stimulating thought and action among students and faculty concerning the U.N., to integrate the 325 foreign students from thirty-seven countries into the University activities and to bring campus personnel closer together by virtue of common interests. Students are now registering for membership on the various commissions.

As part of a project the Rutgers University Forum, a weekly round-table discussion, has devoted a number of its sessions to international affairs. Students of the University have taken part; a United Nations bill was recently staged to further international interest among the student body.

The organization of the United Nations is a living reality to students at Kansas State College through their own campus "International Security Assembly," patterned after the U.N. Now a year old, the student-initiated assembly is studying the same problems that now confront the real Security Council in New York.

These examples concerning student life and government on college campuses of different regional sections today show several different lines of action: A desire for more authority of student life in the hands of the student government, a desire to have an expression of opinion in all matters pertaining to their welfare, a return to the old established mores which proved good, a process of re-evaluation, and introduction of innovations interrelated with the mores of the larger society.

The interest in having the origin, history, and functions of various extracurricular activities reviewed and the organizations of the present-day campus revised to meet the new situation shows a desire on the part of students to meet change on the campus. Their desire for a student government functioning under a new system of behavior patterns as a regulator of student conduct would indicate a need for change. All their desires seem to indicate a struggle on the part of the students for a more democratic pattern in their ways of doing and a willingness to assume the responsibility involved. When the pattern of cooperation becomes developed in the new type of student government, viz., that of "International Security Assembly," the old mores concerning violation of student rules and regulations, hazing practices, and other provincial mores of dominance may give sway to a new pattern of mores centered around student thought and action in a larger concept than just the college campus.

There is some evidence, too, of the desire on the part of administration to seek student opinion, to appoint joint student-faculty-administrative committees, and to seek wider functions in the student body of the established administrative system. The traditional college social system seems to be moving into new patterns of relationships, not only student-student but student-faculty and student-faculty-administrative. New responses on the part of students are being noted; this very often provides a clue to what their teaching has been. New patterns in teaching may underlie the present-day trend in student government. Change is inherent in all these new responses.

IMPACT OF A NEW SOCIAL SYSTEM

A new social system seems to be evolving on our college campuses, brought about by new conditions and recognition of the importance of meeting needs in new ways. Ritual in indoctrination, selective mechanisms, and ways of living are, in some cases, being changed abruptly; in others, there are signs of gradual changes or changes in some parts. Prestige values to different forms of social behavior are being granted; new groups are receiving status which had not been recognized before; the usual culturally patterned behavior expected of certain positions in student life is likewise being changed. Because of the exigency of change, it is to be expected that mistakes will be made in the process.

In the daily newspaper of a large Northern university, dated October 17, 1946, under an article entitled "Sophs Will Serve with Traditions," one reads: "Organized to foster traditions, the traditions commission has developed a program for *orientation* of freshmen." "The Goon Squad, the group formerly in charge of frosh hazing, was part of the traditions commission until it was *disbanded* this year, due to the unusually large number of older students in the freshman class." According to newspapers from other college campuses, freshman hazing and initiation practices continue, except that returned veterans are exempt from wearing caps and ties.

It might be well to note the latter initiation practices. When the veterans are excluded from initiation, they are set apart as a separate group; when initiation is required of younger students, they likewise are set apart as a separate group. They are subject to practices to which another similar group is not subjected. It would seem that initiation practices should be found in which all heterogeneous units could participate in some pattern of unity. Such practices might include knowledge of the patterns of the college culture and the cultural expectancies, an understanding of the importance of social interrelationships, a discussion of the interests which unify the student body of the campus, a knowledge of the importance of social issues, and the philosophy and functions of the college's student government.

Regarding the new groups that are receiving social status on the campus, a dean of women of a strong denominational liberal arts college in the Middle West told how organized sorority-fraternity life versus the organized independent society as a part of campus life was assuming new directions in that college. The membership in the college is split in two—half are members of fraternities, half are non-members. The prestige of the independents is steadily increasing; they get offices and recognition, and definitely have a role on the campus. Some outstanding girl leaders and popular girls on the campus have been independents of their own choice. One of them had been warned when she first came to the college that "she would never amount to anything on this campus unless she was a sorority girl." She took up this challenge and joined the independents, and became one of the finest leaders on the campus.

The student newspaper of a large Midwestern university, dated July 20, 1946, announced that "Beautiful ———, sophomore, was crowned queen of the Summer Prom last night after winning one of the closest elections in campus history by four votes." The queen elected was a sorority pledge while her opponent was a member of the independents, made up of non-sorority girls. The closeness of this vote shows the rising prestige of an organized independent non-fraternity group, a prestige which is spreading from campus to campus because of the demand of a larger segment of college youth than ever before for an organization that will be more democratic in membership than the fraternity and sorority.

An innovation in fraternity life has been started at Marietta College, where a new fraternity has been founded, open to both men and women, without regard to race or religion. The society, Eta Tau Delta, was organized by a group of students who look for the development of a strong fraternal order based upon democratic principles. The traditional secrecy of Greek-letter societies was declared "out." Laying down the principle that no one would be discriminated against "because of race, religion, nationality, or sex," the society announced that it would welcome as members representatives of all groups, would seek to promote individual personality development and appreciation of all types of peoples, and would "further the efforts of the nation in forming a brotherhood of countries."

This innovation in the fraternity life of a campus is an example of what MacIver[8] proposes for a new group life in meeting the needs of our civilization. He declares that the controlling factor is the need for social education, for social re-education. The trouble, according to MacIver, lies essentially in social attitudes; the accent must not be on differences. It is not a question of the assimilation of differences, nor a question of the toleration of differences; it *is* the *reception* of the differences into the unity of the whole society, that is, each member is accepted for his own individual worth and contribution, regardless of what race etc., he might represent.

In a conference with a student from one of the older Southern colleges for women, the student remarked, "A girl can usually get into a sorority on the campus if she really wants to join. It's too bad, though, for the Jewish girls as there is no Jewish sorority on the campus." This is not a particular social attitude on the part of this one girl, who like many other college girls, is groping for an understanding of racial prejudices and who awaits encouragement from leadership to re-evaluate fraternity mores and ritual which permit a toleration of differences but do not receive the differences into the unity of the whole society. Religious and racial stratification do exist in our larger society. One has to face the fact that the college, being a community, will not be any different from the societal community. However, one should expect a college community with its higher level of intelligence and leadership to move in more democratic social directions.

A personnel worker in a large cosmopolitan college has related how a constructive attack on the problem of racial discrimination was taken by a Jewish sorority on that campus. In the constitution of their sorority it was written that "only Jewish girls can belong." Because discriminatory practices were being discussed by this campus student body, this sorority asked one of the faculty personnel workers to discuss the issue at one of their meetings. The personnel worker emphasized strongly that complaints were heard quite frequently from Jewish girls concerning discrimination by various Gentile social sororities and organizations on the campus, although a survey of many of their charters shows that discrimination

[8] R. M. MacIver, *Civilization and Group Relationships*, p. 165–169. Copyright, 1946, by Harper & Brothers.

against the Jews was not officially written in them. "It *was* officially written, however, in the Jewish constitution that only Jewish girls are to be invited into their sorority. It *is* now time to clear their own doorstep before criticizing others." The Jewish sorority then began a series of discussions; the pledge group, the actives, and the alumnae thoroughly discussed the issue. It was then taken to a near-by college whose chapter also discussed it. Finally, they all favored bringing pressure on the National Office to have this discriminatory phrase removed. They went to a national convention and were successful in having it removed from the national charter.

Personnel workers should observe especially the techniques used in this constructive process—the mediation of a strong personnel worker, the technique of discussion, and the cooperation of a group on a neighboring campus. Mainly, however, it was the technique of full discussion by everyone concerned, those in college and out, that brought to pass this constructive measure. This incident also has particular import in showing how the good functioning of a campus group can change an undemocratic selective mechanism in its own mores, and also influence the mores of a national organization which is not in line with its thinking. Since it is a national sorority organization which usually exerts its influence on a local chapter, the above incident might be termed an innovation in the sorority world.

The New York Times' survey in 1946 indicates that national intercollegiate fraternities are again playing an active role in college life. According to this survey the postwar college fraternities will be more mature; many are seeking means of bridging the gap between the fraternity and non-fraternity man. More emphasis is to be placed on scholarship and less on social activities. This trend has been caused to some extent by the return of the veteran to the college campus. At different universities and colleges over the country new inter-fraternity advisers' councils and a new inter-fraternity council constitution have been established, defining the place of the fraternities in the college. Under this system hazing is abolished, a more democratic rushing procedure has been developed, and an improvement of physical facilities is urged to meet the competition of university-operated dormitories. Greater emphasis is put on academic record. According to *The New York*

Times' survey, some presidents express themselves as follows: "Under appropriate direction the fraternity can offer a rich experience in communal living; it can play an important role on the campus, if operated on a different philosophy."

It would seem from this survey that a good start has been made in re-evaluating the fraternity mores of the college world. It remains to be seen how far the fraternity will proceed along these lines. Some definite starts for more democratic mores have already been made. It is possible, however, that the diffusion of wealth in the larger society will have its effect, as it did in the 1920's, in helping to create a snobbishness in the fraternity world.

Interviews with many deans and personnel directors yield much evidence that other new social patterns, new ways of doing things, are also in the picture of the present-day campus. Examples such as the following may be cited.

An assistant dean of a small denominational university relates that she can see certain patterns of popularity arising. Many of the girls seem particularly desirous of following certain social practices, such as drinking, because they feel the new type of man on the campus likes that, and since they have been on a "manless" campus or "man-minority" campus for several years, it is now necessary to adopt whatever pattern of popularity the occasion may demand.

This situation, in reverse, however, is shown by the remark made by a dean from a Southern Negro institution who spoke of the complaints of veterans, particularly those who had been on the campus before, against the "forwardness of their college girls." Frequent remarks were: "They weren't like this before"; "We don't want them like this"; "What has happened to the feminine grace of ———— College?"

A head resident of a girls' dormitory in a large state university stated that she noticed during the previous year that quite different types of girls had entered, girls who had been employed, or girls whose mothers had been employed. As a result, quite a different set of courtesy mores existed. Many of the social graces which college girls practiced ordinarily were lacking; an obvious example was the omission of introduction of parents and boy friends to the resident head.

In the student daily of a Midwestern campus one reads: "Last spring the Student Council started research on a marriage course to be offered by the University. A poll was taken to determine what students wanted in such a course and fairly detailed plans were drawn up for its opening in the fall. We can beat the divorce figures with education. That is the aim of students on this campus as they plan for the future and hope for a happy married life."

In the newspapers of the college world, mention is often made of the married student and his family. The struggle for role and status on the part of married students on the campus is likely to be overlooked today in studying the social patterns of student life. Riemer[9] portrays the married student as caught between two well-established patterns. First, the recreation and leisure-time activities on the university campus center around courtship between the two sexes, and the folkways of dating and dancing have been built around the tension of mate selection. Second, the married college couples find themselves without access to the "young married set" in either the professional or business world. Consequently, the married student has to arrange his social life on a more or less individual basis, which results in either almost complete isolation or making his apartment a meeting place for spontaneous gang formation among non-fraternity and non-sorority students. After the birth of their first child they select friends who struggle with similar difficulties in their everyday life. At this stage they become group conscious, and the wives organize themselves into what is usually called "Dames Club." Riemer found in case studies of married students on the campus that they were aware of the special obligations and sacrifices that were necessary because of their marriage. They expected adjustment difficulties and outright crises to arise from the clash of the different roles.

A dean of women in a denominational liberal arts college in the Middlewest related that there was an outstanding social-cleavage habit on their campus—the fraternity men date sorority women and independent men date independent women. When the fraternity veteran returned he made a change in the social system by dating and inviting to dances nice-looking girls, whether they

9 Svend Riemer, "Marriage on the Campus of the University of Washington," *American Sociological Review*, 7 : 810–815, December 1942.

were sorority girls or not, and as a result many independent girls have been attending fraternity dances. The veterans have also urged that the doors be open on dance nights to all students. "Let anyone come who wants to do so." However, civilian students, most of them students of theology and officers of the Pan-Hellenic Association, turned down this innovation. New officers have been elected with veteran representation, and the dean feels a change to a more democratic social life between fraternity and independent members will result.

One can see from these various incidents that class distinctions are being broken down by the new standards of veterans toward more democratic ways of doing things. One also can see that social patterns on the campus are being shaped by the family culture which the student brings, by behavior symptomatic of a strong sense of insecurity in regard to popularity on the campus, yet by a strong desire for stability in marriage. In an interview with a veteran who had seen three years of service in the Armed Forces, the veteran remarked that in the great diverse student body today on the campuses, which includes students of many heterogeneous experiences, a good *re-thinking* process might take place in discussions among cross sections of a student body. The thought could center around, first, *What did happen?* in which an analysis could be made of their experiences, their looseness of conduct, if necessary, and an effort to understand why *that* had happened, in other words, the social and economic forces back of behavior. Second, the thought could be centered on *What do I want?* in which efforts would be made to clarify and formulate what can come from their experiences, and how they can rehabilitate themselves and set their standards. Third, a discussion of *What ought to be?* could follow, from which youth would realize that they are the builders of tomorrow. Finally, some actual techniques should be devised from which would materialize a *plan of action*. The married students, having greater representation on the campus than ever before, need likewise to be considered in any plan. It is first of all necessary that the married student recognize that he is one of a group in the campus environment. He should be given opportunities to assemble on the campus, and the use of recreational facilities should be thrown open to his married partner who is not enrolled in the college. Cooperative efforts on a group basis may assist the individual couple to meet economic crises that develop in a situation threatened by many insecurities. The building of constructive mores on the part of *all students* is essential. Personnel workers and educators must realize more than ever that these are the young people for whose *dignity and worth* they are striving.

PRESENT-DAY IMPACT OF CAMPUS POLITICS

According to the student newspapers of twelve outstanding colleges and universities, the occasion for college politics during the summer of 1946 seemed to be the election of Summer Prom Queens, the queen candidates in each case representing the organized factions of sororities and fraternities and the non-fraternity independents. On one campus one reads of the withdrawal of candidates because of the intimidations of some of the campus political manipulators. The editor of one student campus paper sums up the political campaign as follows:

Campus leaders of the organized and independent parties each run their own organizational politics. Whenever there is a campus election, these leaders pick the persons who have been loyal to the party and seem fitted for the job to run for office. In the Independent party, a powerful political machine run by several "Independent Independents" keeps a finger on the unorganized affairs. Other independents on the campus who run contrary to the machine find their political futures are jeopardized unless they swing over to the bandwagon. The organized parties are run in much the same way. Viewing the events of the past few days from the impartial viewpoint of a newspaper editor, we would say that "When you dig up dirt on one side in any political battle, you might as well dig it up from the other side because it's always there."

One can agree with another student editor when he writes about the political situation of his campus in the following way: "The ins and outs of campus politics have long been a puzzle to many students who have not been able to see the whole picture and really the mechanics of the operations are just national politics on a smaller scale." It is true in many colleges that the campus political mores parallel those of our American society, but again the question is posed: Is it not possible for the college to create more democratic mores? Should the students not be able to see the whole picture? Need an intelligent electorate be so sluggish in its political responsibilities?

In contrast to this situation is that in a college on a university campus where a more democratic approach to elections has been worked upon. In answer to the question, "What seems to be the most significant event around which student life is centered and certain mores established?" the residence director of this college replied, "Student government association and democratic approach to elections." In answer to the query, "When and why did this event become important in student life?", the director explained how ten or more years ago the sorority social system had gained the balance of power on the campus and a veritable "spoils system" and "high-powered politics" evolved. Sorority leaders were forcing freshmen and other members to vote for a certain list of girls for student association officers, saying, "If we vote for these girls as officers, our sorority girls will be favored with such and such a position and honor." This system of politics went on until an outstanding freshman girl became a leader in the situation; she refused to vote for the list of girls presented for student government, saying, "They are not efficient people for the office." The upper classmen tried to use coercion but the freshman leader persisted in her views. Further, she called a meeting of the freshman class, asked others if they had been advised as to voting, and persuaded the class, which was the largest on the campus, to "clean up the crooked politics." The Independents, non-sorority girls, joined the freshmen. The sorority girls, realizing they were outnumbered, called a mass meeting of the entire student body; the political situation was "thrashed out." Finally, they decided to set up a plan on the order of Civil Service. An examining board consisting of five to seven members of the faculty from other schools on the university campus was set up. It was the function of this board to examine the fitness of new candidates. Girls wishing to become candidates voluntarily presented themselves for the roster. The examining board gathered information about the nominees from as many sources as possible; personnel workers sent all records available concerning the student nominees to the committee; health, ability, training, character were all considered. If none of the candidates was fit, a new name was selected by the committee.

One of the requirements for prospective candidates was a knowledge of Parliamentary Law. A Law faculty member was asked by the students to give this course on the campus. In this manner an undemocratic political system was broken up.

What were the dynamics of the second situation? First, an outstanding student leader with unflinching courage came out of the ranks. Second, a non-fraternity electorate, the "sinned against," was willing to become dynamic. Third, faculty became effectively cooperative. Perhaps a personnel worker should look into the background of this student leader. Where did she come from? What pre-collegiate influences had she experienced? What constructive forces were evident in her family life? Qualities of leadership should be studied on every campus—what are the qualities that meet situations like these? Here, the interaction of one dynamic personality in the student life of an institution was the apex in establishing a new set of democratic mores.

HOUSING PROBLEMS

In this migratory decade, a left-over from the war when men and families moved from one part of the country to another for Army Service or for work, we seem to be faced with a homeless generation. Family loyalty cannot be built on a secure solid basis which is centered around the home and privacy when people live in one half of an apartment with another family in the other half, when three or more married members of families plus the parents share homes which are usually far too small, having been built for only one family. The educational world as well as the local community or larger society is tested by this situation.

The changes which are taking place in housing on the college campuses will be bound to bring about a migratory life with its new mores in living and social life. The overcrowded dormitories, the trailers, quonset huts, auto courts, army barracks, and homettes which are being used to house the influx of students tell the story of a homeless college generation.

These changed living conditions will have destructive as well as constructive effects. Closely crowded living conditions are health hazards; they are the cause of lack of adequate rest and opportunity for meditation, and often prevent rather than promote good friendship and sociality. They may, in fact, cause actual neuroses to develop in students who have been used to privacy; they necessitate adjustments which some individuals cannot make. On the other hand, the trailers, small apartments, and homette form of living may make the college more conscious of living conditions, and students may receive more helpful suggestions as to diet and health, which they would not otherwise receive. It may promote more lasting and wholesome friendships; the families living in the small units may create a wholesome environment for the single students. Perhaps, if the college is alert to the situation, a nursery may be provided for the children of these families which would be of benefit not only to them but to the college youth interested in the care and study of children. The trailer students could organize their own government with a town hall recreation center.

Can the college community meet this situation? What can counteract this lack of family solidarity, family privacy, family loyalty, and individual development? Perhaps here is the chance to make group living a dynamic reality. Group loyalty might take the place of old-time family loyalty. A collective form of living might be worked out. Perhaps here is the great chance to work with a "down-to-earth" occasion for building up a collective way of life.

There is also a chance to structure good group relationships, and to interrelate their functioning with the actual problems of campus life. Perhaps the stern necessity of living together will help to break down clique structure and social hierarchies, which have so long existed on American campuses. This migratory and crowded type of living on college campuses today may offer one of the greatest opportunities for a group actually to *live* its relationships.

Besides these general problems of housing the great influx of students on the campuses today, there are other problems peculiar to certain campuses. The impact on the campus of this special housing problem is shown in the following incident taken from the student daily of a large university, dated July 13, 1946. The headline of the article read, "———— Court Order Forces Eviction of Veteran." The story was stated in somewhat the following manner:

The Veteran concerned saw action in New Guinea, Philippines, Leyte, Okinawa, and Japan; he received the purple heart three times, was awarded the silver star for bravery in combat during Leyte campaign; he was married and had a two year old daughter. He tried to enter this university in January, 1946, but could not find a place to live with his wife and daughter and was not admitted. Following an extensive search, the veteran found one room with kitchen privileges at $12 per week. The twenty-one year old veteran moved in in March. His landlady asked him to move shortly afterwards so that a relative might come to visit her. The ex-GI moved out, the relative arrived, and stayed one week. The landlady rented the room afterwards to a single man. The veteran then went to a new apartment above a garage which had been approved by the building inspector; it was located in a zone where apartments were forbidden except for domestic servants. The veteran's landlord made an arrangement whereby the veteran would help to maintain the grounds, and his wife would help the landlord's wife with housework and her four children. The landlord was called before court for violating the city zoning ordinance for Zone A which states: "No building to be used as a dwelling or tenement house shall be constructed or altered in the rear of or moved to the rear of a building situated on the same lot." But a clause in the same section of the ordinance reads: "These provisions shall not be construed, however, as preventing the erection, alteration, and maintenance of dwelling quarters in connection with an accessory building upon the rear of the lot, when the persons occupying such quarters are employed in domestic services on the premise." The landlord had already been given a permit to erect a garage, and to construct one room and a bath over the garage to be used by servants. The landlord was given the order by the Judge in the court "to repair the garage-apartment to conform with the original permit, allowing the erection of a garage, and on the further condition that the defendant have the family evicted from the structure."

The student paper continues:

That concludes the story up to the present, but the finish has not yet been written. We think the court has placed too much emphasis on legality in place of liberality in ordering the eviction of the veteran and his family. The veteran and his wife paid no rent, and rendered domestic services in exchange for the apartment. Yet the judge, who lives in the same zone, based his ruling on the fact that he did not consider them domestic servants.

The VA has pledged itself to back the veteran. Now they have a chance to perform a real service to one, and to all interested citizens who believe in the things for which veterans fought.

In a student newspaper from the same university, dated July 17, 1946 one reads:

Since our front page editorial on the ———— eviction case appeared last Saturday, most of the leading papers throughout the state have carried the story and backed up ———— strongly on their editorial pages. The press and radio have also publicized the case, due mainly to the efforts of the VA president. A prominent attorney and member of the legislature who won fame in the war agreed to appear as counsel in his interest. The VFW organization has also pledged its full support in fighting the eviction.

Although the end of this housing episode is not yet known, it may end in an old-fashioned "town and gown" riot. In this age of improved means of communication, this kind of a riot may have disastrous consequences. Here college students are refusing to let one of their number be a victim of a conflict between the town's aristocratic mores of Zone A and a patriotic citizen's mores. Here the impact of a housing situation in a college community may cause the institutional mores of a college to come out from the midst of "cloistered walls" and become interested in civic mores.

In the newspaper of the same university, dated July 13, 1946 appears an article entitled "Trailer Court Troubles," which affords another interesting sidelight on the impact of housing on the college community.

Of all the students attending the University, the inhabitants of the local trailer court seem to have three of the most legitimate gripes we have yet heard. First is the matter of rent. Each veteran pays $10 monthly for trailer space in accordance with a contract that he signs with the University prior to taking up residence in camp. The $10 gives him the privilege of setting up his trailer in a marked off area measuring 24 x 30 ft. and includes electricity (for lights only), water, and use of the wash-bath house. There are 44 trailers on the lot at present, which means that the University takes in $440 monthly. It cost something to erect the bathhouse and fix the grounds, but the present upkeep is very little.

The greatest of these inconveniences is the lack of an adequate drainage system. Everytime it rains the harried campers are forced to get out and hurriedly dig ditches in the hardpacked ground to turn the water away from their trailers.

The third inconvenience is that they have no telephone. If they want to make a call, it is possible for them to walk over to a dormitory but there is no possible way for anyone to call them. The wife of one of the veterans is expecting a child and has returned to her home. He has no way of receiving a phone message. There will be 50 more trailers added soon to the present site. The contract signed by the trailer owner with the University has a section that reads: "That party of the second part [the owner of the trailer] will cooperate in maintaining the trailer camp as an attractive, clean, comfortable, and desirable community. Failure to do so will lead to cancellation of the contract by the party of the first part [the University]."

The student paper writes:

Yet the party of the second part faces near-inundation every time it rains, has no telephone communication, lives in crowded conditions, and combats other inconveniences—such as no mail delivery—for a $10 monthly rental fee—the same amount of room rent paid by some students for the privilege of living in a fraternity house and enjoying all of its benefits and comforts. Many of the veterans have children to care for besides going to school and handling the other problems of homelife. In many cases both husband and wife are attending the University. The only way they can come to school is by living in a trailer. They are doing so and making the best of it. Why not give them a break?

The above quotation indicates an innovation in college mores. Here we have students challenging institutional mores for the purpose of satisfying fellow student needs and retaining constructive student mores. The right kind of interaction and interrelationship between institutional mores and student mores in this situation will create a more satisfied and integrated student.

In a student periodical of another university, dated July 3, 1946, one reads:

Plans for a new Student House is the biggest news at the Baptist Student Union at the moment. The state secretary of ——————— waxes enthusiastic when that subject comes up. Until the new house is completed, the Baptist Student Union will continue its present activities at the old location. The state secretary considers the organization completed for the summer semester, but stresses the need for more of the one hundred new Baptist students on the campus to make use of the facilities. He issues a cordial invitation to all Baptist students on the campus to come to the student house at any time and to take part in other activities of the Union.

This quotation shows how denominational mores which help a particular set of students may create a partisan identification and social cleavage on a college campus. No doubt these Baptist students are being greatly helped, but does their Student House afford a unifying influence on the campus as a whole? Should a state university's mores afford one certain group of students special privileges when, as its title indicates, it should serve on an equal basis students of all faiths, religion, races, socio-economic statuses?

Another student paper, dated July, 1946, gives an account of seventy-five men student residents of X dormitory on a university campus, who salaamed before the door to the Governor's office in the Statehouse in a demonstration against X dormitory being turned over to women residents in the fall. The men, mostly veterans of World War II, shouted the name of the hall and made sounds vaguely representing Arabs, as they covered themselves with blankets, fell upon their knees and, with arms extended, bowed repeatedly toward the open office door. Two hundred men made the trip to the statehouse from the campus in three street cars and several automobiles. They carried placards reading: "Fox holes for rent," "Nothing is too good for the Vet," "1919 no beer, 1946 no dorm," "Don't trust the trustees," "Bored of Trustees," "Residence Halls: Vets 0, Girl 6." A student in the college of commerce, a former aviation cadet, proclaimed: "We would like to have the governor recommend to the Board of Trustees of the university that X dormitory not be turned over to women in the fall. We want somebody to do something and nobody seems to want to do anything about it." A University spokesman said that it is doubtful whether the temporary housing, which is being constructed for veterans will be ready for occupancy by October first, but "there might be a miracle." The buildings, being provided by the federal government, are coming in and being erected daily and the university has priorities on materials for the project, but great difficulty has been encountered in acquiring copper wire, plumbing joints, and other materials necessary.

Another headline read: "Veterans Pitch Tents in Mock to July 4th." "Three hundred GI students clad in bathrobes and pajamas pitched tents on the campus Oval at eight last night in a "direct mock" to Independence Day. The veterans, occupants of X dormitory, planned to sleep on the ground until noon today in protest to the ruling which they consider unfair, that the dormitory must be vacated to girl students August 31."

"We're all veterans," a student at the University's law school said shortly after the students settled down in the center of the Oval. "We never thought we were coming back to things like this." This student is the publicity chairman for the committee of veterans that pleaded vainly with the university board of trustees and the governor that X dormitory, built for men with men's facilities, be kept as a men's dormitory.

This student declared that the majority of women students at the University favored the retention of X dormitory by veterans. If the five hundred men occupants are "turned out, they will be relegated to the slums," the student said. "This is not what we fought for, and not what we were promised. The substitute which the trustees propose for X dormitory is barracks. These will be ten miles from the university—and barracks! How can a man study in barracks after living in them for years under trying conditions? Psychiatrists say this is unsound."

The board refused to change its decision; the bivouac brought no results and the governor stated that the matter was up to the board. Another factor which influenced the board in its decision was the fact that the only additional housing available for students was for veterans, and women had to be taken care of through the university's own facilities.

Additional housing for approximately five hundred men was open to veterans at ————— barracks, which were formerly used by the Navy. Applications have filled the officers quarters, which house about one hundred, but only thirty-five students have asked for quarters in the former enlisted men's barracks. Making it difficult for the board to change its decision now was the fact that approximately five hundred fifty women had been notified that they would be housed in X dormitory in the fall and a change of mind would have made it necessary to notify them of the change and find new housing. Later reports of this problem stated a settlement by decree of court in favor of the university board's decision.

All such instances of present-day housing impacts on the college campus show that institutional mores of the past must be more fully adjusted to present-day student needs. The housing incident at the above institution is one that might happen on any campus. A first analysis might indicate a veteran versus girls cleavage, but on second consideration one sees in it a much deeper problem of veteran resentment and emotional disturbance. The repulsiveness of the barracks is deep-seated with the veteran. It implies regimentation, lack of freedom, inspections, and much of the part of life that he is trying to outlive. Having to give up something that "had belonged" to them was disillusioning. An appeal perhaps to their chivalry in not pushing the girls into barracks life, and a recognition on their part of the opportunity to obtain a college education may have been factors for thought and discussion on the part of the veterans. These disturbing situations in student life test the mores of administrative power. Understanding and discussion between the administration and students of all factors in disturbing situations would seem an administrative necessity. The inability to obtain building materials demonstrates rather forcefully how the housing problem of the larger society intermeshes with that of the college campus.

In answer to letters sent out by an undergraduate college in a Northern university during the war, great fear was shown among students in service, a fear that stretched all the way from the Valley of the Po to the Gulf of Leyte, that the people back on the campus, staff and students, would not take as good care of Alma Mater as her absent sons desired. They seem worried that the things they had loved about the old school had been harmed by the effects of the war or neglected by careless stewards. The fact that veterans did not want change back home was universal; home, school, church, and other ties were the only things they could see clearly in a devastating war period and in their minds were symbols of security.

According to a personnel worker in a denominational liberal arts college in the Middlewest, the housing impact on that particular campus brought about changes in the established mores of social stratification which had long existed between sorority and non-sorority girls. The crowded living conditions put girls of different sororities and even non-sorority girls together; the housemother of these particular groups remarked about the friendliness which existed; cliques were broken up; the girls from different sororities and independents or non-sorority girls dated men of the same fraternity, which was unheard of before. This housing situation, however, was being opposed, according to the dean, by a national sorority association which wants a sorority's own members to have a separate house and live together. This again affords an example of the culture of the wider community intermeshing with that of the college and creating a particular kind of mores.

Another interesting change due to the housing situation has been brought about in student sorority life in a small liberal arts college for women situated in a Middle Atlantic state. At this particular college, according to the head of a dormitory, there are six national sororities who do not have houses but rent rooms in the city for their meetings and quarters. The housing situation has lately become so complicated and there has been so much demand for rooms that they have been financially unable to hold rooms they once had. The college is in the small store section of the city; the business district is expanding toward the college and thereby advancing rents. The college in question is in the process of changing its location and new buildings are being built. The college administration would not clarify its stand on sororities, and give assurance that there would be a future for them on the new campus but the consensus of the faculty, although not openly expressed, seemed unfavorable toward them. Because of this stand of the college, the housing impact of the city, and inability of girls to meet their expenses, one of the sororities is being disbanded this year. There is not a sorority versus non-sorority cleavage on this campus, but sorority versus sorority and a great deal of rivalry for positions exists between the sororities. The present-day housing impact, however, has lessened somewhat this seemingly destructive cleavage. Besides, a lack of integration in the student body is also being brought about because of the change of the college site which has made it necessary for the girls to be placed in three different locations. As a result the student body are losing their college spirit, are complacent about world problems, and are too interested in their own little social affairs.

A staff sergeant and chief psychiatric social worker in the Army who is now teaching brought out rather forcibly the impact of housing today on the effectiveness of teaching. Many instructors are not able to move their families to the communities in which they teach. This situation is bringing about unhappy teachers, and their work with students is thereby being affected.

These housing situations present constructive and destructive practices. For the first time, perhaps, in residence history, cooperative housing and cooperative living become a dynamic reality on the college campus. Constructive group mores and relationships in these closely crowded facilities become necessary for survival. Status will depend upon each one considering duties and rights for the concern of all. The good old "tradition of the house" will vanish, and student creativity, originality as to successful ways of functioning socially, will be the focal points in building new mores.

Impact of Campus Thought and Action on the Wider Community

Throughout this chapter descriptions have been presented from both social and academic realms showing the present-day campus impacts on the wider community. More specific examples of campus thought and action in its wider context will be presented in this section.

In the July 3, 1945, edition of a university student newspaper the headline reads: "OPA Death Brings Campus Protests." Action of several types has been taken by various campus groups, notable among these that taken by veterans in sending telegrams to senators and representatives just before the President vetoed the bill passed by Congress. An article headed "We and the OPA" states:

There is one thing that we believe can be done locally. Much has been mentioned in the last few days of 'buyers' strikes'; it is possible to refuse to buy high priced items of clothing, household furnishings, and sundries. It is even possible, if the local merchants let their prices soar, to immediately establish a cooperative buying union among the students, which would buy food from smaller towns in the surrounding area. What must be done if we are to protect ourselves in any measure is to serve notice on the City Council that we are ready to take organized action should the necessity arise and it now seems quite clear the necessity has arisen.

But whatever we do must be cohesive, the action must be unified, the action must be publicized and the action must be effective.

In another university student newspaper dated April 26, 1946 one reads the following student exhortation: "Save the OPA. Write or Wire. Complacency Today Means Rising Prices, Boom, Collapse, Chaos Tomorrow."

The headlines of the same student newspaper, dated March 26, 1946, show something of the interaction of the students of this college in national and international events.

Survey tomorrow polls campus on conscription; veteran's ballot to be counted separately.

American Youth for Democracy Forum Friday on Franco Spain.

Faculty panel tonight on Labor-Management Forum; Peace committee will continue activity in permanent body.

Student Association to inaugurate a bi-weekly student opinion survey, starting next week.

Emergency council students to determine elections procedure; Investigate Winston Churchill demonstration.

We cannot help but develop a decided preconception of the definitely undemocratic character of any group belonging to an organization such as AYD.

The AYD and the Trotskyite Smokescreen.

In another student newspaper, dated October 31, 1946, one reads this student indictment against alumni:

No amount of explaining will now change the ideas of the hundreds of students who attended last Saturday's game to sit in the controversial students' seats, only to see townspeople and alumni with the choicest seats in the stadium. The college administration may present perfectly legitimate reasons for their policy, but that won't change the minds of the students. If the administration wants the students' love of his college to remain a tradition, it must run the college for the students, not for the *alumni*. An impersonal college, run as a business with business interests coming first, cannot capture the heart of any man.

This is an unusual departure from tradition in this college, as students formerly accepted the fact of favoritism to alumni.

Implications for Personnel Workers and Educators

Counts states that "Education is always a function of some particular civilization at some particular time in history."[10] Today education becomes a function of a civilization which has been subjected to the confusion, chaos, dislocations, and disillusionment of five years of war. This is indeed a time in college history when old norms will be shaken and new norms will develop. From the excerpts in this chapter dealing with student life on various campuses, it would appear that students today are creating a new way of thinking, are more adequately concerned with the stubborn necessities of modern life and society, and are actually taking action to bring to pass certain events. Some college administrators likewise are developing new mores by defining their administrative problems and policies to students and by seeking their opinions. Innovations in instructional areas can also be noted. Needs of students are being more directly stated by the students themselves to the administration and courses are being suggested also by them to meet their needs. New student mores are arising, better attuned to student needs in meeting and interacting with the impacts of the larger society. Although some old traditions and ceremonies are being retained and respected, in the main new norms in student life are in the process of being formed.

In the college world at this time it would seem opportune for educators and personnel workers to submit their institutional culture to a thoroughgoing scrutiny and analysis. New conditions create new emphases, new philosophies, new techniques of control, and new problems. The various impacts of student life—the heterogeneity of the student population, with the diversity of cultural strains and value-systems, the special adjustments to be made because of the varied type of experiences encountered, the needs of many types of students and varied ways of meeting them, the accelerated maturity and, at the same time, uncertainty and insecurity of students, the desire for more power through the student government association, the reverberations from housing situations, the questioning of the values of the college fraternity and

[10] George Counts, *Education and the Promise of America*, p. 23.

similar groups, the interest in social problems of society—all be-speak a change in the customary college student mores and the beginning of new norms for student life.

All these postwar strivings of youth have great significance for instruction, administration, guidance, and campus living. Students today, through the force of campus politics, campus thought, and action on national social events, and through the discussion of housing problems, problems of discrimination, and student government practices and aims are seeking to express themselves in the life of the campus and in that of the wider community. Personnel workers and educators should strive in this unusual swing of student life to set up well-planned goals in behalf of increasing an economic, political, and cultural democracy, not only in campus life but in life in the wider community. The campus problems involved in the above student actions are similar to problems of the larger community, that is, insufficient housing, higher living costs, increased tuition, race discrimination, and undemocratic politics. Students should feel the need to exercise their basic civil rights and to share in making decisions which affect them. Here is a chance for personnel workers and educators to work toward the social maturity necessary to win a political democracy on a campus and to play a part in securing a more democratic political world. Today when college campuses are crowded with students from working-class families, students with wives and children, students with part-time or full-time work experience in unionized industries, students who have labor and consumer problems, who have fought in other parts of the world and observed their economic systems—this would seem a more opportune time than ever before in college history to train and work for an economic democracy. Also, today when racial and religious discriminations, social stratification and social cleavages, and selective mechanisms are operative and a student body is not so rigidly trained in matters of social etiquette, it would seem opportune to develop practice toward a cultural democracy. Groups which have a fully democratic purpose should be encouraged to function.

It would seem, on this present-day campus, that no pattern dare become common policy. Considering the three aspects of personnel work, according to Lloyd-Jones and Smith[11]—the student personnel point of view, the student personnel administration, and the student personnel services—the present-day campus, in its struggle for new norms, offers the following challenges. As to the personnel point of view, the personnel worker and educator must carefully reassess their own mores in order to handle without bias the social mores of a heterogeneous student body. They must have a social understanding of student backgrounds, needs, and experiences, as well as a social sensitivity to many kinds of behavior. They must be able to visualize the kinds of cooperation needed in a social system for compatible human relationships. As to the administrative aspect, the personnel worker and educator must see structure and function in mutual relationship, and sponsor the organization which is necessary for functional campus living. They must be able to evaluate critically the purposes, rules, and norms of the groups on the campus. They should see that all campus clientele, resources, and potentialities are used. Coordination, integration, and cooperation will be needed in guidance, administration, campus living, and instruction. There is an opportunity today to overcome an "administrative-complex" by breaking away from what has been a persistent consciousness of long established rules and regulations. Personnel counselors will have delicate responsibilities; they must recognize and reconcile conflicting points of view among many types of students.

Administrators will find it advisable to define and discuss problems with students and with faculty. Flexibility in methods and policies, balance between rigidity and change, and relativity in values will become administrative necessities. As to personnel services, they must now include many more activities of compelling interest—activities which will give status, prestige, and role to many more students than was formerly the custom. The social life and extracurricular activities of all kinds for students must be further evaluated and developed. The present and future campus must offer potentialities for leadership, a laboratory for community living, and a chance for living right relationships. Students of all backgrounds must share in building the future mores.

[11] Esther Lloyd-Jones and Margaret Ruth Smith, *A Student Personnel Program for Higher Education*, p. 21.

Butts[12] has mentioned the great controversies existing in the college world—"The Great Tradition versus Social Intelligence," "Discipline versus Freedom," "The Ivory Tower versus the Watchtower," "Culture versus Cash," "Traditional Studies versus Modern Studies," "Aristocratic versus Democratic Conception of the College," "Religious versus Secular Conception of the College," "General Education versus Specialization," "The Elective versus Prescribed Studies." In his book he points up "typical conflicting points of view that have appeared in answer to the several persistent controversies in the field of college education. This has been done in the hope that it will aid citizen and educator alike to judge more adequately among the various proposals and to engage more intelligently in making policy."[13]

The college beset by all these controversies, which eventually become not controversies in ideologies but controversies between personalities, becomes blinded to the needs of its own students. If colleges, as typified in Sarah Lawrence, could study the life problems, experiences, and needs of students, their psychological attitudes and emotional patterns, perhaps better institutional mores could be developed in line with student mores, and vice versa. With helpful guidance students could then chart the course of the college if the progressive attitude is to be developed which Butts outlines so carefully after a discussion of each controversy, and if the student-life guidance program is to become an inseparable part of the educational structure of the college.

Bibliography

Butts, Freeman. *The College Charts Its Course.* New York: McGraw-Hill Book Company, Inc., 1939. 464 p.

Cantril, Hadley. *The Psychology of Social Movements.* New York: J. Wiley and Sons, Inc., 1941. 274 p.

Counts, George S. *Education and the Promise of America.* New York: The Macmillan Company, 1945. 157 p.

Crabtree, Edith. "Mutual Suspicion Blocks Full Attainment." *Themis of Zeta Tau Alpha,* 43 : 97, March 1945.

[12] By permission from *The College Charts Its Course,* by Freeman Butts, Copyrighted, 1939, by McGraw-Hill Book Co., Inc. p. 417–427.
[13] *Ibid.,* p. 417.

Crosser, P. K. "Social Change and School Adaptability." *School and Society*, 55 : 184–187, February 14, 1942.

Efron, Edith. "Old Jobs, or New Ones, for the Veterans." *New York Times Magazine*, 94 : 11, Section IV, March 18, 1945.

Efron, Edith. "The Two Joes Meet—Joe College, Joe Veteran." *New York Times Magazine*, 95 : 21, Section IV, June 16, 1946.

Hale, Lincoln B. and Hartshorne, H. *From School to College*. New Haven: Yale University Press, 1939. 446 p.

Lloyd-Jones, Esther and Smith, Margaret R. *A Student Personnel Program for Higher Education*. New York: McGraw-Hill Book Company, Inc., 1938. 322 p.

MacIver, R. M. *Civilization and Group Relationships*. New York: Harper and Brothers, 1946. 177 p.

Ogburn, W. F. *Social Change*. New York: B. W. Huebach, Inc., 1923. 365 p.

Plant, James S. *Personality and the Cultural Pattern*. New York: The Commonwealth Fund, 1937. 432 p.

"Results of the Survey of Social Life at Dartmouth College." *School and Society*, 43 : 664–665, May 16, 1936.

Riemer, Svend. "Marriage on the Campus of the University of Washington." *American Sociological Review*, 7 : 810–815, December 1942.

Rosander, A. C. "The Economic Stratification of Youth and Its Social Consequences." *Journal of Educational Research*, 32 : 592–604, April 1939.

Shelley, P. "Reconversion on the Campus." *Progressive Education*, 22 : 12–13, March 1945.

Sherif, Muzafer. *The Psychology of Social Norms*. New York: Harper and Brothers, 1930. 209 p.

Strang, Ruth. *Behavior and Background of Students in College and Secondary School*. New York: Harper and Brothers, 1937. 515 p.

Thrasher, Frederic M. "A Three-Year Program for the Fraternities of Dartmouth College." *School and Society*, 48 : 15–16, July 2, 1938.

Todd, John E. *Social Norms and the Behavior of College Students*. New York: Bureau of Publications, Teachers College, Columbia University, 1941. 190 p.

Waller, Willard. *The Veteran Comes Back*. New York: The Dryden Press, 1944. 316 p.

Warner, W. L., Havighurst, R. J., and Loeb, Martin B. *Who Shall Be Educated?* New York: Harper and Brothers, 1944. 190 p.

Warner, W. Lloyd and Lunt, Paul. *The Social Life of a Modern Community*. Yankee City Series, Vol. 1. New Haven: Yale University Press, 1941. 460 p.

Young, Kimball. *Social Attitudes*. New York: Henry Holt and Company, 1931. 382 p.

Young, Kimball. *Social Psychology*. New York: F. S. Crofts and Company, Inc., 1946. 558 p.

VIII

CONCLUSION

The FIRST premise of this study is: "The mores are ways of doing things to satisfy human needs." These ways of doing things suggest modes of behavior on the part of students in a college community. Modes of behavior may be characteristic of students as individuals or as groups. Individual ways of doing things, however, are not independent, self-contained modes of behavior, but are responsive to group-sustained mores. Descriptions have been given throughout this study to show that social behavior arises from satisfaction or frustration of the basic personality needs. The particular form which role, prestige, and status assume on a campus results from an effort to satisfy ego-integrative needs; in-group versus out-group, social stratification, and selective mechanisms operate for satisfaction of social-status needs. Traditions, customs, and folkways prevail to give status, security, and stability to student life. Innovation, invention, and diffusion take place to satisfy the need for new experiences and the need for recognition. Interpersonal relations among members of a college community are basic to the satisfaction or frustration of the need for response, the need for security, and the need for recognition of the individual. Group activities, their organization, structure, and functions contribute to the satisfaction of basic needs, such as the need to function, the need for a sense of personal worth, the need for security, or the need for social recognition. The intricate social system of every college, with its academic and student structure, and sometimes with its stratifications, cleavages, and selective mechanisms, is likewise the result of the social status needs of its constituency.

Personnel workers and educators may feel that all these individual and group activities and relationships will automatically take care of the satisfaction of student needs on their campuses. The question is: To what extent are these activities meeting the needs? Are situations for the satisfaction of the student's basic needs being studied and directed into socially desirable directions so that constructive mores will predominate in a college social system? Are these needs being satisfied through democratic rather than autocratic ways of doing things? Is the need for social recognition being satisfied through social mobility rather than through caste and class structure? Are the needs being satisfied on an intragroup basis only and not through intergroup relationships?

The second premise of this study is: "Culture sets the chief framework within which the individual learns to function with his fellows; the mores grow out of this culture." It has been hoped from this study that personnel workers and educators will see more clearly a picture of their college as a culture-matrix. The culture-matrix of each college is different from every other, depending upon its particular history, the composition of the student body, the geographical location, the special social heritage, and various other factors. The mores are indigenous to the culture of each college; there may be similarities in the cultures of certain colleges but there are likewise certain consistent differences which only the students of one particular campus will share. The genetic origin, founding, and beginning of every college have established a cultural order which leaves its imprint throughout the years of its history. This cultural order is founded on certain values and goals which become ingrained and operative in the members of a college community though folkways, faiths, codes, beliefs, philosophies, and ways of living either in one large group or among several small groups. These values, goals, and ways of doing things in a college community become modified by the culture which new students bring, by the continuity or discontinuity of the social heritage and established culture of the college as an institutional system, by the culture of the wider community, and by the physical and material equipment of the college. The mores of a particular college campus are the result of its whole cultural order. Culture is the widest context of human behavior and develops in an effort to satisfy the whole range of basic human needs. The question arises: How can personnel workers use the various cultural influences in their work with students and the college community? Too often administrative fiat is issued regarding social behavior instead of studies being made of the persistent patterns of habits, ideas, attitudes, and values. Young says, "Culture sets the chief framework within which the individual learns to function with his fellows."[1] What kind of framework does the college have? Are personnel workers conscious of the particular culture of their campuses? Are they permitting incoming groups of students to be molded by the same undesirable patterns that have persisted year after year? Do parents still pick for their newborn babies colleges which they have never seen?

The third premise of this study is: "The mores are structured by a college social system which defines positions in the system and the culturally patterned behavior expected of these positions." The very structure of a college community is itself, from the standpoint of both the faculty and the students, a matter of culture. Typical ways of behaving are reflected in the institutional structure of a college social system. Each person occupies a particular position in the social system and certain behavior is expected of him in his role in that position. The positions the various members of a college community occupy determine their participation in the culture of the campus. Sometimes these positions are structured by means of systems of prestige, selective mechanisms, material equipment, social stratification, racial cleavages, class and caste, and create mores particular to each situation. A social system usually produces what happens on a campus. Its structure and function are related: always there is *what it is* and *what it does*. What is the social system, considering its academic structure and student structure, doing to create an *esprit de corps*? Is there a systematic basis for analysis of all complaints for the purpose of establishing better morale? Is the social system promoting on the part of students democratic functioning and democratic living? What do selective mechanisms and social cleavages imply?

Does the social system function for the building of social maturity on the part of students? Social maturity implies self-support and self-management, moral responsibility, and intel-

---

[1] Kimball Young, *Social Psychology*, p. 8. Copyright, 1946, by Appleton-Century-Crofts, Inc.

lectual integrity. Physiological maturity develops naturally but social maturity must be acquired. Social adulthood is a learned mode of behavior in the social environment, a system of habits acquired. Will the college social systems of tomorrow be prolonging infancy or educating for adulthood? A social system could be planned by a college. Some blueprints must first be worked on. In this plan the totality of efforts and relationships on the part of all would be directed toward constructive values, goals, and behavior which would create mores that would be elements of force for good social control of a campus.

The fourth basic premise of this study is: "The mores are strongly conditioned by the interrelationships of persons and groups on the campus." To understand better disturbing events on a campus, the significance of a study of all interrelationships in the total picture of the college community has been stressed. Friendly, congenial relationships between administration, faculty, and students will bring about satisfaction of the basic personality needs. Leadership is a part of interpersonal relationships and contributes to the effectiveness of the group as a bearer of constructive mores. It is advocated that leadership and interpersonal relations be continuously studied by all techniques possible. It is well known that good interpersonal relationships are the *sine qua non* for constructive attitudes, good social functioning, and development of values. The question always for study in this connection is: "How can satisfactory interpersonal relationships be developed in a college community?" What structural arrangements best promote good interrelations between faculty-faculty, student-student, and student-faculty? What arrangements are made within the existing structure for meeting social-status needs, the need for recognition and response, and the ego-integrative needs? What are the techniques by which good interrelations can be effected? Are organization, functions, and activities set up for such a program? What efforts are being made toward developing college spirit which has as a basic aim good interpersonal relations?

The fifth premise of this study is: "The mores spring from the organization, structure, and functioning of groups." The types of charters, ideologies, social norms, activities, personnel, and functions which the various groups present on a campus have been emphasized as needing study. Exclusive, inclusive, and overlapping memberships of groups have likewise been stressed for consideration. Intergroup, as well as intragroup relations, have been mentioned as a field for analysis. A plan for the study of the unsupervised, spontaneous groups on a campus, which have a culture of their own and structure the campus mores uniquely, should constantly be in operation. It has been shown that the mores of students will be profoundly affected by the groups in which students participate. The style and manner of living of the group, its organization, structure, function, and social norms, should all be considered by the personnel worker as important data for understanding the mores. Personnel workers and educators are particularly urged to use all means possible in studying group behavior. Not only should they know how to describe group behavior, but they should study also the *process* of group action—the antagonisms, rivalries, coercions, cooperations, and methods of interaction by which the interests of all members of the group are served.

The question for thought on the part of the personnel worker and the educator might be: What new goals can be set up for more democratic group-sustained mores on the college campus of the future? For achieving these goals the present is a time of great challenge and leadership—a time for understanding, for courage, for tolerance on the part of all groups and classes. As MacIver says,

> We have to think in terms of new standards and new goals, and we should think of a charter, a sort of charter of human relations that needs to be set up. Our age needs a new, a somewhat different charter, a charter that will think not of the relations of individuals, but of the relations of groups, so that groups may be unified freely without loss, without prejudice within the whole.[2]

Sumner also believes that "A really great and intelligent group purpose, founded on correct knowledge and really sound judgment, can infuse into the mores a vigor and consistent character which will reach every individual with educative effect."[3] What is the great group purpose on the campuses today?

[2] R. M. MacIver, *Civilization and Group Relationships,* p. 169. Copyright, 1946, by Harper & Brothers.

[3] W. G. Sumner, *Folkways,* p. 64. Copyright, 1906, by Ginn and Company.

The preceding chapter has been devoted to a picture of present-day campuses in which the needs of the heterogeneous student bodies will have to be satisfied in many different ways and in which the varied experiences of the student body will lead to new ways of doing things. It has been pointed out in this chapter that the mores of the present student culture will need more careful study. Because of the rise in social mobility since the war, many parents who formerly could not send their children to college can now do so. The present student socio-economic base is thus wider than that in prewar times. The mores of the institution will therefore need critical evaluation. Certain customs and traditions may not satisfy the needs of the new student body. A new college spirit may have to evolve or a former college spirit may have to be revived. Much in the cultural heritage may have to be interpreted again and again in terms of present-day needs. Institutional structure, organization, and functions in keeping with "ways of democracy" may have to be reconstituted. New mores of control, built on a pattern of cooperation, responsibility, and good interrelationships between faculty and students, may have to be created. The cultural processes of innovation, invention, and diffusion will almost certainly operate to bring changes in the student mores.

As to the mores of the wider culture, this postwar era is the age of atomic energy. The world is becoming a more tightly organized world; greater struggles are being made for equalities, racial, economic, and religious, and for a science of human behavior. These mores of the wider culture should have new meaning for the campus culture, the group life, the social relationships, the town and gown relationships, the interests of alumni, the influence of national organizations, and the influence of society at large. The college might be built more into the lives of the people in the outside culture; an opportunity might arise for carrying higher culture to the "folks"; problems of the larger society peculiar to a geographical location might enter the horizons of student life. If social conditions of society at large are studied in the curricular and extracurricular activities, more insight might be gained into the social behavior of students. Group life could evolve into living relationships rather than exist on competitive in-group and out-group basis. Perhaps more clubs, such as the following which were

discovered in the yearbook of one college could be established:
Union Club, *inclusive, coordinate* social club for *all* upperclass
women; and the Lagunita Club, *inclusive, cooperative* social club
for *all* upperclass women. The words "selective," "exclusive," do
not appear here.

In the preceding chapter it was shown that this is the time in
college history when old norms are being shaken and new norms
are developing. As to the new cultural elements that are appearing on the campus, one might get help from the statement which
Linton makes:

> Actually, every element of culture has qualities of four distinct, al-
> though mutually interrelated kinds: i.e., it has form, meaning, use, and
> function. . . . The form of a trait complex will be taken to mean the
> sum and arrangement of its component behavior patterns; in other
> words that aspect of the complex whose expressions can be observed
> directly. . . . The meaning of a trait complex consists of the associa-
> tions which any society attaches to it. Such associations are subjective
> and frequently unconscious. . . . The use of any culture element is an
> expression of its relation to things external to the social-cultural con-
> figuration; its function is an expression of its relation to things within
> that configuration.[4]

The refusal of the veterans at the university cited in Chapter VII
to follow the freshman initiation rules and the old-line student
controls is an illustration of a new element of culture on a campus.
Its form was indifference and defiance of former student customs
and traditions. The meaning of this veteran action to the particular college campus where it occurred consisted of the association
which students on that campus attached to it. To the college
sophomores who were non-veterans on that campus, this action was
a violation of being "collegiate." The sophomores had always used
this custom of domination to keep the freshmen in tow, to satisfy
their desire for the dominance which had been denied them when
they were freshmen. To the veteran who had had one to five years
of war domination, the custom was silly, and he saw no use for it
at all. Certainly it had no function in his life; he was behind in his
schedule of education and was seriously eager to get on with his
learning.

[4] Ralph Linton, *The Study of Man*, p. 402–404. Copyright, 1936, by Appleton-
Century-Crofts, Inc.

How is the personnel worker and educator to work with these two conflicting groups? Perhaps he or she would be wise to review the functions of some of these prewar customs. Many of these student rules and other prewar mores will probably become obsolete because they have no function on the campus today. How, then, shall the need for dominance, for prestige, for status be met? Perhaps student mores of entirely new forms and new meanings need to be considered; a new structure may be necessary. Perhaps the needs of students for dominance, for security, and for social approval can be met by respect for work patterns demonstrated in work experiences, by respect for a social maturity that will arise out of service, not only to the college community but to the larger community outside the college. Perhaps the former rigidly controlled tendencies can be diverted, not only to democratic rights and privileges but also to democratic duties or to responsibility shared by all. The college can work for community participation projects sponsored by student government which can make a contribution of time and energy to the common good. Would it be impossible on the postwar campus with its heterogeneous population to divert the efforts of all students to some common ideal and practice, such as building together a new program of education and adult social living in the college community in which they share membership and in the larger community in which they will later live? Perhaps this will give to the non-veteran experience in the sterner realities of life and to the veteran, who has seen only strife and the stern reality of facing death, something of the joy in facing life with its opportunities in community living. Lynd says, "We watch culture change and say that 'it changes.' But culture does not 'work,' 'move,' 'change,' but is worked, is moved, is changed. It is *people* who do things, and when their habits and impulses cease to carry an institutional folkway, that bit of the culture disappears."[5] This statement of Lynd has significance in the change of traditional college institutional structure and traditional student customs which no longer can meet the standards and goals of democratic living on a campus. However, it is people who do things, and if democratic goals mean enough to people in a college

[5] Robert Lynd, *Knowledge for What?* p. 38.

community, they will bring about the collapse of autocratic structure.

For the conflicting groups on the campus today perhaps the college community needs more occasions which create unity in differences, such as *interfaith* fellowships, *intergroup* functioning, and a greater degree of congenial interrelations of all kinds. For these purposes perhaps more effort should be spent in all-college affairs that cut across ordinary group formations. Some colleges have found such affairs highly successful. For example, the daily coffee hours, the all-college breakfasts on the desert sponsored at the Junior College, Phoenix, Arizona, bring together successfully the faculty and all students. At Denison University faculty and students participate equally in the "March of Dollars Drive" to collect funds for philanthropic purposes, such as the World Student Service Fund, the Red Cross, the Sister Kenny Fund, and other worth-while projects. Another unique all-college event is the Convalescent Home Day at Leland Stanford Jr. University, when students visit a convalescent home for children and take full charge for one day, mending children's toys and helping to refurnish the home. As has been mentioned previously, another outstanding example of good all-college interrelationships is the Ham and Egg Show at Fort Valley State College, an event which brings the students, faculty, and community together for the expressed purpose of educating the community and the students who go back into the rural communities; an event which includes a folk festival when the folklore of the Negro in the particular rural section is reproduced by parents, children, and students, who join in folk dancing. For the same purpose, but of a different nature, is the Presidents' Club of Christian College, Columbia, Missouri. There the presidents of the college clubs meet to discuss leadership, plan the calendar of events, and take care of the many service projects. In the Christian movement of Elizabethtown College, Pennsylvania, students representative of all faiths participate, not only in the large group association but also in all special work committees. Other notable examples might include such events as the boat ride of Goucher College when the faculty and students charter a boat and go down the bay afternoon and evening; the all-college picnics and dances on the concrete slab at Sam Houston State Teachers College, Texas; the Clodhopper Dance of the Agricultural and Technical College of North Carolina, at which faculty and students alike wear overalls and gingham dresses; the Snow Picnics on the mountains at La Sierra College, Riverside, California, which all students and faculty attend. *Integration* can result from all such activities.

Will a new superstructure of mores take place on the college campus? Conferences with many personnel workers indicate that former routines and pre-established equilibrium have been shaken. It is possible that student life is in the process of a major social movement. It is possible that a new social system with germinal ideas and a new ideology is emerging. At the heart of every movement is some restatement or re-emphasis of values. The time seems ripe for this restatement. When we study this new movement on the campus, we are studying the particular way students will respond to new value claims, according to their needs, their situations, and their prior indoctrinations. Sumner states that, "The goodness or badness of mores consists entirely in their adjustment to the life conditions and the interests of the time and place."[6] "The mores change because conditions and interests change."[7] But, "the element of persistency in the mores is always characteristic of them."[8] "No less remarkable than the persistency of the mores is their changeableness and variation."[9]

It would seem from accounts of college student life today that the mores of a student body are a strange composite of social heritages from diverse groups and of new usages called into existence by the needs of the time. Many immature customs must give way to new and, it is hoped, more mature ways of doing things which will have greater significance for the different experiences and interests of youth today. The needs of the industrial world call for changes in curricula and differently trained young people. The difficulty of knowing the nation's social and economic needs may confuse academic and personnel programs. Compulsory military training will certainly distort the tenor of undergraduate college life until it can be fitted into an educational scheme. Today the cultural patterns are changing. Today the values of many tra-

[6] W. G. Sumner, *op. cit.*, p. 79.
[7] *Ibid.*, p. 84.   [8] *Ibid.*, p. 80.   [9] *Ibid.*, p. 84.

ditions are being questioned, yet there is also seen on some campuses an urge to have them maintained. Status and role are indefinite, and groups that were broken up during the war period are having trouble getting re-established. Their old norms are not sufficient to meet the new needs. Student bodies are clamoring for a different type of teaching from that which they are receiving. Teachers are still retreating to the abstract and absolute instead of studying the society in which they live. A persistence of the traditional mores of teaching still prevails and yet it is known that changeableness and variation in the mores can occur. As Lynd says, culture is changed but it must be done by people. What a challenge for the college community—a community which represents the highest form of education, which is comprised of persons who should be flexible, adaptable, interested in change! Teachers must fit into the mores of the situation but at the same time must work, not only to transmit the social heritage and mores but also to criticize and reform them.

There is no doubt that a new social situation has developed on the college campus. A disintegration has taken place in housing conditions, old rules and regulations are being questioned, faculty personnel has changed, curricular programs are crowded and upset, and old philosophies and methods of teaching are questioned. There is indeed the problem of adjustment of institutional equilibrium. There is the problem of renewing vitality and at the same time maintaining stability. The two characteristics of the mores—persistency and variability—hold the solution of the present crisis. The whole problem involves a process of experimentation, development, adjustment, and an evaluation of past experiences in the light of current conditions. On this point Benedict postulates that

It is only the inevitable cultural lag that makes us insist that the old must be discovered again in the new, that there is no solution but to find the old certainty and stability in the new plasticity. The recognition of cultural relativity carries with it its own values, which need not be those of the absolutist philosophies.[10]

Perhaps an entirely new sense of direction, a design for an entirely

10 Ruth Benedict, *Patterns of Culture*, p. 278. Copyright, 1934, by Houghton Mifflin Company.

new social system on the campus, can be worked out. Legislation, to be strong, must be consistent with the mores; since the mores are in a state of flux, legislation therefore should be flexible until a new social system on the campus is formed. Linton says,

Patterns are derived from behavior and may be modified by it. If a new social situation develops . . . the behavior between individuals standing in the new relationship will at first be unpatterned. However, the possible behavior . . . will be limited and circumscribed by the pre-existing patterns of the system. In time those standing in the new relationship will develop forms of behavior which are simultaneously effective in the new relationship and compatible with pre-existing patterns. . . . Finally, these new developments in behavior will be reduced to a pattern and incorporated into the social system.[11]

What will these new behavior patterns be? Here lies a challenge for great opportunities to the college world to build what they want, to create real community living with an interaction and assimilation of diverse groups, and to have a chance to live relationships even amid crowded conditions.

Social behavior is learned and acquired; constructive mores are built through the cooperation of the whole college community and all the influences that impinge upon it: the trustees, the president, the faculty, the students, the parents, the alumni, the local community, the national organizations, and the wider culture. A college community should consider itself a society in that it is an organized group of people who have learned to work together. As a society, it is also working for a way of life, or a culture which is an organized group of behavior patterns. What are the behavior patterns that will build the future mores and make them factors of social control of student life on a campus? These will depend upon the personnel workers' and the educators' understanding of the mores, and their ability to discern elements in them, particularly the elements of force. This is a time in the history of a college community that calls for new plans, new techniques, new vision, new mores. According to the periodicity of swings in patterns, ten or twenty years from now the social situation may change radically again. Different plans, different techniques, and different mores will be developed in the process of changing the social system that

---

[11] Ralph Linton, *The Study of Man*, p. 106.

is being formed today. Personnel workers and educators must be alert to change, to an understanding that mores must fit into life conditions and interests. They must be aware that the mores have persistence and yet variability, two qualities which make them strong factors for social control. They must understand them, study them, and if necessary work for their modification. What are the multifarious workings of the mores in your college community?

Bibliography

Benedict, Ruth. *Patterns of Culture.* Boston: Houghton Mifflin Company, 1934. 290 p.

Boaz, Franz. *Anthropology and Modern Life.* New York: W. W. Norton and Company, Inc., 1932. 255 p.

Linton, Ralph. *The Science of Man in the World Crisis.* New York: Columbia University Press, 1945. 532 p.

Linton, Ralph. *The Study of Man.* New York: D. Appleton-Century Company, Inc., 1936. 503 p.

Lynd, Robert S. *Knowledge for What?* Princeton: Princeton University Press, 1939. 268 p.

MacIver, R. M. *Civilization and Group Relationships.* New York: Harper and Brothers, 1946. 177 p.

Ogburn, W. F. *Social Change.* New York: B. W. Huebsch, Inc., 1923. 365 p.

Parsons, P. A. "A State University Reaches Out." *Educational Record,* 12 : 450–459, October 1931.

Sumner, W. G. *Folkways.* Boston: Ginn and Company, 1906. 692 p.

Young, Kimball. *Social Psychology.* New York: F. S. Crofts and Company, Inc., 1946. 558 p.

Appendix

Appendix

PLANS AND TECHNIQUES FOR RESEARCH ON THE MORES OF STUDENTS ON A COLLEGE CAMPUS

An Outline for the Study of the Physical and Material Culture of the College and the Composition of Student Body

A. The college setting
   1. Physical data.
      a. Location—compactness of college unit.
      b. Material culture—types of buildings.
      c. Adequacy of rooming and boarding facilities—furnishings.
      d. Relation of location of college to its environment.
         (1) Cultural facilities.
         (2) Cities accessible, etc.
      e. Recreational facilities of college. What is the use of the social room?
   2. Historical data.

B. Composition of student body (various ratios)
   1. Classification by age, sex, married, non-married.
   2. Classification into dormitory groupings, off-campus residence, commuters, etc.
   3. Classification by home residence—state, region, cities, rural.
   4. Classification by socio-economic status.
   5. Classification into fraternity and non-fraternity.
   6. Classification into curricula or course pursued.
   7. Classification by extracurricular participation.
   8. Classification by work status (part-time, full-time).
   9. Classification into groups whose parents were college graduates, non-college graduates, alumni of this college.

Note: To obtain the information as classified under B, one can use personnel cards, registrar's office records, and other objective records which may be available.

Schedule on Community Environment*

1. How many students live in its homes?
2. How many students work in its enterprises?
3. How many students mingle in its social life?
4. How many students patronize its amusements?
5. How many students attend its churches?
6. Is there an attitude of hospitality or exploitation?
   What evidences? ....
7. Is the town considerate of student welfare?
8. What types of social places are provided?
9. Do churches and other organizations plan programs and socials for students?

Schedule on College Culture Complex

(Interviews with faculty, students, alumni; analysis from historical
accounts, records, newspaper, etc.)

1. What elements in the student culture were taken over through imitation of other college campuses?
2. How has diffusion of borrowed cultural elements taken place?
   a. Are elements taken over because they are useful?
   b. Is it in *form* or in *meaning*, or in both, that borrowed elements become integrated into the new culture?
   c. What adaptive changes are made? What new interpretations are made and to serve what new ends?
3. What elements are revived in the student culture by re-emphasis?
4. Is there borrowing between groups on the campus?
5. What will each group allow others to borrow?
6. What maladjustments or group discontents exist within this college culture? Do they arise through:
   a. Presence of newly invented customs or innovations?
   b. Observation of other college cultures?
   c. Internal origin—within the culture itself?
   d. Conflict between culture and its environment?
   e. Factors of change, such as influence of the automobile, radio, etc.
7. What are the needs to which the new customs are responses?
8. Who are the innovators and imitators? Why are they discontented with their *status quo*? Is it lack of prestige? Subjection to inferior status? For practical advantage? Mobility of group?

* *Note:* This information can be obtained from the community agencies, from the deans of students, from students, and records.

9. What is the extent of receptivity?
   a. What groups accept? What do not?
   b. What are the elements accepted? Rejected?
   c. Why are elements rejected?
   d. What are the *particular* interests which dominate the life of the receiving group?
   e. Does the prestige of the donor group have anything to do with acceptance of new elements?
   f. What "minor fads" are received wholesale without question of their utility or prestige?
10. Where do new cultural elements disseminate?
   a. Is there a dissemination to certain categories, as age groups, sex groups?
11. In what way are they disseminated?
   a. Do students with less prestige take over elements of higher prestige?
   b. Do students with more prestige take over elements of lower prestige?

Schedule on Mores Due to Control Through Indoctrination, Authority, Exploitation, etc.

(Interviews with student leaders, and faculty sponsors)

1. What groups rival or compete with one another?
2. What is the ultimate source of authority for this group? Leader of the group? Faculty sponsor? President of college?
3. By whom was the authority delegated?
4. What democratic procedures are used?
5. What are the admissions criteria and qualifications for prospective members?
6. What is the compulsive dominance of the group?
   a. Punishment of those who do not conform? Instruments and means used to elicit and suppress behavior?

Questionnaire on Student Government Submitted to Student Government Executive Officers

1. What considerations enter into the choice of student representatives on student government bodies?
   .... Previous scholarship.
   .... Weight of present schedule.
   .... Participation in other extracurricular interests.
   .... Representative of college classes, i.e., freshman, sophomore, etc.
   .... Representative of social groups, i.e., fraternities, clubs.
2. In the following list, place an (x) before each item on which the student government organization holds power, adding any other items at the end of the list:

.... Development of an honor system.

.... Handling of fire prevention and other safety provisions.

.... Promotion of student participation in extracurricular activities.

.... Regulation of student life as regards conduct.

.... Handling of chaperonage.

.... Supervision of church attendance.

.... Supervision of chapel attendance.

.... Handling of student organization funds.

.... Regulation of student absences.

.... Publishing of handbooks.

.... Handling of disciplinary cases.

.... Control over dormitories, clubs, and fraternities.

.... Other ....

3. List, in order, the three items checked in question above which receive the greatest amount of attention from the student government organization: 1st ....
Most attention   2nd ....
3rd ....

4. Check which: Does the college undertake to handle dishonesty and dishonorable conduct on the part of students:

.... 1. By individual faculty watchfulness?

.... 2. By cultivation of unfavorable sentiment within the student body?

.... 3. By student honor system?

.... 4. By no formal means whatever, leaving the matter to college traditions, student opinion, and personal attitude?

5. Is your self-government organization a member of a similar intercollegiate organization? Yes ...... No ...... If so, which one ....
....

6. What is the present attitude of the faculty toward self-government?
...... very favorable ...... favorable ...... neutral ...... opposed
...... strongly opposed.

7. Can you detect any difference in the attitudes of seniors and freshmen toward self-government? ......

Schedule on Student-Alumni Relationship

(Questions asked of leaders of each group)

1. What force is exercised by national chapters or alumni upon your group?
2. Do alumni suggest members for your group?
3. Does the group transcend the authority of the alumni?
4. Do the alumni grant rewards, prizes, etc., for events held by your group?
5. What influence do faculty alumni exert?
6. What money raising methods do they advocate?

Schedule on Relationship of Student Mores to Societal Influences

(Faculty interviews: Members of faculty, deans, president. Also analysis of handbooks, yearbooks, newspapers)

1. What has been the influence of societal pressures on students over 5- to 10-year periods since you have been at this college?
2. What changes came about with the use of the automobile, radio, cigarettes? What restrictions, if any, on the radio, automobile, and cigarettes?
3. What student habits changed during and after World War I? World War II? The depression?
4. What changes are now taking place?
   a. Types of curricula chosen by students.
   b. Democracy of student elections.
   c. More pleasure activities or less.
   d. Individualism or collective action.
   e. Rules—regulations—chaperonage—class-attendance system.
   f. Morale of student body.
   g. Interest in religion.
   h. Social mingling.
   i. Most popular diversions.
   j. Role of women on the campus.
   k. Interest in political or labor events.
   l. Interest in international affairs.
   m. Tendency among groups for larger scale planning than formerly.
   n. More leadership in the last ten years? Less or more organization?
   o. More or less social cleavage, class consciousness?
   p. More or less sense of security on the part of students?
   q. Hobbies in evidence on campus which parallel societal influences.
   r. Slogans on the campus which are reflections of some underlying social condition in society at large.
5. Effect of outside community upon social problems of the campus.
   a. Use of leisure time.
   b. Number of students living in the town community.
   c. "Control" culture of campus a reflection of the outside community.

Schedule on Social Structure

(Use of Chapin's Sociological Graphs and Moreno's Sociogram)

Graphs
1. Amount of participation of members in groups.
2. Number holding offices on the campus.

3. Honors received:
   Membership in honorary societies.
   Dean's list.
   Athletic awards, etc.
4. Scholastic standing.
5. Popularity Index:
   a. Number of "isolates" or "stars of attraction."
   b. Number of members attending dances.
   c. Number of boy friends and girl friends each member has.
   d. Type of social functions attended.

Sociometric Technique (Could be administered to each group)

Questions
1. With whom in this group would you like to attend a movie?
2. Beside whom would you like to sit at your table in the dining-room?
3. With whom in this group would you like to work on a committee?
4. Whom would you like to help you represent this group at a faculty committee meeting?
5. With whom would you like to share a room?
6. With whom outside this group would you most like to associate?

Schedule on Ceremonies and Ritual

(Interview *before* the rite takes place)

Old members:
1. What do you expect of the group from this ritual?
2. What faiths, beliefs, rules will be established?
3. What is the role of the novitiate? Will it heighten or subordinate his status as a newcomer?

Novitiates:
1. What do you expect from this ceremony?
2. Have you ever been in a ceremony before?

(Interview *after* the rite takes place)

Novitiates:
1. How did you feel about the ceremony?
2. In what way did the ceremony most impress you?

Further Things To Be Observed During Ceremony:
1. What evidences of cohesiveness are evident and how are they furthered by the ceremony? What ceremonial oaths, prayers, lighting effects, etc.?
2. What do the symbolic acts reflect? Religion?

3. What does the novice promise? Are promises made to fellow members only, or are they made to non-members also? Is there only in-group morality?

4. To what pattern does the motif of the ceremony belong?

5. With what doctrines or principles does the society or group seek to indoctrinate the novitiate?

6. What follows the ceremony? Are there lectures? What values are inherent in them?

7. What are the interrelations of the words and actions with the symbols and signs?

Schedule for Members of Sororities, Fraternities and Non-Fraternity Members

(Social Class Structure)

Name of group ....

Date ....

Persons interviewed ....

Remarks ....

1. What proportion of girls attending your fraternity dances are local college girls? ....

2. If girls invited are not local college girls, from what college are they invited? ....

3. What percentage of town girls, not college students, are invited? .... Outside towns? ....

4. What proportion of girls attending your fraternity dances are sorority girls? ....

5. Girls from what sorority are chosen most often for your dances? ....
   ....

6. How many of your fraternity members attend all-college, non-fraternity dances? ....

7. What girls do the men of your fraternity most often date?
   a. College girls ....
   b. Local town girls ....
   c. Out-of-town college girls ....
   d. Out-of-town non-college girls ....

8. How do they entertain their dates?
   a. If a date with a college girl:
      (1) spend the evening at the dormitory ....
      (2) attend the movies ....
      (3) go out-of-town ...... by bus ...... by automobile ......
   b. If a date with town girl:
      (1) spend the evening at girl's home ......
      (2) attend the movies ......

(3) go out of town ...... to movies ...... other places ......

(4) attend college affairs ......

9. What is approximately the amount of money spent?

   a. For corsage for a college girl .... sorority .... non-sorority ....

   b. For date expenses with college girl .... sorority .... non-sorority ....

   c. For date expenses with town girl ....

10. What proportion of your men are invited and attend?

    a. Sorority dances .... What sorority ....

    b. Non-sorority affairs ....

    c. Parties by town girls ....

11. What proportion of your men are invited but do not attend?

    a. Sorority dances .... What sorority ....

    b. Non-sorority affairs ....

    c. Parties by town girls ....

12. What are some criteria in the estimation of men for popularity of women on this campus?

(This same form can be used for sorority, and non-sorority, and non-fraternity with changes in wording.)

Note: Further verification of this schedule's results can be made through analysis of social registers of clubs, and rooming residences where permission records are kept of students' activities.

Schedule for Interrelation of Persons and Groups

Student's name ....

Club membership ....

Type of residence ....

Class: ....

Socio-economic status: ....

1. Are you a member of the clubs you want to join? Yes ...... No ......
   If not, why not? ....

2. Are you receiving from these clubs what you would like to have received?
   Yes ...... No ...... If not, why not? ....
   ....

3. Is there competition in the group to which you belong? Yes ...... No
   ...... State the form of competition ....
   ....

4. What clubs did you want to join that you have not already joined? ....
   ....

5. Why did you want to join these clubs or club? ....

   Note: Socio-economic status will be that defined by Personnel Record Form.

6. Do your club meeting-places serve as a retreat? Yes ...... No ......
Explain ....

7. Of what class do students exert a dominating influence over you? ....
....

8. What freshman hazing practices did you most dislike? ....
.... Why? ....

9. If an upperclassman, what hazing practices do you insist upon? ....
.... Why? ....

10. What are the goals of students here? ....

11. What students do you like most here? (You may designate individuals or groups.) .... Why? ....

12. What students do you respect most here? ....
Why? ....

13. What fraternity do you like most? ....
Why? ....

14. What sorority do you like most? ....
Why? ....

15. What are the things which most unite students on this campus? ....
....

16. What are the things which separate most the students on this campus?
....

17. What discrimination, if any, exists on the campus? Among students ....
.... Among faculty ....

18. Do you have as many dates as you want? ...... Yes ...... No ......
Why not? ....

19. Which experience in your student life has been most pleasant to you?
....

20. Which experience in your student life has been most unpleasant to you?
....

21. Do you know your faculty as well as you would like? Yes ...... No ......
If negative, why not? ....

22. What faculty do you like most? ....
Respect most? .... Why? ....

23. Do you have as much money as you would like to spend? ....

24. How much do you spend a week for pleasure? ....

25. Have you had experience in your extracurricular work in initiating and carrying out plans? ...... In completing a task successfully ...... Explain ....

26. Are there social conventions here which seem to handicap you? ......
Explain ....

Schedule on Evaluation of Leaders

(Evaluation by members of groups; evaluation by faculty sponsors)

1. Do the members faithfully report to meetings of the club, of various committees, and for other functions? Yes ...... No ......
2. Are there habitually complaints and grievances? Yes ...... No ...... What kind of complaints ....
3. Can the leader of this group handle difficult individuals? Yes ...... No ......
4. Does he encourage initiative from the group? ......
5. Does he know how to distribute responsibility? ......
6. Can he manage conflicts between sub-groups? ......
7. Can he coordinate efforts? ......
8. Is there cooperation in the group? ......
9. Does the leader have a dominating attitude? ......
10. Does the leader have a submissive attitude? ......
11. Has the group had contacts with other groups? ......
12. Is the group as self-directing as its stage of development makes possible? ......
13. Is the group showing itself capable of selecting leaders? ......
14. Does the leader make a positive contribution to the group's activities? ......
15. Does the leader represent constructive values? ......
16. Is the leader sincere with this group? ......
17. Is the leader sensitive to the personal needs of members of the group? ......
18. Is the leader accepted by the group? ......
19. Does the leader follow the ordinary customs, traditions, etc.? ......
20. In what respects does the leader fall down? ....
21. Which leader do you most esteem on the campus? ....
22. What faculty are most esteemed as leaders? .... Why? ....

Schedule on Evaluation of Groups

Faculty at large .... Sponsors ....
....
    Student members of groups   Students at large
1. Which groups carry out best their purposes?
....
2. Which groups perform functions efficiently? ....
3. Which groups most meet the needs of their members for:
    a. Prestige on the campus? ....

b. Self-development? ....

c. Practical usefulness in later life? ....

4. Which group develops the most capable leadership? ....

5. Which groups are self-centered, snobbish? ....

6. Which groups have the best social habits? ....

7. Which groups best develop cooperation within the group, cooperation with other groups, and cooperation with the college as a whole? ....
....

8. Which groups have good control and influence on the campus? ....
....

Note: For evaluation by group sponsors and group members, questions should be worded, "Does This Group? ...."

Schedule on Folkways

(Interviews with students falling under various classifications as outlined on page 279)

A. Folkways of Spending

1. When and where do "eating" dates occur?
2. What is the usual refreshment?
3. Are refreshments "dutch treat" or on the men?
4. What group of girls are more likely to go "dutch treat" with the men?
5. What group of men expect girls to "dutch treat"?
6. Do girls buy their own tickets for college amusements?
7. What are the occasions for a "must" in corsage giving? To what girls must the man give corsages?
8. Are there some groups which have special spending practices?
9. Must members be of the "right kind" before money is spent?
10. What is the extent of "room" parties? What groups particularly have them?
11. What vending machines and how many are in the different dormitories?
12. On what occasions must one spend money?
13. Are the same compulsions for spending exercised by students working their way through college?

B. Reading Habits

1. What popular magazines are most read? Check with librarian:
   a. Books read which are not used for courses—fiction and non-fiction.
   b. Amount of periodical reading.
   c. Reading habits.

C. Smoking and Drinking

1. When does one feel a social obligation to smoke?

2. Where are the places where one always smokes?
3. Where does one not smoke?
4. Where is drinking likely to take place? Among what groups?
5. What is the social obligation in drinking habits?
6. Is there a universal attitude against drinking?

Note: Town opinion and faculty opinion should be secured, if possible, on habits of college students.

D. Habits of Discussion
   1. What are the topics most discussed outside formal group meetings?
   2. On what questions is there strong feeling?
   3. Where are the most interesting discussions likely to take place?
   4. How do different persons and groups face questions?
   5. What are the burning questions today?
   6. What is the respect of each sex for the other on opinions?

Note: Follow-up with analysis of college newspaper articles and themes of English classes.

Outline for the Description of Groups*

I. Identity
   1. Group limits.
      a. Exclusive; as by age, locality, sex, social status.
      b. Restricted; as when members must subscribe to certain conditions. (Subscribe to a creed, conform to certain conditions.)
      c. Inclusive; open to all.
   2. Entrance and exit; voluntary, involuntary, by election.
   3. Identification of members; how recognized, as by name, garb, insignia.

II. Composition
   1. Size or number of elements, i.e., persons or units; kinds of elements.
   2. Homogeneity or diversity of membership; degree of common membership in other groups; social distance.
   3. Stratification or uniformation; classes, social distinction.
   4. Permanent or shifting membership; stability or instability.

III. Intergroup Relationships
   1. Independent and autonomous.
   2. Federated, semi-autonomous.
   3. Chartered—controlled.
   4. Degree of dominance.

* Dwight Sanderson, "Group Description," *Social Forces,* 16:313, March 1938. Reprinted with the permission of the publishers, The Williams & Wilkins Company.

IV. Intragroup Relationships
  1. Forms of interaction between members.
    a. Personal or impersonal, representative, fiduciary.
    b. Contacts—frequency and character of.
    c. Participation—forms and degree of.
    d. Quality or type of participation—competitive, cooperative, domestic, fraternal, etc.
    e. Solidarity—degree of awareness.
    f. Group control of behavior of members—degree of primary loyalty.
    g. Group folkways and mores.
    h. Language peculiarities.
    i. Place of role of certain individuals.
  2. Spatial relationships.
    a. Area covered.
    b. Density or dispersity of group.
    c. Place of meeting.
  3. Temporal relationships.
    a. Temporary, continuous, or seasoned group.
    b. History and traditions.

V. Structure and Mechanism
  1. Leader, type and origin (how selected and if from group).
  2. Subgroups, committees.
  3. Stated aim and purpose, with or without; unity or diversity, broad or specialized.
  4. Code of behavior for members, definite or lacking.
  5. Means of consensus: meetings, discussions, journal, parliamentary procedure, etc.
  6. Means of developing and maintaining morale.
  7. Extent of institutionalization—ritual, ceremonial, insignia, custom, initiation.
  8. Mechanisms for group maintenance or preservation.
    a. Through history and traditions—records, histories.
    b. Through means for homogeneity—party whip, tithing man, committees to secure acquaintance and participation.
    c. For preventing aggression—price agreements, strikes, lockouts, funds, alliances.
    d. For preventing crisis—vice-president, constitutions, parliamentary procedure, reserve funds.
    e. For securing adaptation, or revision of organization—inventory, surveys, conventions, special committees.
    f. For secrecy or privacy—oath, password, grip, etc.
  9. Physical basis or essential physical equipment.

Bibliography for Social Research

Bickham, M. H. "Making Social Analyses of College Communities." *Journal of Educational Sociology,* 2 : 514–519, May 1929.

Brown, Clara M. "A Social Activities Survey." *Journal of Higher Education,* 8 : 257–264, May 1937.

Chapin, Francis Stuart. "Research Studies of Extra-Curricular Activities and Their Significance in Reflecting Social Changes." *Journal of Educational Sociology,* 4 : 491–498, April 1931.

Chapple, E. D. "Measuring Human Relations: An Introduction to the Study of the Interaction of Individuals." *Genetic Psychology Monographs,* 22 : 3–147, February 1940.

Coyle, Grace. *Studies in Group Behavior.* New York: Association Press, 1937. 258 p.

Ellsworth, Allen S. and Bogardus, Emory S. "Measurement in Group Work." *Sociology and Social Research,* 23 : 62–70, September–October 1938.

Fry, C. Luther. *The Technique of Social Investigation.* New York: Harper and Brothers, 1934. 315 p.

Hulett, J. E. "Interviewing and Social Research; Basic Problems of the First Field Trip." *Social Forces,* 16 : 358–366, March 1938.

Johnson, Alvin D. "An Attempt at Change in Inter-Personal Relationships." *Sociometry,* 2 : 43–48, July 1939.

Katz, Daniel. "Attitude Measurement as a Method in Social Psychology." *Social Forces,* 15 : 479–482, May 1937.

Odum, Howard W. and Jocher, Katharine. *An Introduction to Social Research.* New York: Henry Holt and Company, 1929. 488 p.

Rice, Stuart A. *Methods in Social Science: A Case Book.* Chicago: University of Chicago Press, 1931. 822 p.

Sanderson, Dwight. "Group Description." *Social Forces,* 16 : 309–320, March 1938.

Strang, Ruth. *Group Activities in College and Secondary School.* New York: Harper and Brothers, 1941. Chap. XII, pp. 292–300.

Thrasher, Frederic M. "How to Study the Boys' Gang in the Open." *Journal of Educational Sociology,* 1 : 244–254, January 1928.

INDEX

Academic structure, 108–116
  Effect on student mores, 114, 115
  Intellectual status in, 113
  Place in,
    Departmental, 108, 109
    Institutional, 108
    Personal, 109, 110
  Prestige mores of, 140
  Roles in, 111
  Social status in, 111
  Status in, 110–115
Adjustment. *See* Veteran adjustment
Administrative fiat, 21, 23, 50, 147, 266
Administrative mores
  Controls as shown in,
    Denominational colleges, 54, 55
    Liberal arts college's catalogues, 51–53
    Regulations, 66
    Selective mechanisms, 141
    Southern state college for women, 55
    Western university, 53, 54
  Impacts on,
    By alumni, 84
    By faculty, community, and students, 90, 91
    By students in northern university, 234, 235
  New trends of, 238, 259
  Significance of campus in transition for, 261, 262
  Student needs and, 255
  Students' challenge to, 251, 252
  Test of, 255
  Veterans' complaints against, 220
Admissions. *See* Alumni, influence of; Selective mechanisms, student structuring and
Age-sex and social group system
  See Social system, description of, on a large campus
Agricultural colleges
  In South
    Clodhopper Dance of Agricultural and Technical College of North Carolina, 272, 273
  In Southwest
    Ways of arousing college spirit, 44

Allen, Frederick Lewis
  See Society at large, 1920's and 1930's in colleges
Alumni
  Implications for personnel workers and educators of, 85
  Influence of, 79–85
    In admission programs, 82, 83
    In denominational colleges, 84, 85
    In relationship to college, and vice versa, 81, 82, 83, 85
    In undergraduate relations, 80, 81, 82
    Schedule for study of, 282
    Student indictment against, 258
  Regressive tendencies of, 84
Antioch College, 7
  Design for living at, 206
Architectural designs and social-cultural patterns. *See* Fraternity-sorority world
Athletic activities
  Group unity and, 177, 178
Attitude formation
  In ceremonies, 58
  Faculty attitudes and, 20
  Interpersonal relationships and, 169
  See also Bennington College
Authoritarian mores
  Breakdown of, 91

Barnard College
  Curricular innovations, 230
Benedict, Ruth
  Cultural lag, 274
Bennington College, 7
  Attitude formation in, 18–21
  See also Change of mores
Blake, Patricia
  College girls' dress, 16, 17
Borrowing, 15–16, 17
  Practical dominance in, 15, 16
  Psychological dominance in, 16
  Schedule for study of, 280
Bucknell University
  Faculty-student Congress at, 7
Butts, Freeman
  Controversies in college world, 262

Campus in transition
  Implications for personnel workers and educators of, 259–263
  Old norms and new, 259
    Scrutiny of institutional culture, 259
    Significance for instruction, administration, guidance, and campus living, 260–263
Canby, Henry S.
  Interactive influences of town and gown, 88, 89
Cedar Crest College
  Change in mores, 232
Ceremony and ritual, 58–61
  Dangers of, 66
  Group unity in, 59
  In-group morality of, 60
  Psychological aspects of, 58
  Schedule for study of, 284, 285
  Social dynamics of, 60, 61
    In junior college of Southwest, 61
Change of mores, 17–23
  Alertness for, 276
  Attitudes and, 169
  Cultural processes and, 11–17
  Established college members and, 23
  In Bennington College community, 18–22
  Overt expression in, 21
  Patterns and periodicity of swings in, 21–23
  Who brings about, 17, 18, 271
  See also Administrative fiat; Curricular innovations
Chapin, Stuart F.
  See Groups on a college campus, structure of, sociological graphs; National organizations, importance of
Characteristics of mores, 10
  Goodness or badness of, 273
  In veteran adjustment, 222, 223
  Persistency and changeableness, 273
  Solution of present crisis, 274
Choice analysis, 162, 163
  Contact range, 162
  Purpose, 163
Christian College, Columbia, Missouri
  Presidents' Club of, 272
City College of New York
  Curricular innovation, 230, 233
Cliques
  Building structure and, 132
  Constructive housing impact on, 255, 256
  Faculty, 185

Cliques (Cont.):
  Implications for personnel workers and educators of, 204, 205
  Informal structure in, 183–186
    Positive and negative aspects of, 184
  Interrelationships based on, 146
  Spontaneous groups and, 179
Cole, Luella
  See Cliques, faculty
College as a culture-matrix, 27 ff.
  Challenge to personnel worker of, 265
  Need for analysis of institutional, 259, 260
  Three interactive elements of, 27 ff.
    Culture which student brings, 28–34
    Physical and material culture, 68–75
    Summary and implications of, 74–76
    Traditional and established culture of college, 34–68
      Mores of control in, 51–68
      Social heritage of, 34–51
College of William and Mary
  Tradition from the outside, 36
Colleges
  Eastern
    Cultural inferiority in, 16
    New impact of student government in, 236
    Selective mechanism in, 127
  Midwestern
    College spirit of "friendliness," 42, 43
    Marriage course at, 244
    Prestige of new group "Independents," 240
  New England
    Alumni influence and, 83
    Social cleavages in fraternities of, 123
    Veterans and traditions of, 83
  Pennsylvania
    Conflict between "Joe College" and "Joe Veteran" in, 221–224
    Culture complex of, 52
    Illustration of new cultural element in, 270, 271
    Location and problems of larger society in, 68
    War mores vs. civilian mores in, 158, 159
  Rural
    College spirit of "honesty" in, 41
    Cultural backgrounds in, 30, 31
    Doctrines of community and, 86
    Emotional effect of student liberalization, 148

Colleges, Rural, (*Cont*.):
  Failure in student government of, 64
Southern
  Selective mechanism in, 128
  Veterans and social maturity, 214
Southern College for Women
  College spirit of "self-government," 42
  Student statement of sorority life in, 241
College spirit, 41–45
  Development of the individual. *See* Negro colleges
  "Face values." *See* Junior colleges, Phoenix, Arizona
  "Friendliness." *See* Colleges, Midwestern
  "Honesty," 41
  "Loyalty to old river." *See* Denominational colleges, Southwestern
  "Oscar P." *See* Agricultural colleges in Southwest
  "Religion." *See* Denominational colleges, Western
  "Self-government." *See* Colleges, Southern College for Women
  "Social-mindedness." *See* Cosmopolitan colleges
  "Tolerance." *See* Denominational colleges, Eastern
  "Unwritten constitution." *See* Universities, Southern
  See also State Colleges, Southern State College for Women
Composition of student body
  Implications for personnel workers and educators of, 271
  Outline for study of, 279
  Present-day heterogeneity in, 212–214
  Role in conditioning college culture of, 29
  Significance of diversity in, 213
  Understanding of mores and, 33
Constructive mores
  In campus housing, 248, 249, 257
  In cooperative interrelationships, 153
  In curricular innovations, 233
  In explanation of administrative actions, 153, 154
  In fraternity-sorority world, 93, 94
  In high spirit and morale, 156, 157
  In interaction between school and local community, 91
  In interaction of campus with wider community, 102, 103

In minimum of social discriminations, etc., 154
  Student government and student, 63
  Techniques used in, 242
Constructive processes
  Cooperation and, 275
  Techniques in breakdown of racial discrimination, 242
  Trends in post-war fraternities, 242, 243
Cornell University
  New impact of student government at, 237
Cosmopolitan colleges
  College spirit of "social mindedness" in, 43
  Constructive attack on sorority racial discrimination, 241, 242
  Cultural factors in, 29
  Discriminatory practices of, 124, 125
  Group prestige in, 136, 137
  Interrelationships in, 146, 147
  New impact of student government in, 237
  Secret cliques in, 184
  Totality of interrelations in disturbing event, 151, 152
  Types of leaders in, 156
Cowley, W. H. and Waller, Willard
  Alumni and tradition, 83, 84
  Points for study of college culture, 27
  Selective practices of student social groups, 129
  Student behavior from control patterns of past, 56
Coyle, Grace
  Evaluation of leadership, 157, 158
  Levels of ritual, 65
Crawford, Mary M.
  See Folkways and customs, student spending and recreation at Indiana University, 1940–1941
Cultural change
  The college in transition, chap. VII.
Cultural conditioning, 8–9
  Cultural lag, 274
  Town and college, 92
Cultural controls, 9
Cultural factors in colleges, 8
  Significance to personnel workers of, 33–34, 75, 76
  Spontaneous groups, 187
  Student culture
    In cosmopolitan colleges, 29
    In denominational colleges, 30–31
    In University of Oregon, 31

Culturally patterned behavior, 108, 115, 116, 118, 120, 229
Of a complex social system, 118, 266
Cultural processes of change, 9–17, 22, 23
Present-day curricular innovations, 229
Schedule for study of, 280, 281
See also Borrowing; Diffusion; Discovery and invention
Culture complex, 52
Group, 174
Schedule for study of, 280, 281
Culture of the wider community
Failure in student government due to mores of, 64
Impact of present-day campus thought and action on the, 257–259
Influences of,
See Alumni; Local community; National organizations; Society at large
Postwar era in, 269
Schedule on relationship of student mores to, 283
Curricular innovations, 229–234
According to college's particular philosophy, 233
Cultural change and, 229
Examples of abrupt change in, 231, 232
In colleges of the U. S. during 1946–47, 229–234
Excerpts from New York Times (1946–1947) on, 229–233
Meaning of, 232, 233

Dartmouth College
New impact of student government, 237
Deans
See Academic structure, status in, 110–113
Democracy in a college community
A major commitment, 141
Campus a laboratory of experience for, 203, 204
Cooperative intergroup relations for, 206, 207
Cooperative interrelationships and, 153
Democratic approach to elections, 247
Development of mores of, 159
Economic, political, and cultural, 260
Emphasis for promotion, 115, 207
Stanford University administrators and, 37, 38
Student struggle for democratic patterns, 238

Democracy in a college community (Cont.):
What personnel staff can do for democratic mores of control, 67
Denison University
March of Dollars Drive, 272
Denominational colleges
Eastern
Clash between church and, 86, 87, 88
Patterns of popularity at, 243
Social cleavages in, 123
Spirit of "tolerance" in, 44
Student culture in, 30, 31
Midwest
Change in fraternity-sorority cleavage, 244, 245, 255, 256
New groups receiving prestige at, 240
Southwestern
College spirit of "loyalty to old river," 43
Western
Church regulative control in, 55
College spirit emanating from president, 44
Custom of "continually keeping vigil on health," 39
Influence of alumni in, 84, 85
Departmental structure, 108, 109
Faculty cliques in, 185, 186
Heads of, 112
Rivalry in, 114, 115
Destructive mores
Administrative fiat in, 147, 148
Faculty cliques and, 185, 186
In campus housing, 248, 249
Lack of good interrelationships and, 167
Lack of leadership and, 156
Prestige mores as, 140
Selective mechanisms and, 130
Dickinson College
Physical culture, 72, 73
Differences in colleges, 8, 9, 15, 69, 70
In cultural demands, 116
In culture-matrix, 265
In group structure and function, 191
In symbols of social prestige, 191
Diffusion, 14, 15
Schedule for study of, 280, 281
Discovery and invention, 11–15
Discrimination, 123–126
Constructive change of, in Jewish sorority, 241, 242
Implications for personnel workers and educators of, 141, 142

Discrimination (*Cont.*):
Kinds of,
National, 125
Racial, 123, 124
Religious, 123, 124, 125
Successful integration of racial groups,
142
Techniques in constructive change of,
242
Disturbing events, 152, 153, 167
See Interrelations, plan of studying
Dormitory
Housing problems in X, 253–255
Social structuring of students and
structure of, 130, 131, 132
Student's adjustment and, 177
Dress mores
See Blake, Patricia

Efron, Edith
Adjustment of veteran and civilian stu-
dents, 221
Reasons for veteran's not returning to
old job, 226, 227
Elements of culture
Qualities in, 270
Schedule for study of, 280, 281
Significance on present-day campus of,
270
Elizabethtown College, Pennsylvania
Christian Movement of, 272

Faculty mores
Department heads. *See* Academic
structure, status in
Faculty club and faculty wives, 110
Faculty precedence, 112
Group stereotypes and, 141
In Eastern college, 52
Mores of curricular practices, 227
Pro- and anti-veteran camps of, 222
Relationships and recognitions in, 113
Role of student with prestige ad-
ministrative positions, 113
Suggestive control of, 55, 56
Teaching mores, 274
Traditional teacher morality, 36
Veterans' revolt against teaching prac-
tices, 220
See also Selective mechanisms, selection
of faculty staff members
Fashions, fads, etc., 47
Characteristics of those insensitive to,
18
Types of, 18
Flexibility of methods, 261, 274

Florida Southern College
Curricular innovation, 231, 233
Folkways and customs, 45–48
"Fish-Day" at Texan college, 57
Schedule for study of, 289, 290
Some specialized folkways, 47
Student spending and recreation at
Indiana University, 1940–1941,
45–47
Followers and imitators, 16
See Leaders and leadership, dominance
and
Football movement
See Cultural processes of change; Dis-
covery and invention, 11–14
Fort Valley State College
Ham and Egg Show, 272
Fraternity-sorority world
Architectural designs and social-cul-
tural patterns in, 132
Changes in, 240, 241, 242, 243
Collective representations in, 182
Constructive trends in post-war, 242,
243, 244, 245
Dynamics of a democratic approach to
elections in, 247, 248
Gangs in, 183
Housing impact on change in, 255,
256
Politics and, 178
Prestige of independents in Mid-
western college, 240
Responsibilities to-day in, 93, 94
Schedule for study of social class
structure of, 285, 286
Social attitudes of, 241
Social stratification in, 120, 121
Status in, 133
See also Discriminations, national and
religious; National organiza-
tions; Present-day campus
politics, organized and in-
dependent parties; Selective
mechanisms, in fraternity world
in Eastern colleges and in stu-
dent social groups; Social cleavages, between fraternities in New
England college
Functioning of groups
See Groups on college campus

Gang, 180–188
Characteristics of, 180
Culture of, 187

Gang *(Cont.)*:
Implications for personnel workers and educators of, 204, 205, 206
Mechanisms of control in, 181, 182
Natural leader and, 183
Nature of, 180
Organization of, 181
Personality and action patterns of, 182, 183
Pressure in fraternities of, 182
Redirection of, 204, 205
Role and status of members of a, 180
Structure of, 182
See also Social grouping, informal organization in plan for study of

G. I.'s and G. I. Bill of Rights, 30, 31, 211, 222, 226

Gist, Noel P., *Cultural Patterning in Secret Society Ceremonials*, 59, 60

Goucher College
Boat ride of, 272

Group description
See Sanderson, Dwight

Group diaries, 199–200

Group record, 198, 199

Group thinking
In heterogeneous student body, 245
Procedures of, 159

Groups on college campus
Classification of, 175, 176
Culture complex of, 174
Each student a product of, 3
Receptivity or rejection of new cultural elements, 280, 281
Functioning of,
Internal and external. *See* Social grouping, informal organization in, plan for study of;
Interrelationship of structure and, 203
Group images, 204
Group-sustained mores,
Challenge to educator of, 268
Fraternity group opinion in, 182
More democratic, 271
Structure, function, and organization of groups in, 174
Implications for personnel workers and educators of, 202–207
Interrelations of,
Failure of a group in total, 150, 151
Opinion of. *See* Gang, mechanisms of control in

Organization of,
Charters, personnel, norms, activities and function in, 189, 267, 268
Questions for analysis of, 190
Satisfaction of needs, 188
Examples from Harvard, 188, 189
Types of,
Formal, 175, 176–179
Assembly, 178
Classroom, 178
Departmental, 178
Resident, 177
Social, 178
Informal, 179–188. *See also* Gang
Prestige in, 136–138
Group prestige ratings, 137–138
Responsibility to a group, 206
Schedule on evaluation of, 288, 289
Structure of,
Analysis of, 190
Importance of study of, 191
Schedule for study of, 283, 284, 291
Sociological graphs for study of, 190, 191
Techniques in studying groups, 195–200. *See also* Group description, outline for; Group diaries; Group record; Group thinking; Groups on college campus, structure of, sociological graphs for study of; Leadership techniques; Malinowski, group organizational diagram; Social grouping, informal organization in, plan for study of
Unity of,
In ritual and ceremonies, 59

Guidance in colleges
Administrative aspects of, 261
"Culture-consciousness" in, 74, 75
Personnel point of view in, 261
Personnel services in, 261, 262
Post-war strivings of youth and, 260
Progressive attitude and, 262
Reassessment of tradition and controls for, 75

Hand, Harold C.
Students' adjustment and resident group, 177

Hartshorne, Edward Y.
Group diaries, 199, 200
Parental letter, 148–150

Hartshorne (*Cont.*):
  Plan for study of informal groups, 186, 187
Harvard and Yale colleges
  Football games of, 12
  Intellectual similarities, 70
  Regressive tendencies, 84
  Student ranking in, 135
  Tradition from the outside, 36
Harvard College, 7
  Family background in, 126
  Practical dominance in, 15
  Social stratification in, 184, 185
  Social structuring due to material equipment of, 130, 131
  Societal influences in Business School of, 98, 99
  See also Groups on college campus, organization of, examples from Harvard; Prestige, seniority at Harvard; Selective mechanisms, student precedence and rank; Morison, S. E.; Social cleavages, "Yard and Gold Coast"
High school of Midwestern state
  See Local community, town and school interactive
Hollingshead, A. B.
  Academic selection, 129, 130
  Social control, 23
Housing problems, 248–257

Imitation
  See Blake, Patricia; Tardé, Gabriel
Implications for personnel workers and educators, 33, 34, 48, 49, 50, 65–68, 74–76, 85, 91, 92, 96–98, 102, 103, 139–143, 166–169, 202–207, 259–262, 264–276
Independent organizations
  Campus politics in, 246
  Democratic approach to elections in, 247
  Democratic change between fraternity and, 244, 245
  Housing situation and breakdown in cleavage between fraternity and, 255, 256
  Prestige of, 240
Indiana University
  Curricular innovation, 230
  Student recreation and spending in, 1940–1941, 45–47
Indoctrination, assimilation, and culturally transmitted attitudes,

Indoctrination (*Cont.*):
  Mores of honor system and initiation practices, 56, 57
  Schedule for study of, 281
Informal organization, 179–188
Informal spontaneous groups.
  See Gang; Informal organization
In-group and out-group
  Group ego of in-group, 56
  Group images and, 204
  In-group morality, 60
  In-group status in academic structure, 110, 112
  Loyalty of in-group, 67
Initiation practices, 57
  Northern University, 239
Innovators and innovations, 16, 17
  Innovations in college mores, 252
  In fraternity life, 240
  Schedule for study of, 280, 281
Instructional mores
  Persistence of traditional, 274
  Present-day student needs and, 227
  Significance of campus in transition for, 260
  Veterans' complaints against, 220
  See also Curricular innovations
Integrative all-college events, 272, 273
Inter- and intra-institutional pressures, 108
Intergroup relations, 193–196
  All-college events and, 272
  Implications for personnel workers and educators of, 207
  Intergroup morality, 205, 206
  Need for, 141
  Qualitative, structural, and functional approaches, 193–196
  Transmitted and direct, 194, 195
Interpersonal relationships
  Attitudes and, 169
  Challenge to educator of, 267
  Content of, 167
  Explanation of, 154, 155
  Importance in personality growth of, 155, 168
  Leadership techniques in studying, 160–163
  Need for study of, 168–169
Interrelations
  Implications for personnel workers and educators, 166–170
  Plan of studying, 152
  Schedule for study of, 286, 287
  Situations for constructive, 153, 154

Interrelations (*Cont.*):
Totality of, 150–153, 167, 267
Failure of group to function, 150, 151
Situation in large cosmopolitan college, 151–153
Types of
Parent-student
Parental letter, 148, 149, 150
President-student. *See* Destructive mores, administrative fiat in;
Student-faculty, faculty-faculty, student-faculty-administration, 152, 153
Student-parent-college
Liberalization in denominational college, 148
Intragroup relations, 196, 207, 291

Jameson, S. H.
See Cultural factors in colleges, student culture in University of Oregon
Janney, J. E.
Fad and fashion leadership, 17, 18
Jennings, Helen
Choice analysis, 162, 163
Junior colleges
In Midwest
Impact of physical housing situation, 71. *See also* Social cleavages, in student structuring
In West, Phoenix, Arizona
All-college breakfasts, 272
Daily coffee hours, 272
Spirit of "face values," 44, 45
Tradition of "The Masque of the Yellow Moon," 38
Veterans' group in, 228

Kansas State College
Innovation in student government, 237, 238

Landecker, W. S.
Intergroup relations, 193
LaSierra College, Riverside, California
snow picnics of, 273
Leaders and leadership
Analysis of, 166
Between veterans and civilians on Pennsylvania campus, 158
Criteria for evaluation of, 157, 158

Leaders and leadership (*Cont.*):
Dominance and, 163–167
Followers, 165, 166
Unique individual leaders, 164–165
Function and importance of, 156
In crisis situation, 248
In interpersonal relationships, 155, 156, 267
In student government, 67
Mapping of, 162
Schedule on evaluation of, 288
Types of, 156
See also Gang, natural leader and
Leadership techniques, 160–164
Choice analysis, 162, 163
Other aids, 163
Sociometric test, 161–162
Confidential popularity index, 162
Group formation, 161
Psychological currents, 161
Questions which might be used in, 162
Significance of, 162
Liberal arts colleges
Eastern
Regulative control in, 51, 52, 53, 54
Middle Atlantic
Housing impact on sororities of, 256
Middle West
Breakdown of social cleavage in, 93
Southwestern Junior
Emotional ceremony and ritual in, 61
Tradition of "Grey Lady Walking," 39, 40
Lincoln University
Curricular innovation, 231
Linton, Ralph
Discovery and invention, 11
Elements of culture, 270
Positions and culturally patterned behavior, 107
Status, role, and prestige, 132, 133
See also Social system, definition of
Lloyd-Jones, Esther
Three aspects of personnel work, 261
See also Social understanding, lack of
Local community
Implications for personnel workers and educators of, 92
Influence of, 85–93
Aristocratic mores in, 250–251
Citizens' committee in, 147
Conflict between doctrines of college and, 86

Local community (*Cont.*):
Conflict in "town and gown" ethics in, 87
Negro college in South and, 87
Town socially a leech, 85, 86. See also Morison, S. E.
Interaction of college and,
"Town and gown" interactive, 88, 89
Ham and Eggs Show and Folk Festival of Southern negro state college, 89
Town and school interactive, 89, 90
See also High school of a Midwestern state
Schedule for study of, 280
Social class distinctions by college men in, 87
Lynd, Robert
Change of culture, 271

MacIver, R. M.
New group life, 241, 268
Social process, 202
Struggle of groups, 203, 204
Value-systems of individual and of group, 173
Malinowski, Bronislaw
Group organizational diagram, 188–189
Marietta College
Curricular innovations, 230
New fraternity, 240
Marks, Percy
See Academic structure, place in, personal
Married students
Married veterans' housing problems, 250, 251, 252
Social patterns of, 244
Status of married veteran, 216
Struggle of, for role and status, 244
Types of, 213
Marshall College
Curricular innovation, 229
McKown, H. S.
Student government selection of members, 62
Military mores
Conditioning from, 219–221
Mississippi girls' school
Tradition of "Grey Lady Walking," 39, 40
Mississippi Southern college
Curricular innovations, 231

Moreno, J. L.
See Leadership techniques, sociometric test
Mores of control
Implications for personnel workers and educators, 65–68
Regulative and suggestive control, 51–57
Analysis for educators of, 66
Student regulative control, 56
See also Administrative mores, controls as shown in
See also Ceremony and ritual; College as a culture-matrix, traditional and established culture of; Democracy in a college community, what personnel staffs can do, etc.; Indoctrination, assimilation, and culturally transmitted attitudes; Student government
Mores of the future, 24, 25
Challenge of, 271–276
Innovations and, 233
Reassessment of traditional mores, 75
Morgan, J. H.
See Dickinson College
Morgan, W. H.
Swings in student religion, 21–23
Morison, S. E.
Boston a social leech on Harvard, 85, 86, 107
Cultural pattern in football, 11–14
Seniority at Harvard, 134–136
Student precedence in order of parental social rank, 126
See also Harvard College

National organizations
Implications for personnel workers and educators, 96, 97
Importance of, 97
Influence of, 93–98
In Negro colleges, 95, 96
In sorority and fraternity competition, 93
In student religious groups, 94, 95
Y.M.C.A., Y.W.C.A. and others, 94, 95, 96
Negro colleges and state colleges in the South,
Cleavages as to geographical origin, 123
College spirit of "development of the individual," 44

Negro colleges (*Cont.*):
  Selective and political mechanisms in, 126
  Town environment and social mores of, 87
  Tradition of Ham and Egg Show and Folk Festival, 39
  Veteran complaints of feminine social patterns, 243
  Veterans' impact for good in, 226
  See also Local community-"town and gown" interactive
Newcomb, Theodore
  See Change of mores, in Bennington College community
New Rochelle College
  Curricular innovation, 231

Ohio University
  Curricular innovation, 231, 233
Olmstead, J. G.
  Study of alumni achievement, 80
Organization of groups
  See Groups on college campus

Parental domination and influence, 29, 31, 34
  Group stereotypes in family mores, 141, 142
  See also Interrelations, parent-student
Parental letter. *See* Hartshorne, Edward Y.
Physical and material culture, 68–75
  Equipment and architectural design in, 72, 73
  Implications for personnel workers and educators of, 74
  Material objects and symbols,
    Physical objects of rivalry, 73
    Traits of material culture, 73, 74
    See also Dickinson College
  Outline for study of, 279
  Problems of the larger society and, 68
    Effect on student mores. *See also* Slosson, Edwin E.
  In Pennsylvania college, 68
  Social-cultural patterns in dormitory housing, 72
  Social structuring due to material equipment, 130–133
Political movements, 102
Prescott, Daniel A.
  Importance of personal relationships, 168

Present-day campus politics
  Democratic approach to elections, 247
  Organized and independent parties, 246
Present-day college girls
  Need for security, 214
  Status of, 216, 217
Present-day housing problems
  Constructive and destructive practices in, 257
  National organization's old mores and, 255, 256
    In denominational liberal arts college, 255, 256
  Nostalgia for the old, 255
  "Trailer court troubles," 251, 252
  Veterans' desire for "X Dormitory," 253, 254, 255
  See also Married students, married veterans' housing problems
President
  Autocratic vs. democratic leadership, 115
  See also Academic structure, status in
Prestige
  Ascription of behavior in positions of, 137–138
  Athletics and, 177, 178
  Differences in social, 191
  Mores due to seeking, 134–136
  Occupational, 119
  Recognitions and expectancies in, 111, 112, 136–137
  Seniority at Harvard, 134–136
  Social, 117, 118, 120, 121
  Ways of obtaining, 137
  See also Destructive mores, prestige mores as; Groups on college campus, prestige in, group prestige ratings
Price, Louise
  Development of student-life at Stanford, 37
  Genetic process of studying group life, 163
  Regulative control at Western university, 53, 54
Princeton University, 7, 70
  Nassau Club of, 69
  Physical culture and its effect on student mores in, 71
Psychological geography of college community, 161, 162

Radcliffe College
  Curricular innovations, 229

Regulative and suggestive control
    See Mores of control
Religion
    See Morgan, W. H.; Y.M.C.A. and
        Y.W.C.A.
Research on mores, 279-292
Riemer, Svend
    Marriage on campus of University of
        Washington, 244
Rollins College
    Curricular innovation, 231
Roucek, Joseph
    Culture patterns of campus a field for
        for study, 27
    Social processes, 200, 201, 202
Russell Sage College
    Curricular innovation, 229
Rutgers University
    Forum at, 237

Sam Houston State Teachers College,
        Texas,
    The concrete slab at, 272
Sanderson, Dwight
    Plan for description of group, 196-198,
        290, 291
Sarah Lawrence College, 262
    Curricular innovation, 231, 233
Scholarships, fellowships, and other aids
    Town committee and athletic, 147
    Types of competition and pressures in,
        114
    See also Selective mechanisms, student
        structuring and, in scholarships,
        fellowships, and student aids
Segmental patterns
    Denominational mores and, 252, 253
    In religion, 96, 97
Selective mechanisms
    Implications of, 141
    Student structuring and, 125-130
        In fraternity world in Eastern col-
            lege, 127
        In honor societies, 128
        In Negro Southern college, 126
        In scholarships, fellowships, and stu-
            dent aids, 128
        In selection of faculty staff mem-
            bers, 129, 130
        In student admissions, 127, 128
        In student precedence and rank,
            126
        In student social groups, 129
Sherif, Muzafer
    Social norms, 211
Slosson, Edwin E.

Slosson, Edwin E. (Cont.):
    Differences between Eastern and West-
        ern colleges, 68-72
    Invention at Leland Stanford Univer-
        sity, 13
    Physical culture and geographical loca-
        tion, 68, 71
Social attitudes
    See Attitude formation; Fraternity-
        sorority world; Interpersonal re-
        lationships; Young, Kimball
Social behavior
    Analysis of student body's, 245
    Learned and acquired, 275
    Phenomena of, 173
    Source of, 2, 102, 264
Social cleavages
    Breakdown between two groups, 151
    Housing situation in sorority groups
        and, 255, 256
    Implications for personnel workers and
        educators of, 141
    In Armed Forces, 225, 226
    In student structuring, 122-126; be-
        tween:
        Conscientious objectors and Armed
            Services men, 123
        Dormitory and town girls in state
            university, 122
        Football players and non-players,
            123
        Fraternities in New England college,
            123
        Protestant and Jewish, Protestant
            and Catholic, 122
        Residential sections in Midwestern
            junior college, 122
        "Yard" and Gold Coast" at Harvard,
            86
Social configuration
    Campus interrelations and, 146
    In college social system, 142
    The mores and, 7
Social control
    Interaction of town and students in,
        92
    Interrelationships in, 169
    Mores and their function in, 1-27, 48,
        56
    Organization of people, essence of, 23
    Organization of students and, 173
    Pressures from the outside and, 9
    Responsibility for, 221
    Stanford University student life and,
        37
    Traditions and, 48, 49

Social-cultural patterns
  Location of student union and, 132
  See also Fraternity-sorority world,
    architectural designs and social-
    cultural patterns
Social education
  Civilian's need of, 218
  Need for, 241
  Today on campuses, 218
  Veteran's need of, 218
Social grouping
  Classifications in, 175, 176, 177
  Formal organization in, 176–179
  Informal organization in, 179–188
  Plan for study of, 186–188
Social heritage, 34–51
  Folkways and customs, 45–48, 75
  Implications for personnel workers and
    educators, 48–51
  Traditions, 35–45
  See also College as a culture-matrix,
    three interactive elements of
Social maturity
  College girl and, 214
  Necessity for definition of, 223
  Relationship of social system to, 266,
    267
  Veteran and, 214, 223
  Wacs and Waves and, 214
  Young high school graduates and, 214,
    215
Social mobility, 211
Social patterns
  Change in curricula, marriage course,
    243, 244
  Married students', 244
  New trends in, 243
  Patterns of dating, 244, 245
    In denominational liberal arts col-
      lege, 244
Social processes in group work, 10, 198,
  199, 200, 201, 202
  Assimilation, 201
  Competition, 201
  Domination and exploitation, 201
  Stratification, 201
Social relationships
  Interaction with total social bonds of
    college community, 146
Social stratification
  At Harvard, 184, 185
  Influence of alumni in, 82, 83
  In student structuring, 120–122
  Schedule for study in fraternities of,
    285, 286
  See also Local community, social class

Social stratification *(Cont.)*:
    distinctions by college men in
Social structuring
  Implications for personnel workers and
    educators, 139–143
  Schedule for study of, 283, 284
  See also Academic structure; Physical
    and material culture, social
    structuring due to material
    equipment; Prestige; Status and
    role; Student structuring
Social system
  Challenge of, 266, 267
  Configuration in, 142
  Data for understanding of, 139
  Definition of, 106, 107
  Description on large campus of, 116,
    117, 118
  Impact of a new, 239–246
    Tradition change in Northern uni-
      versity, 239
  Implications of, 139, 140, 142
  Interrelations in, 4
  Knowledge of norms of behavior im-
    posed by, 140
  Positions in and culturally patterned
    behavior expected, 108, 118
  Possibility of new, 273
  Re-emphasis of values in, 273
  Structural and functional aspects of,
    107, 142, 266
Social understanding
  Lack of, 202
  Of heterogeneous student body, 218
  Student backgrounds, needs and, 261
Society at large
  Implications for personnel workers and
    educators of, 102–103
  Influence of, 98–103
    1920's in the colleges, 98, 99, 102
      Diffusion of wealth, 99
      Emancipation of women, 99, 102
      Fight against Bolshevism, 98
      Veneration for business, 99
    1930's in the colleges, 99, 100, 101,
      102
      Campus a reflection of outside
        society, 100, 102
      Campus cooperatives, 101
      Fatalism, 100
      Pecuniary purpose, 101
      Security, 100
  Schedule for studying student mores
    and influences of, 283
Socio-economic base

Socio-economic base *(Cont.)*:
Characteristics of students of lower, 43
Implications of, 269
Present-day broadening of, 211, 212, 269
Sociometric test, 161, 162
Questions for, 162, 284
Southwestern College, Memphis, Tennessee
Curricular innovation, 230
Stanford University
Discovery and invention in, 13
Kinship of "Stanford Farm," 37
Physical culture in, 69
Regulative control of "rough tradition," 53, 54
Students' Day at Convalescent Home, 272
Traditions of, 37
State colleges
North Central State campus
Selective mechanism in, 127, 128
Southern State College for Women
Administrative control in, 55
College spirit of, 43
Tradition of "Old Maids' Gate," 38
State universities
Lack of courtesy mores at, 243
Students' complex social system of, 117, 118
Scale of campus social values, 117, 118
See also Present-day housing problems, veterans' desire for X dormitory; Social cleavages, in student structuring
Status and role
Achieved and ascribed, 139
Active and latent, 133, 134, 192, 193
Implications of, 140, 141
In definition of social system, 106, 107
In social classifications of student positions, 132, 133
Role of individual to college, 138
Social grouping and, 174
Social status and role
Fulfillment of, 3
New groups today receiving, 240
In Midwestern college, 240
Student's total of, 193
Within each group, 191–193
Food, clothing, and recreational equipment for, 192
Uncertainty of, on present-day campus, 215, 216, 217
Witness of importance of, 133

Status and role *(Cont.)*:
See also Academic structure, status in
Structure of groups
See Groups on college campus
Student backgrounds
See Composition of student body; Social understanding
Student body
See Composition of
Student culture
See College as a culture-matrix, three interactive elements of
Student editor excerpts from college newspapers
On campus politics in university, 246
On student government in Eastern college, 236
Student government, 61–65
Failure in effective functioning of, 63, 64, 65
New impact of, 235–239
At Dartmouth, in faculty-student committee, 237
At Williams College, in honor system, 237
In large cosmopolitan college, 237
In lines of action, 238
In model organization of U.N.— Cornell and Kansas State, 237, 238
In old Eastern colleges, 236
In Southern university, 235
In weekly round-table discussion, Rutgers, 237
Questionnaire for study of, 281, 282
Report from thirty personnel workers of strength of, 62
Types of representation in, 62, 63
Student morale, 43, 49, 147, 157, 228
Student needs
Assumption of college patterns and, 139
Challenge to personnel worker of student's basic, 265, 271
Heterogeneous student body and, 214
Informal clique and, 184
Invention and, 14
Peculiar to family, 33
Rural students and, 131
Satisfaction of, 264
Structural arrangements for, 267
The mores and, 2–5
Ego-integrative needs, 4
Physical needs, 4
Social status needs, 3, 4
Veterans' return and, 227

Student newspaper excerpts on student impacts,
  In campus politics, 246–248
  In thought and action on wider community, 257, 258
  On administrative measures, 234
  On housing problems, 248–257
  On new social system, 239–245
  On student government and student body, 239
Student recreation, 45, 46
Student religion
  Hillel Foundation, 95
  Interfaith fellowship, 97, 272
  Newman Foundation, 94, 95
  Reassessment of, 97
  United Student Christian Council, 95
  World's Student Christian Federation, 95, 97
  See also Change of mores, patterns and periodicity of swing in; National organizations, influence of, in student religious groups; Segmental patterns, denominational mores and; Y.M.C.A. and Y.W.C.A.
Student responsibility, 64, 65
Student spending, 45, 46, 47
Student strikes
  In large Northern university, 234, 235
Student structuring, 115–130
  Culture patterns and positions in, 116
  Classroom group and, 178
  Departmental clubs and, 178
  Social campus groupings and, 178
  Social classifications in, 115
    Age-sex and social group system, 116–119
    Occupational choice, 119, 120
    Optional relationships and residential, 119–130
Students
  Commuting, 28
  Interaction in national and international events of, 258
  Needs stated by, 259
  New groups of, 212, 213
  On present-day campus, 215, 216
  Regulations of, 66
  Rural, 28, 30, 31
  Superstructure of constructive mores and, 91
  Value-systems of, 32, 33, 213
  See also Social stratification
Students' cooperatives, 101, 102
Summer prom queens

Summer prom queens (Cont.):
  Occasion for campus politics, 246
Sumner, William G.
  Definition of mores, 2, 173
  Group purpose, 268
  Mores and status, 111
Swarthmore College, 7, 21
  Compulsory change in, 21
    Student pressure against fraternity snobbishness, 21

Tardé, Gabriel
  Laws of imitation, 16
The mores
  Definition of, 2–7, 173
  Formation of, 9, 10
  Group-sustained. See Groups on college campus
  Indigenous to a particular culture, 8
Thomas, W. I. and Znaniecki, F.
  Four patterns of wishes, 2
Thrasher, Frederic M.
  See Gang
"Town and gown," 86, 87, 89
  Conflict of, 201
  Housing problem of veteran and, 250, 251
Traditional culture of the college,
  See Folkways and customs; Mores of control; Social heritage; Traditions
Traditional patterns
  Grandfather-father-son, 28, 83, 141
  Grandmother-mother-daughter, 38
  Second Generation Club, 80, 82
Traditions
  Continuation of, 49
  Definition of, 35
  Elimination of, 50
  Forms of existence, 48
  Implications of, 48–51
  Influence of, 35–36
  Origin of, 49
  Purposes they serve, 49
  Questioning of, 273, 274
  Reasons for existence, 48
  Three classes of, 36–45
    Almost entirely indigenous, two types
      Pervasive, 40
        College spirit, 41–45
      Specific, 40
    From outside, 36
      College of William and Mary, Harvard, Yale

Traditions (*Cont.*):
  In part from outside, in part from within, 36–40
  "Grey lady walking" of Western Mississippi College, 39; Ham and Egg Show and Folk Festival of Southern Negro State College, 39; Masque of the Yellow Moon at Junior College in West, 38; Old Maid's Gate at Southern State College for Women, 38; Springtime Customs at Vassar, 38; Stanford farm, 37; strong religious faith of western denominational college, 39
  See also College spirit
Trailer court problems
  See Universities, large, housing problems in
Trustees
  Present-day student government and, 235, 236
  See also Academic structure, status in

Universities
  Large
    Housing problems in, 249–257
    Denominational mores of, 252, 253
    Trailer court troubles, 251–253
    Veterans' struggle for X dormitory, 253–255
    Impact on wider community of, campus thought and action, 257–259
  Midwestern
    Prestige of new group "Independents," 240
    Selective mechanisms in, 129, 130
  Northern
    Change in tradition in, 239
    Student impact on administrative measures in, 234, 235
    Veterans' nostalgia for the old in, 255
  Southern
    College spirit, "the unwritten constitution," 41
    New impact of student government in, 235, 236
  Western
    College spirit of "individualism" in, 43, 44
    Regulative control, "man viewpoint" in, 53
    Social stratification in, 124

Universities (*Cont.*):
  Successful integration of Oriental women in, 142
University of California
  Greek theater of, 69, 71, 72
University of Denver
  Curricular innovation, 231, 233
University of Michigan
  Curricular innovation, 230, 233
University of New Hampshire
  Change in mores, 231
The University of Notre Dame
  Curricular innovation, 230
University of Oregon
  Adjustment problems in, 31
University of Pennsylvania
  Physical culture and its effect on student mores, 69, 70
University of Washington
  Social life of married students at, 244

Value-systems, 23, 32, 33, 173, 273
Vassar College
  Change in mores, 232
  Diffusion-custom of "Daisy Chain," 15
  Historical customs and traditions at, 38
  Innovations of, 230, 233
Veteran adjustment, 221–228
  Conflict between "Joe College" and "Joe Veteran," 221, 222, 223
  Difficulty of women veterans in academic, 223, 224, 225
  Faculty views in, 222
  Nostalgia for the old, 226
  Suggestions for successful, 228, 229
Veteran problems, 226, 227
  Challenge to educator in civilian vs., 271
  In housing, 248–257
Veterans
  Change in tradition for, 239
  Change of dating patterns by, 244, 245
  Impact of, 219–229
    In adjustment on campus, 221–228
    In conditioning from military mores, 219, 220, 221
      Revolt against teaching methods, 220
    In veterans' groups, 228
      In junior college in West, 228
  Impact on wider community of thought and action of, 257, 258
  Action in national and international events, 257, 258
  Fight for O.P.A., 257, 258

Veterans (*Cont.*):
  Influence in breakdown of class distinctions by, 244, 245
  Need for security of, 214, 215
  Nostalgia for the old in, 226, 255
  Problems of, 226–229
  Reasons for not returning to old job, 226–228
  Status of married, 216
  Strong impact for the good, 226
  Uncertainty of statuses and roles of, 215, 216, 217
  See also Composition of student body, present-day heterogeneity in; Social cleavages, in student structuring, conscientious objectors and armed services men
Veterans' wives,
  Dubious role, 217

Wacs, Waves, Spars
  Academic adjustment of, 223, 224, 225
  Differences in experiences of, 225
  In student body, 213
  Security needs of, 214
  Status of, 216
Waller, Willard
  Treatment of veterans' groups, 228
  See also Ceremony and ritual, social dynamics of; Social system, description of, on large campus
Warner, W. L., Havighurst, R. J., and Loeb, Martin B.
  Student social status, 32
Warner, W. Lloyd and Lunt, Paul S.
  Plan of studying interrelationships, 152

Warner, W. Lloyd (*Cont.*):
  Total social configuration, 146
Warren, Roland L.
  Analysis of student groups, 178
Wellesley College
  Curricular innovation, 230
Wesleyan University
  Change in mores, 232
  Curricular innovations, 230
Widener, H. W.
  College a victim of pecuniary culture, 101
Williams College
  Change in mores, 232
  Honor system, 237
Wilson College
  Change in mores, 232
  Curricular innovation, 230
Wilson, Gertrude
  Group processes, 198–199
  See also Group record
Wilson, Logan
  See Academic structure, place in, departmental and personal

Yale College
  Alumni and physical equipment at, 69
  See also Canby, Henry S., interactive influences of "town and gown"; Harvard and Yale colleges
Young, Kimball
  Attitudes and change of relationships, 169
Y.M.C.A. and Y.W.C.A., 20, 94, 95, 96, 97, 175, 191, 194